Panasonic
Microwave Oven Cookbook

Welcome to the world of convenient, time saving microwave cooking. Finally, you have found a way to prepare delicious meals and still lead the active on-the-go life-style so common today. Soon you'll wonder how you ever survived without this invaluable appliance.

To help insure success in microwave oven cookery, please read the operating instructions and the first section of this book. A basic understanding of your oven is an unwritten ingredient in every recipe. Also, you will find many techniques and helpful hints to guarantee a smooth transition from conventional cooking to the modern microwave oven way.

The recipes in this cookbook have been chosen and tested to provide you with a wide variety of flavorful dishes. As you master microwave oven cooking you will find the charts and hints helpful in adapting your own favorite recipes. As your experience grows, we know you will be as excited and pleased with this unit as the day you purchased it. Enjoy your microwave oven and all its delicious benefits.

Patricia R. Quarles

Patricia R. Quarles, National Home Economist

All foods photographed were prepared and heated according to recipes in this cookbook. Some recipes were increased for photographic reasons.

Full page and cover photography by Laszlo Studio, New York, New York

Please direct all inquiries to:
Consumer Affairs Division
PANASONIC COMPANY, Division of
Matsushita Electric Corporation of America
One Panasonic Way
Secaucus, N.J. 07094 U.S.A.

In Canada:
Panasonic Home Economist
Matsushita Electric of Canada Limited
5770 Ambler Drive, Mississauga, Ontario L4W 2T3
TEL.: (416) 624-5010

TABLE OF CONTENTS

Understanding how your microwave oven works and realizing the benefits over conventional cooking will reinforce your decision to become a microwave oven cook.

Having carefully reviewed the operating instructions, settle down with a cup of tea or coffee and read what cooking with this amazing unit is all about... and plan dinner for tonight.

COOKING WITH MICROWAVE ENERGY

Microwaves are a form of high-frequency radio waves. This energy is the same type that is necessary for radio (including AM, FM and CB) only having a shorter wave length. They are emitted from a magnetron tube which converts electrical energy into microwave energy. The microwave is approximately four to six inches long and has a diameter of about one-fourth inch. Microwave energy can be:

REFLECTED   TRANSMITTED   ABSORBED

Reflection

Microwaves are reflected by metal just as a ball is bounced off a wall. This is why the oven interior is epoxy coated metal. A combination of stationary (interior walls) and rotating metal (turntable or stirrer fan) helps assure that the microwaves are well distributed within the oven cavity to produce even cooking.

Transmission

Microwaves pass through some materials such as paper, glass and plastic much like sunlight shining through a window. Because these substances do not absorb or reflect the microwave energy, no change takes place. This is why these are ideal materials for microwave oven cooking containers.

Absorption

When microwaves come in contact with moisture they are absorbed and cause the food molecules to vibrate. This vibration causes friction between molecules. Friction causes heat much like rubbing your hands together on a cold day to warm up. This action causes the food to heat and become cooked. Microwaves can penetrate foods up to a depth of one inch. The internal cooking of larger food masses is done by conduction of the rapidly vibrating molecules toward the center. Because microwaves dissipate, much like sunlight as it reaches the earth's surface, they cannot be stored in the foods.

POWER SELECT SETTINGS

Your microwave oven is equipped with multiple Power Select settings:
HIGH (100%), MEDIUM HIGH (90%), MEDIUM (70%) MEDIUM-LOW (50%), LOW (30%), WARM (10%) and DEFROST (35%).
While most foods can be heated on HIGH (full power), certain types of foods, milk for example, will benefit from heating with a reduced amount of energy over a slightly longer time.
This variety of settings offers you complete flexibility in microwave cooking.

HIGH setting is full power and is used to heat foods high in moisture or that require fast cooking for best quality and time efficiency—

- Boil water
- Brown ground beef for casseroles
- Cook fresh fruits and fruit desserts
- Cook poultry (up to 3 lb.)
- Cook fish
- Cook vegetables
- Heat beverages (not containing milk)
- Make candy
- Preheat Browning Dish (accessory)

MEDIUM-HIGH setting is best suited to reheat pre-cooked foods and frozen foods—

- Heat frozen foods, not containing eggs or cheese
- Cook casseroles   • Heat canned foods
- Reheat leftovers   • Warm baby food

MEDIUM setting is invaluable for cooking meats and recipes with delicate ingredients—

- Bake cakes   • Cook meats
- Cook shellfish   • Prepare eggs
- Prepare recipes with delicate ingredients, such as eggs, milk and cheese

MEDIUM-LOW setting gives a low, gentle heating for finer texture foods—

- Bake muffins   • Cook custards
- Melt butter and chocolate   • Prepare rice

LOW setting offers the possibility to cook less tender cuts of meat allowing food to simmer and flavors to blend without overcooking—

- Prepare less tender cuts of meat
- Simmer stews, etc., to develop flavor
- Soften butter and cheese

WARM setting has a unique heating ability not available in most conventional cooking—

- Keep foods at serving temperature
- Raise yeast breads   • Soften ice cream

DEFROST setting is for all thawing. Refer to Defrosting Charts within each chapter for specific times and procedure.

PROGRAM COOKING

Program cooking is setting your microwave oven to cook up to three different operations at the same time. You do not have to wait until the first time has elapsed to set the second and third power and cooking time desired.

By utilizing this feature, one program can DELAY the START of cooking. Prepare a recipe, then set the length of time to postpone the beginning of microwave cooking. This feature is also helpful when cooking sauces, pot roasts, stews, etc. The ingredients are first brought to a boil at Power Select HIGH, then cooked at a lower power, MEDIUM or LOW, to allow flavors to blend or meats to cook tender. STAND time, necessary at the end of most microwave recipes, can also be set in the same operation as the cooking power and time.

Your microwave oven is also equipped with a special WARM setting to keep foods at serving temperature. With all these possibilities for program cooking, consult the operating instructions for complete information to ''program'' the unit.

The part of each recipe that can be programmed may be the first heating times. However, in some instances, foods are heated separately (ground beef-browned, butter-melted, etc.) before the program can be set. All cooking powers are listed at the top of each recipe. The powers to be programmed together will be connected with an arrow (→) and printed in blue (High→Medium). Also, within the recipe instructions, the powers that can be programmed together are printed in blue.

Look for the symbol 🎛 to indicate which recipes can be set for Program Cooking.

We have included a variety of recipes that benefit from three program cooking. These instructions can be adapted for your own recipes. Just follow the basic information below:

- Select DELAY/STAND to postpone the beginning of microwave cooking.
- Use Power Select HIGH to bring ingredients to a boil. Follow HEATING LIQUIDS CHART page 22 for an approximate time to set.
- Set Power Select LOW for the second cooking power when cooking less tender cuts of meat. These need about 20 to 30 minutes per pound to cook until tender and should be cooked with a minimum of 1 cup liquid per pound of meat.
- Choose MEDIUM-LOW Power Select when heating to blend flavors. Timing for this second cooking is a matter of preference.
- Program in the necessary STAND time at the end of each recipe. If a recipe calls for ''STAND covered'', and this step can be done in the microwave oven, it is not necessary to cover the food if the recipe was heated uncovered.
- Use Power Select WARM to keep foods at serving temperatures.

To insure the best results, it may be necessary to stir a recipe once or twice during the first or second program timing. These instructions are given, if needed, in each recipe.

TEMPERATURE SELECT SETTINGS

Various recipes throughout this cookbook give instructions for use with the temperature probe. If your unit is not equipped with a probe, use the approximate time given in each recipe or the time (per pound) indicated in the charts.

A conventional meat thermometer may be used to check the internal temperature of a food item. However, DO NOT USE A CONVENTIONAL MEAT THERMOMETER IN FOOD WHILE HEATING IN THE MICROWAVE OVEN. A microwave oven safe thermometer may be used during heating.

The probe can be used in foods other than meats and poultry. The following is a list of such foods with the appropriate temperature and Power Select that can help you further utilize the benefits of cooking by temperature. (Roasting charts for meat and poultry using the temperature probe are found in the respective chapters.)

ITEM	POWER SELECT	TEMP. SELECT
Baby Food (heating)	MEDIUM-HIGH	115°F to 130°F
Beverages (steaming) with milk with water or juice	MEDIUM HIGH	160°F 160°F
Casseroles	MEDIUM-HIGH	145°F to 160°F
Canned Foods	MEDIUM-HIGH	160°F
Dips—with meat with seafood or cheese	HIGH MEDIUM	145°F 145°F
Fish, whole	HIGH	175°F
Leftovers	MEDIUM-HIGH	160°F

Helpful Information for Using Temperature Probe

- Use the clip to hold the probe in the center part of the cooking container. (FIG. 1)
- Insert the probe at least one inch into the food to insure accurate temperature reading. (FIG. 2)
- Insert probe into meat as horizontally as possible. (FIG. 3)
- Poke probe through plastic wrap into center of food when heating a dish covered. (FIG. 4)
- Do not use the probe in frozen foods or with the browning dish accessory.
- Remove probe from oven cavity receptacle with pot holder.
- Clean probe with mild detergent and a soft cloth. DO NOT immerse in water or wash in dishwasher.

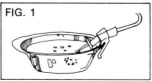

FIG. 1

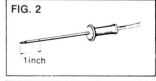

FIG. 2

1 inch

Fig.3

FIG. 4

COOKING EQUIPMENT

Microwave cooking opens new possibilities in convenience and flexibility for cooking containers. There are new microwave accessories constantly being introduced, but do not feel you need to purchase all new equipment. Many items you already have can be tested to see if they are microwave oven safe. You'll be surprised at the numerous things you have around.

Glass, Ceramic and China

Most of these utensils are excellent for use in the microwave oven. Many manufacturers now identify microwave oven safe dishes with either an asterisk (*) or a note in the accompanying product literature. Heat resistant glassware, unless it has metallic trim or decoration, can most always be used. However, be careful about using delicate glassware since it may crack, not from microwave energy, but from the heat of the food.

The most well known microwave oven safe glassware is Corning® products. Corning now marks their products ''good for microwave'' or ''good for range and microwave.'' The Centura® cookware line (by Corning) bearing an asterisk (*) is microwave oven safe. However, the Centura tableware is generally not acceptable. A few Centura accessory items are marked with the asterisk symbol. Corelle® Livingware (by Corning) with the exception of the close handle cups is microwave oven safe.

Pyrex® (by Corning) without metallic trim is microwave oven safe and offers unique pieces in their new line. Other manufacturers of glass utensils that are also microwave oven safe include Fire King® (by Anchor Hocking), French Cookware® (by Marsh Industries), Glassbake® (by Jeannette Glass), Glass Ovenware® (by Heller Designs) and oven ware by Federal Glass®. Dinnerware such as Temper-Ware® (by Lenox®) and Franciscan® Casual China that is marked ovenproof is usually safe to use in the microwave oven.

With all these possibilities, just remember a few basic things...

DO NOT USE:
- utensils with metallic trim or parts (i.e. bands, screws, etc.)
- dishware with cracked glazes
- ceramic mugs or cups with glued on handles
- delicate glassware

WHEN IN DOUBT...DO THE SIMPLE DISH TEST

How to Test a Container for Safe Microwave Oven Use:
Place glass measure of water in the microwave oven along with the container to be tested; heat two minutes at Power Select HIGH. If the container is microwave oven safe, it should remain cool and the water should be hot. If the container is warm, it has absorbed some microwave energy and should not be used.

JARS AND BOTTLES can be used to heat foods provided any metal lids are removed from the glass container. This is only for heating food to serving temperature, i.e., reheat leftovers, warm baby foods, etc. Cooking cannot be done safely because most of these containers are not heat-resistant and during extended heating times, heat from the food would cause cracking or breaking.

Here is a list of heat-resistant glass cookware we find invaluable in microwave cookery. You probably have many of these items on your shelf already:

- glass measuring cups
- custard cups
- glass mixing bowls
- glass loaf dish
- covered casserole dishes
- oblong baking dish
- cake dishes, round or square
- glass pie plate

Paper

For short cooking times and for foods with a low fat or water content, paper is a convenient container for the microwave oven. NAPKINS, WAXED PAPER, PAPER TOWELS, PLATES, CUPS, FREEZER WRAP and CARDBOARD all are handy utensils. Avoid wax coated paper goods. Foods that reach high temperatures can melt the wax. Wax paper, however, can be used effectively to prevent spatter when cooking.

Paper is also used in microwave cooking to absorb fat and excess moisture. Cooking bacon on a paper plate, between layers of paper towel is a common example of this.

CAUTIONS: Some recycled paper products may contain impurities which when combined with hot fat could cause sparking (arcing) or fires when used for cooking in the microwave oven.

Plastics

Plastic dishes, cups, some freezer containers and plastic-coated paper products may be used in the microwave oven. There are numerous types of plastic products available so choose carefully; some can become soft, disfigured or pitted from the heat of the food. ''Dishwasher Safe'' is a good sign that the container will also be microwave oven safe. Containers made from and labeled Polysulfone plastic are very durable in microwave cooking. Plastic dishes should not be used for cooking over an extended period of time or with foods having high fat or sugar content.

- Freezette® storage containers by Republic Molding can be safely used in the microwave oven for baking or reheating
- Melamine dishes are NOT microwave oven safe.
- Tupperware® is NOT recommended for microwave oven cooking.

COOKING BAGS designed to withstand boiling, freezing or conventional heating are safe to use in the microwave oven. The pouch should be slit (small slits near the top of bag) to allow steam to escape. When sealing a cooking bag with the enclosed metal twist-tie, make sure the ends are securely wrapped around the closure and do not stick up. DO NOT TRY TO COOK IN PLASTIC STORAGE BAGS.

Using twist-tie on cooking bag

PLASTIC WRAP can be used to cover dishes in most recipes. Over an extended heating time, some disfiguration of wrap may occur. When using plastic wrap as a casserole dish cover make a few small slits in the top to allow some steam to escape. When removing plastic wrap ''covers'', as well as any glass lid, be careful to remove it away from you to avoid steam burns.

Straw, Wicker and Wood

Straw and wicker baskets may be used in the microwave oven for short periods of time to warm rolls or bread. Large wooden utensils, such as bowls or cutting boards should NOT be used for prolonged heating as the microwave energy may cause the wood to become dry and brittle.

Metal

Metal containers or utensils and those with metallic trim should NOT be used in the microwave oven. Since microwave energy is reflected by metal, foods in metal containers will not cook evenly.
There is also the possibility of ''arcing''. This is a static discharge or spark between gaps in the metal or between the metal and the interior of the oven. If arcing occurs, turn the unit off and transfer food to a non-metallic container.
Although metal utensils must be avoided in microwave cooking, some metal can be helpful when used correctly.

Using foil when cooking chicken

ALUMINUM FOIL can be used safely if the amount of food cooked is much greater than the amount of foil. Because it reflects microwave energy, foil can be used to an advantage in some recipes. It can be used to prevent cooking. Small pieces of foil are used to cover areas such as chicken wings, tips of roasts or other thin parts that are cooked before the rest of the recipe is finished. Foil is used in these cases to slow or stop the cooking process and prevent overcooking.

FOIL LINED CONTAINERS, either cardboard or plastic, should NOT be used in the microwave oven. Foil lined milk cartons, frozen orange juice concentrate containers, or baking containers included in some cake mixes are examples of things to be avoided.

FROZEN DINNER TRAYS can be used in the microwave oven, but results are only satisfactory if the container is no higher than ¾-inch. In metal containers, all the heating takes place from the top; the metal container reflects the energy directed to the sides and bottom. See Heating Convenience Foods, page 138.

METAL RACK, see Accessory information, page 8, regarding microwave oven safe roasting racks. DO NOT USE METAL RACKS DESIGNED FOR OTHER PURPOSES SUCH AS CAKE COOLING RACKS OR BROILER PANS IN YOUR MICROWAVE OVEN.

METAL SKEWERS can be used if there is a large amount of food in proportion to the amount of metal. Take care in the placement of the skewers to avoid arcing between the skewers or between the skewers and the sides of the oven. Wooden skewers are the best and can be easily purchased at your local market, grocery store or in the housewares section of many department stores.

TWIST-TIES enclosed in cooking bags may be used if they are securely wrapped around the closure and do not stick out. (See illustration this page.)

THERMOMETERS are available for use in microwave ovens. See Accessory information, page 8, regarding microwave oven safe thermometers. DO NOT USE CONVENTIONAL MERCURY CANDY OR MEAT THERMOMETERS in food while heating in the microwave oven.

Special Accessories for Microwave Ovens

As more and more consumers are turning to microwave cooking, more and more special accessories are being introduced in the market place. Check to see accessory is easy to handle, fits your needs and is dish-washer safe.
The more popular are explained on next page.

BROWNING DISHES are used to sear chops, meat patties, steaks, etc. The dish is first preheated for several minutes in the microwave oven at Power Select HIGH.
A special coating on the bottom of the dish absorbs the microwave energy and becomes very hot. When foods are added to the dish, the result is a seared affect.

- Preheat dish according to directions accompanying accessory.
- If using oil or butter, add after preheating.
- Add food to be seared and heat according to recipe or personal preference.
- Use pot holders to remove dish from microwave oven.
- Clean in dishwasher or with hot, sudsy water. For burned-on food, use mild cleanser. Do not use plastic mesh pads, steel wool, etc.
- Do not use browning dish on conventional gas or electric surface units, in oven or under broiler.
- Do not use browning dish and temperature probe together.
- Check information included with browning dish for detailed instructions and heating chart.

CAKE BOWLS are available to insure success in baking with microwave energy. Generally, a microwave oven cake is best when baked in a tube shape. Special plastic cake bowls are designed to meet this need.

- Lightly grease before each use.
- Fill ½ full or use about 2 cups batter (a single layer cake mix)
- Do not use in conventional gas or electric oven or expose to heat above 230°F.
- Wash by hand or on upper rack of dishwasher.

Note: *10 to 20 cup cake bowls are available and can be used to bake an entire mix.*

CUPCAKERS are handy when baking cupcakes, muffins and many other surprising things. When making cupcakes, small custard cups can be used to support the batter-filled cupcake paper. During baking, these cups must be rearranged once. Using this plastic ''muffin pan'' simplifies this task and eliminates the need to wash six dishes. The cupcaker can also be used in heating stuffed peppers, baking potatoes, etc.

- Line Cupcaker with cupcake paper.
- Fill ½ full with desired batter (cupcake, muffin, etc.)
- Do not use in conventional gas or electric oven.
- Wash by hand or in upper rack of dishwasher.

ROASTING RACKS, both metal and plastic, have been designed for safe use within your microwave oven. The racks are used inside the baking dish to hold roasts, poultry, etc., out of the drippings that accumulate during heating. An inverted saucer or casserole lid can be used for this purpose. However, the roasting racks hold the item more evenly and securely. DO NOT USE METAL RACKS DESIGNED FOR CAKE COOLING OR BROILING.

- Place rack in glass baking dish.
- Arrange food on rack.
- Cover loosely with wax paper.
- Clean in dishwasher, with steel wool or plastic scrubber.

THERMOMETERS are available for use in microwave cooking, but must be so marked. These specially designed thermometers are used just as regular thermometers are used in conventional ovens. DO NOT USE CONVENTIONAL MEAT OR CANDY THERMOMETERS in food while operating the microwave oven.

PREPARING RECIPES

Ingredients

All ingredients are used as taken from their common storage place, unless otherwise indicated. For example, milk, eggs and butter are used refrigerator cold.
Recipes using canned ingredients include the liquid unless specified DRAINED. Other assumed things unless clarified are:

- flour used is all-purpose
- milk is homogenized whole milk
- sugar is granulated white sugar (100% sucrose)
- eggs are large—Grade A
- amounts given are level measuring units (cup, teaspoon, etc.)

SPECIAL HINT: Pierce the skin or membrane of foods when heated whole in the microwave oven. This allows steam to escape. Forgetting to do this creates the possibility of the food bursting when heated with microwave energy. This is the main reason eggs cannot be hard boiled in their shell. The yolk and white membranes need to be pierced before heating. The same technique is applied to fruits or vegetables with a skin when heated whole (i.e. apples and potatoes).

Browning

Meats and poultry cooked 10 to 15 minutes brown from their own juices. Foods cooked for shorter periods of time can be aided with the help of browning sauce, Worcestershire sauce or soy sauce. Simply brush one of these sauces over the meat or poultry before heating. These sauces do not add or take away from the desired flavor of the recipe. Baked goods do not need long heating times and, therefore, do not brown. When cakes or cupcakes will be frosted, no one will notice this visual difference. For quick breads or muffins, brown sugar can be used in the recipe in place of granulated sugar or the surface can be sprinkled with dark spices before baking.

Spacing

Individual foods, such as baked potatoes and hors d'oeuvres, will heat more evenly if placed in the oven equal distance part. When possible, arrange foods in a circular pattern.

Arrange food in circular pattern

Similarly, when placing foods in a baking dish, arrange around the outside. For example, place six frankfurters around edges of dish; not lined up next to each other. Food should NOT be stacked on top of each other.

Arrange food around edge of dish

Covering

As with conventional cooking, moisture evaporates during microwave cooking. Because microwave cooking is done with time and not oven temperature, the rate of evaporation cannot be as easily controlled. This, however, can be corrected by using different materials to cover dishes. Casserole lids or plastic wrap are used for a tighter seal. Various degrees of moisture retention are also obtained by using wax paper and paper towels.

Unless specified, a recipe is heated uncovered. Heating, covered, refers to a casserole lid or plastic wrap. Other coverings are designated when necessary. When using plastic wrap for a cover, do not seal it tightly around the dish. A small amount of steam must be able to escape: a small slit in the top, or leaving an area around the edge uncovered, meets this need.

Timing

A range in heating time is given in each recipe for two reasons. First, to allow for the uncontrollable differences in food shapes, starting temperature and regional preferences. Secondly, to allow for the differences in electrical volt output power which changes during peak load periods.

Always remember, it is easier to add time to an undercooked product. Once the food is overcooked, little can be done.

In each recipe an APPROXIMATE COOKING TIME is given. If a recipe is cooked in two "batches", the Approx. Cooking Time includes this extra heating time.

Stirring

Stirring is usually necessary during microwave cooking. We have noted when stirring is helpful, using the words once, twice, frequently or occasionally to describe the amount of stirring necessary. It is best to bring the cooked outside edges toward the center and the less cooked center portions toward the outside.

Turning and Rotating

Often it is not possible to stir something to redistribute the heat. At times, microwave energy will concentrate in one area of a food. This is particularly true with meats. Uneven layers of fat will cook faster in the fatty areas if this heating pattern is not broken up. When a dish is rotated, the food will heat more evenly.

In the same manner, some foods should be turned in the container during heating. For example, because of the different thicknesses in the breast and back sections of poultry, a turkey is turned over once during the heating to insure more even cooking.

If your microwave oven is equipped with a turntable, it is not necessary to turn dishes when indicated in various recipes. However, rearranging or turning food over in a dish should be done as indicated to insure a satisfactory end result.

Standing Time

Most foods will continue to cook after the microwave oven is turned off. In meat cookery the internal temperature will rise 5°F to 15°F if allowed to stand, covered, for 10 to 20 minutes.

Casseroles and vegetables need a shorter amount of standing time, but this standing time is necessary to allow foods to complete cooking in the center without overcooking on the edges.

Extra Help

Look for the following symbols. This extra information helps streamline this cookbook to your particular family size and lifestyle.

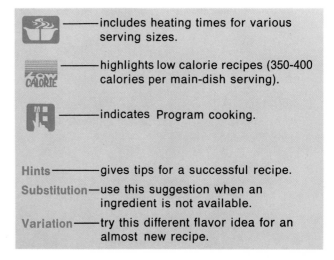

— includes heating times for various serving sizes.

— highlights low calorie recipes (350-400 calories per main-dish serving).

— indicates Program cooking.

Hints — gives tips for a successful recipe.

Substitution — use this suggestion when an ingredient is not available.

Variation — try this different flavor idea for an almost new recipe.

Reheating

Make the best use of leftovers by heating them in your microwave oven. Foods taste fresh and moist when reheated the microwave way.

Below are guidelines to follow when reheating various types of foods. The infinite combinations of foods and amounts to be reheated make it impossible to list all the timing. Just start with this basic information and keep notes on the timings for your common leftovers. You will have no trouble putting leftover foods to good, delicious use.

- Baked goods—Arrange 4 to 6 servings of rolls, biscuits, etc. in microwave oven safe serving container. Heat, covered with paper napkin, at Power Select MEDIUM 1 to 2 minutes. Wrap 1 roll in paper napkin and heat ¼ to ½ minute.

  Hint: *Test baked goods before adding more heating time; when overheated these items become tough and hard.*

- Casseroles—Add a small amount of liquid (stir in if possible) and heat, covered, at Power Select MEDIUM-HIGH. Heat 3 minutes; stir or turn dish, then heat as necessary. If casserole has bread crumb like topping, heat, uncovered, during last part of heating.
- Plates of foods—Arrange food on plate with thicker or larger parts towards rim; top with gravy, butter, etc. Heat, covered with wax paper, at Power Select MEDIUM-HIGH, about 3 minutes.
- Sandwiches—Wrap closed sandwich in paper towel. Heat at Power Select MEDIUM-LOW 1 to 2 minutes. Arrange open-faced sandwich on paper plate; heat, covered with wax paper, 1 to 2 minutes.

Converting Favorite Conventional Recipes

The most difficult decision when converting conventional recipes to microwave cooking is selecting the timing. A basic rule would be to cut the suggested cooking time to one-fourth. It can be very helpful to find a similar microwave recipe and adapt that time and power setting.

Do not salt meats or poultry before cooking. Salt causes meats to toughen and dry out in conventional as well as microwave cooking. Meat can be salted when sliced or as eaten. However, do not hesitate to season meats before cooking with other herbs and spices.

Baked goods rise more when heated in the microwave oven and lose more moisture. Reduce leavening agents by one-fourth (¼) and increase liquids by one-fourth (¼). Refer to Sweets and Treats chapter page 120 for other cake baking hints.

Ingredients for casseroles, stews, etc. should be cut to a uniform size and shape when possible to insure more even cooking.

BEFORE CALLING FOR SERVICE

Many times a service call can be avoided by checking a few simple things. The following conditions are not caused by a defect in the unit itself, so please check the following points before requesting service.

Condition	Time-Saving Checks
No Power	* Oven plugged in? * Check home fuse or circuit breaker.
Oven not operating	* Oven door closed? * Controls set properly?
Oven does not shut off	* Setting of timer or clock (certain models) correct? * Temp. probe properly inserted in food (certain models)?
Takes longer than time in cookbook	* Incorrect power selection? * Low voltage at power outlet? * Starting temp. and shape of foods vary, so simply cook a little longer.
Oven light not illuminated	* Bulb burned out? * Timer set? * Oven door closed?
Uneven cooking	* Rotate food. * Proper wrap or use container for food. * Controls set properly? * For large meat, utilize standing time at room temperature after cooking.
Oven light flickers	* This is normal.
Water condensation around door	* This is normal—merely wipe dry.
Sparks occur	* Metallic wrap or container touching oven wall. * Ceramic ware trimmed in gold or silver.

PRECAUTIONS TO AVOID POSSIBLE EXPOSURE TO EXCESSIVE MICROWAVE ENERGY

(a) **Do not attempt to operate this oven with the door open** since open-door operation can result in harmful exposure to microwave energy. It is important not to defeat or tamper with the safety interlocks.

(b) **Do not place any object** between the oven front face and the door or allow soil or cleaner residue to accumulate on sealing surfaces.

(c) **Do not operate the oven** if it is damaged. It is particularly important that the oven door close properly and that there is no damage to the:
  (1) door (bent)
  (2) hinges and latches (broken or loosened)
  (3) door seals and sealing surfaces

(d) **The oven should not be adjusted or repaired** by anyone except properly qualified service personnel.

If you stop to think about it, our lives are filled with "firsts". And you are about to begin a new cooking experience. Someday soon you will wonder how you ever managed without your microwave oven.

You may not be as nervous as your first driving lesson, but surely you are as excited to see the outcome.

To help you build your collection of favorite meals we have arranged some menu selections for BREAKFAST, LUNCH and DINNER. We have included order of preparation to insure a smooth and relaxed meal. Just complete each meal with coffee, tea, milk, etc. Most menus serve four, unless otherwise noted. See specific recipes or look for symbol for smaller quantity directions.

As your experience grows, it will become easy for you to put together family pleasing meals with this cookbook and some of your favorite recipes you will want to convert for microwave convenience.

Before starting any cooking be sure to read and understand the operating instructions for your microwave oven. Also, the invaluable information in the introduction chapter and in the beginning of each chapter should be read thoroughly. After that...... living is easy!

BREAKFAST

CONTINENTAL BEST

MENU: Assorted Rolls (warmed) and Butter
Breakfast Fruit Tart
Orange Glow (beverage)

ORDER OF PREPARATION:
1. Prepare Breakfast Tart shell according to recipe page 129; heat jam.
2. Heat Orange Glow, page 23.
3. Finish assembling Breakfast Tart.
4. Wrap rolls in paper napkin; heat according to Reheating information page 10.

APPROXIMATE COOKING TIME: 25 minutes

DAD'S FAVORITE

MENU: Welsh Rarebit
Bacon Strips
Cherry Brunch Rolls

ORDER OF PREPARATION:
1. Prepare Cherry Brunch Rolls, page 113; keep covered until ready to serve.
2. Cook Bacon according to chart, page 54. Wrap in paper towel, then aluminum foil to keep warm.
3. Prepare Welsh Rarebit page 88.

APPROXIMATE COOKING TIME: 20 minutes

EARLY BIRD SPECIAL

MENU: Orange Juice
Corn Muffins (from mix)
Saturday's Ham and Egg Scramble

ORDER OF PREPARATION:
1. Prepare Corn Muffins according to chart, page 112. Keep covered until ready to serve.
2. Follow recipe for Saturday's Ham and Egg Scramble, page 87. While eggs are standing, pour juice, set table, etc.

APPROXIMATE COOKING TIME: 20 minutes.

EASY ON THE COOK

MENU: Curried Fruit Compote
Waffles (frozen)
Ham Slices

ORDER OF PREPARATION:
1. Prepare Curried Fruit Compote, page 129. Cover and serve warm.
2. Heat Ham Slices according to chart, page 54. Wrap in aluminum foil to keep warm.
3. Prepare Waffles according to chart, page 138.

APPROXIMATE COOKING TIME: 20 minutes.

MONDAY MORNING EYE OPENER

MENU: Grapefruit Juice
Baked Eggs in Bologna Cups
Raisin Bran Muffins

ORDER OF PREPARATION:
1. Prepare Raisin Bran Muffins, page 116; keep covered until ready to serve.
2. Follow recipe for Baked Eggs in Bologna Cups, page 86. While eggs are heating and standing, pour juice, set table, etc.

APPROXIMATE COOKING TIME: 15 minutes.

WEEKEND SPECIAL

MENU: Orange Juice
Country Breakfast
Baked Apples

ORDER OF PREPARATION:
1. Heat baked potatoes for Country Breakfast, page 104.
2. While potatoes are standing, prepare Baked Apples, page 128. Cover and serve warm.
3. Finish preparing Country Breakfast, page 86. While eggs are heating, pour juice, set table, etc.

APPROXIMATE COOKING TIME: 30 minutes.

Pictured on the preceding page: SUNDAY DINNER— Homemade Gravy, Roast Beef, Fresh Carrots and Green Beans, Mashed Potatoes.

LUNCH ✿✿

LADIES FOR LUNCH

**MENU: Apricot Glazed Chicken
Chicken Flavored Rice (from mix)
Green Beans Amandine
Chilled Chocolate Almond Souffle**

ORDER OF PREPARATION:
1. Prepare Souffle, page 128. NOTE: This recipe requires 3 hours chilling time so prepare early in the day or the night before.
2. Prepare Rice according to chart, page 108. Let stand, covered, until ready to serve.
3. Prepare Apricot Glazed Chicken, page 58. Let stand, covered, until ready to serve.
3. Assemble Green Beans Amandine, page 100 while chicken is heating. Heat beans while chicken is standing.
5. If necessary, reheat rice or chicken 2 to 3 minutes while beans are standing.

APPROXIMATE COOKING TIME: 1 hour

LUNCH FOR THE GANG

**MENU: Hamburgers Your Way
Coleslaw
Apple Fudge Brownies**

ORDER OF PREPARATION:
1. Make favorite coleslaw (or purchase at store); chill.
2. Prepare Apple Fudge Brownies, page 126. Keep covered until ready to serve.
3. Assemble and prepare Hamburgers Your Way, page 90.

APPROXIMATE COOKING TIME: 20 minutes.

PRE-SPORTS SPECTACULAR

**MENU: Tossed Green Salad
Macaroni and Cheese
Marble Brownies with Vanilla Ice Cream
Cape Cod Warmer (beverage)**

ORDER OF PREPARATION:
1. Prepare Marble Brownies, page 126. Keep covered until ready to serve.
2. Make salad while Brownies are heating; chill salad.
3. Cook macaroni for Macaroni and Cheese according to chart, page 106.
4. Assemble Cape Cod Warmer, page 22, while macaroni is heating. Heat Warmer while macaroni is standing; assemble Macaroni and Cheese.
5. Prepare Macaroni and Cheese, page 88.

APPROXIMATE COOKING TIME: 1 hour

RAINY DAY SPECIAL

**MENU: Cup of Split Pea Soup (canned)*
Crispy Croutons
Red Delicious Sandwich
Chocolate Pudding (from mix)**

ORDER OF PREPARATION:
1. Cook Pudding according to chart, page 127; chill.
2. Make Crispy Croutons, page 113.
3. Heat Soup according to chart, page 35.
4. Assemble Sandwiches, page 92, while heating soup. Heat Sandwiches while soup is standing.

APPROXIMATE COOKING TIME: 25 minutes.

***Note:** *If time is available, prepare homemade Savory Split Pea Soup, page 35.*

RODEO LUNCH FOR TWO

**MENU: Round-About Dogs
Pickles Chips
Potato Sticks or Chips
Carrot Spice Cake**

ORDER OF PREPARATION:
1. Prepare Carrot Spice Cake, page 121; keep covered until ready to serve.
2. Prepare Round-About Dogs, page 93.

APPROXIMATE COOKING TIME: 20 minutes.

SATURDAY LUNCH BREAK

**MENU: Tomato Soup (canned)
Meat Loaf Meltwich
Celery Sticks
S' Mores**

ORDER OF PREPARATION:
1. Cut celery into thin strips; chill.
2. Heat Soup according to chart, page 35.
3. Assemble Meat Loaf Meltwich sandwiches, page 91, while soup is heating. Heat sandwiches while soup is standing.
4. Assemble S' Mores, page 127, before eating. Heat after eating, while table is being cleared.

APPROXIMATE COOKING TIME: 11 minutes.

WINTER WARM-UP

**MENU: Brunswick Stew
Tossed Green Salad
Cider Spice Cake with Vanilla Sauce**

ORDER OF PREPARATION:
1. Prepare Cider Spice Cake, page 122; store, covered until ready to serve.
2. Prepare Vanilla Sauce, page 30.
3. Prepare Brunswick Stew, page 36.
4. While stew is heating, assemble salad; chill.

APPROXIMATE COOKING TIME: 1¼ hours.

DINNER ❦❦❦❦❦❦❦❦❦❦❦❦❦❦❦❦❦❦❦❦❦❦❦❦❦❦❦❦❦❦❦❦❦❦❦❦❦❦❦

AFTER WORK HURRY-UP

MENU: **Tossed Green Salad**
Country Ham Casserole
Ice Cream with Hot Fudge Sauce

ORDER OF PREPARATION:
1. Prepare Casserole, page 77.
2. Assemble salad while casserole is heating; chill.
3. After dinner, while the table is being cleared; prepare Hot Fudge Sauce, page 30.

APPROXIMATE COOKING TIME: 40 minutes.

ANY DAY FAMILY FAVORITE

MENU: **Meat Loaf**
Baked Potatoes
Fresh Broccoli
Raisin Bread Pudding

ORDER OF PREPARATION:
1. Prepare Raisin Bread Pudding, page 128.
2. Prepare Midget Meat Loaf, page 46.
3. While Meat Loaf is standing, bake potatoes, page 104. Wrap potatoes in aluminum foil <u>after</u> heating.
4. Prepare Broccoli according to chart, page 97.

APPROXIMATE COOKING TIME: 45 minutes.

BAYOU BANQUET

MENU: **Shrimp Creole**
Rice (instant)
Okra (frozen)
Siesta Cornbread
Pecan Pie

ORDER OF PREPARATION:
1. Prepare Pecan Pie, page 132.
2. Prepare Cornbread, page 114; keep covered until ready to serve.
3. Prepare Shrimp Creole, page 72.
4. Prepare Rice (Instant) according to chart, page 108.
5. Prepare Okra according to chart, page 98.

APPROXIMATE COOKING TIME: 45 minutes.

BEAT THE CLOCK

MENU: **Oven-Fried Pork Chops**
Hot German Potato Salad
Green Beans (canned)
Gingerbread Pear Cobbler

ORDER OF PREPARATION:
1. Prepare Gingerbread Cobbler, page 130. Keep covered until ready to serve.
2. Assemble Potato Salad according to recipe page 103 using canned sliced potatoes. Let stand, covered; serve warm.
3. Prepare Pork Chops, page 51.
4. While Pork Chops are standing, heat Green Beans, page 139.

APPROXIMATE COOKING TIME: 40 minutes.

COMPANY ELEGANCE (*Serving 6*)

MENU: **Vichyssoise**
Beef Bourguignon
Buttered Noodles
Tossed Green Salad
Strawberry Souffle

ORDER OF PREPARATION:
1. Prepare Souffle according to Superb Strawberry Souffle recipe page 128; chill. NOTE: This recipe requires 3 hours chilling time so prepare early in the day or the night before.
2. Prepare Vichyssoise according to recipe page 35; chill.
3. Prepare Beef Bourguignon according to recipe page 41
4. Assemble salad while beef is cooking; chill.
5. Cook Noodles according to chart, page 106, while beef is standing.

APPROXIMATE COOKING TIME: 1¾ hours.

EASY FIXIN'S

MENU: **Ham Steak with Raisin Sauce**
Baked Stuffed Potatoes
Orange Glazed Carrots
Toffee Fondue

ORDER OF PREPARATION:
1. Prepare Stuffed Potatoes, page 102. Let stand, covered, until ready to serve.
2. Prepare Ham Steak, page 50. Let stand, covered until ready to serve.
3. Heat Carrots according to recipe, page 101.
4. After dinner, while table is being cleared, prepare Toffee Fondue, page 125.

APPROXIMATE COOKING TIME: 45 minutes.

Sourthern Hospitality: Short Ribs with Barbecue Sauce, page 15

ENTERTAINING EASE (*Serving 6*)

MENU: **Paella**
Asparagus Spears (fresh)
Caramel Custard

ORDER OF PREPARATION:
1. Prepare Caramel Custard according to variation of Basic Egg Custard, page 127, chill.
2. Prepare Paella, page 80.
3. While Paella is standing, heat Asparagus according to chart, page 97.

APPROXIMATE COOKING TIME: 1¼ hours.

KIDS COOK

MENU: **Tender Crispy Chicken**
Spanish Rice
Carrots (frozen)
Banana Splits

ORDER OF PREPARATION:
1. Prepare Spanish Rice, page 109; Let stand, covered, until ready to serve.
2. While rice is standing, heat chicken, page 62; let stand, covered, until ready to serve.
3. Prepare Carrots according to chart, page 97.
4. After dinner, while table is being cleared, prepare Banana Split Topping, page 29. Serve over favorite ice cream.

APPROXIMATE COOKING TIME: 1 hour.

MID-WEEK CELEBRATION

MENU: **Cornish Hens with Peach Sauce**
Stuffing (chicken flavor mix)
Brussel Sprouts (fresh)
German Chocolate Upside-Down Cake

ORDER OF PREPARATION:
1. Prepare Chocolate Cake, page 123; keep covered until ready to serve.
2. Prepare Cornish Hens with Peach Sauce, page 63; let stand, covered, until ready to serve.
3. Prepare Stuffing Mix, page 65.
4. While stuffing is standing, heat Brussel Sprouts according to chart, page 97.

APPROXIMATE COOKING TIME: 45 minutes.

PLEASING POULTRY

MENU: **Hawaiian Island Chicken**
Buttered Crumb Potatoes
Sliced Zucchini (fresh)
Chocolate Pound Cake

ORDER OF PREPARATION:
1. Prepare Chocolate Pound Cake, page 121; keep covered until ready to serve.
2. Prepare Hawaiian Island Chicken, page 61; let stand, covered, until ready to serve.
3. Prepare Buttered Crumb Potatoes, page 102.
4. While Potatoes are standing, prepare Zucchini according to chart, page 98.

APPROXIMATE COOKING TIME: 50 minutes.

ROMAN FISH BAKE (*Serving 6*)

MENU: **Fillet Provencale**
Spaghetti
Relish Tray
Festive Rum Cake

ORDER OF PREPARTION:
1. Prepare Rum Cake, page 122; keep covered until ready to serve.
2. Prepare Spaghetti according to chart, page 106. Drain; cover until ready to serve.
3. Assemble a relish tray while Spaghetti is heating; chill.
4. Prepare Fillet Provencale, page 70; let stand, covered, until ready to serve.

APPROXIMATE COOKING TIME: 55 minutes.

SOUTHERN HOSPITALITY

MENU: **Short Ribs with Barbecue Sauce**
Corn on the Cob (fresh or frozen)
Chunky Applesauce
Southern Cheese Spoon Bread
Chocolate Rocky Road Pie

ORDER OF PREPARATION:
1. Prepare Chocolate Rocky Road Pie, page 131; chill.
2. Prepary Chunky Applesauce, page 129; chill, if desired.
3. Prepare Short Ribs with Barbecue Sauce, page 45.
4. Prepare Spoon Bread, page 114. Heat while ribs are standing. Let stand, covered.
5. Prepare Corn on the Cob according to chart, page 97.

APPROXIMATE COOKING TIME: 2 hours.

SUNDAY DINNER (*Serving 6*)

MENU: **Roast Beef**
Mashed Potatoes
Green Beans Amandine
Coconut Lemon Meringue Pie

ORDER OF PREPARATION:
1. Prepare Lemon Meringue Pie, page 131.
2. Prepare Roast Beef according to chart, page 40.
3. While Roast is standing, heat Potatoes, page 103; mash then let stand, covered.
4. While Potatoes are standing, heat Green Beans Amandine, page 100.

APPROXIMATE COOKING TIME: 1 hour (with 3 lb. roast beef—MEDIUM).

No longer will it be host in the kitchen and guests in the livingroom! Your microwave oven can free you from the pacing and waiting for hot hors d'oeuvres to finally be ready. Piping hot nibbles will take only minutes to reheat in your microwave oven. And the oven turns off automatically after a set time...no forgotten disasters.

Charm even your youngest visitor with unique hot beverages. We guarantee HOT SCOTCHIE to be a favorite! It is so easy to have something deliciously different, you won't wait for company to treat yourself to a special drink.

APPETIZERS

APPETIZER PÂTÉ

Power Select: HIGH→MEDIUM
Approx. Cooking Time: 7 minutes
Yield: about 1⅓ cups

1 pound chicken livers, halved
½ cup chicken broth
⅓ cup chopped onion
¼ teaspoon thyme
4 slices bacon, cooked (see page 54)
¼ cup butter or margarine, softened*
1 tablespoon sherry (optional)
½ teaspoon garlic salt
Dash pepper
Parsley flakes

Set Power Select at HIGH. In medium glass bowl, combine livers, broth, onion and thyme. Heat, covered, 2 to 3 minutes.
Set Power Select at MEDIUM. Heat 3 to 4 minutes or until livers are tender, stirring once. Drain and reserve ¼ cup liquid.
With electric mixer, blender or food processor, puree liver and onion mixture, reserved broth, bacon, butter, sherry, garlic and pepper until smooth. Spoon into crock or small bowl; sprinkle with parsley and chill. Serve as a spread with crackers.

***Hint:** To soften butter in your microwave oven, see Quick Tips, page 140.*

Assorted Appetizers and Hors d'oeuvres

BACON BITES

Power Select: HIGH
Approx. Cooking Time: 4 minutes
Yield: 8 hors d'oeuvres

4 slices bacon, halved
8 frozen potato puffs, canned pineapple chunks or water chestnuts

Set Power Select at HIGH. Between layers of paper towel on paper plate, heat bacon 1½ to 2 minutes or until partially cooked. Wrap bacon around potato and secure with toothpick. Arrange on paper towel lined paper plate and heat 1½ to 2 minutes.

CHICKEN TOASTIES

Power Select: MEDIUM-HIGH
Approx. Cooking Time: 6 minutes
Yield: 24 hors d'oeuvres

2 cans (5 oz. ea.) boned chicken, drained and flaked*
3 tablespoons mayonnaise
2 tablespoons parsley flakes
2 tablespoons dry bread crumbs
2 tablespoons dried onion flakes
¼ teaspoon curry powder
1 egg, beaten
½ cup dry bread crumbs

Combine chicken, mayonnaise, parsley, 2 tablespoons bread crumbs, onion and curry; shape into 24 balls. Dip each ball in egg and then roll in remaining bread crumbs; chill.
Set Power Select at MEDIUM-HIGH. Arrange 12 on paper plate and heat 2½ to 3 minutes; repeat procedure. Serve, if desired, with curried mayonnaise or mustard sauce.

***Substitution:** Use 1¼ cups cut-up cooked chicken.*

CHILI DIP OLÉ

Power Select: HIGH
Temperature Select: 145°F
Approx. Cooking Time: 8 minutes
Yield: about 2 cups

½ pound ground beef
½ cup finely chopped onion
1 envelope (1¼ oz.) chili seasoning mix
1 can (6 oz.) tomato paste
1 tablespoon sugar (optional)
Corn chips

Pictured on the preceding page: Nuts and Bolts Party Mix, Marinated Vegetable Bites, Stuffed Mushrooms, Café Brûlot, Orange Glow, Cape Cod Warmer, Appetizer Pâté

Set Power Select at HIGH. In medium glass bowl, crumble ground beef; stir in onions. Heat 3 to 4 minutes, or until beef is browned, stirring once; drain. Stir in chili seasoning, tomato paste and sugar.

TO HEAT BY TEMPERATURE: Insert probe into dip. Set Temperature Select at 145°F.

TO HEAT BY TIME: Set time 3 to 4 minutes.

Heat; serve warm with corn chips.

COCKTAIL REUBENS

Power Select: MEDIUM
Approx. Cooking Time: 9 minutes
Yield: 36 hors d'oeuvres

36 slices party-size rye bread
½ cup creamy Russian dressing
¼ pound thinly sliced corned beef
1 can (8 oz.) sauerkraut, drained
6 slices (rectangular) Swiss cheese, each cut into 6 pieces

Set Power Select at MEDIUM. Spread bread with dressing; top with corned beef, sauerkraut and cheese. Arrange 12 on paper plate or serving platter and heat 2½ to 3 minutes or until cheese is melted; repeat procedure.

CRANBERRY GLAZED FANTAIL FRANKS

Power Select: HIGH
Approx. Cooking Time: 9 minutes
Yield: about 36 hors d'oeuvres

1 can (8 oz.) whole berry or jellied cranberry sauce
1½ tablespoons prepared mustard
1 tablespoon lemon juice
1 pound cocktail frankfurters*

Set Power Select at HIGH. In square baking dish, combine cranberry sauce, mustard and lemon juice. Heat 2 to 3 minutes, stirring once.
Meanwhile, cut a lengthwise slit in each frankfurter cutting through at each end. Stir into glaze mixture. Heat 5 to 6 minutes or until heated through, stirring once.
To serve, skewer frankfurters with toothpicks.

*****Substitution:** *Use 1 pound frankfurters, cut into 1½-inch pieces for cocktail frankfurters.*

CRUNCHY VEGETABLE MUNCHIES 🔲

Power Select: HIGH→STAND
Approx. Cooking Time: 8 minutes
Yield: about 24 hors d'oeuvres

1 head (about 1½ lb.) cauliflower*
1 package (2⅜ oz.) Italian flavored seasoned coating mix

Set Power Select at HIGH. Cut cauliflower into about 24 flowerets; rinse. Empty coating mix into plastic bag and coat cauliflowerets. On paper plate, arrange 12 in circular pattern and heat 3 to 4 minutes or until tender. Let STAND 2 minutes before serving; repeat procedure.

*****Variation:** *Use 1 pound zucchini, cut into ½-inch slices.*

HOLIDAY CHEESE BALL

Power Select: WARM
Approx. Cooking Time: 8 minutes
Yield: 1 (6 inch) ball

1 package (3 oz.) cream cheese, softened*
3 cups shredded Cheddar cheese (about 12 oz.)
¼ cup flour
¼ cup white wine
¼ teaspoon onion powder
⅛ teaspoon garlic powder
⅛ teaspoon Worcestershire sauce
⅓ cup finely chopped nuts or parsley flakes

Set Power Select at WARM. In medium glass bowl, combine cream cheese, cheddar cheese, flour, wine, onion, garlic and Worcestershire; heat 5 minutes. With electric mixer, beat until smooth. Shape into ball and roll in nuts; chill.
To serve, heat 3 minutes at WARM or until spreadable.

*****Hint:** *To soften cream cheese in your microwave, see Quick Tips, page 140.*

INDIVIDUAL CHEESE TARTS 🔲

Power Select: HIGH
           MEDIUM→STAND
Approx. Cooking Time: 6 minutes
Yield: 6 servings

2 slices bacon, diced
1½ tablespoons finely chopped onion
6 pastry shells, baked (about 2½-in. diameter)
6 tablespoons shredded Swiss cheese
2 eggs, beaten
½ to ¾ cup whipping cream*
Parsley flakes

Set Power Select at HIGH. In small glass bowl, heat bacon and onion 2 to 2½ minutes or until bacon is crisp and onion is tender, stirring once, drain.
On 12-inch glass plate, arrange shells in circular pattern; into each, sprinkle bacon and onion and then cheese. Add eggs beaten with cream; sprinkle with parsley.
Set Power Select at MEDIUM. Heat 3 to 3½ minutes or until tarts are almost set, turning dish once. Let STAND 5 minutes before serving.

**The amount of cream used will depend upon the actual size of pastry shells.*

LAREDO STYLE NACHOS

Power Select: HIGH
Approx. Cooking Time: 2 minutes
Yield: about 20

Corn, taco or tortilla chips
Canned bean dip
Guacamole dip (optional)
Jalapeno peppers, sliced (optional)
Shredded Monterey Jack cheese

Set Power Select at HIGH. Spread 20 chips with bean dip and guacamole dip; top with peppers and cheese. Arrange on wax paper lined glass oven tray or serving plate. Heat 1 to 2 minutes or until cheese is melted; serve immediately. Repeat procedure as desired.

MARINATED VEGETABLE BITES

Power Select: HIGH
Approx. Cooking Time: 7 minutes
Yield: about 4 cups

4 cups cut-up fresh vegetables (about ½-in. pieces)
½ cup Italian dressing

Set Power Select at HIGH. In oblong baking dish, toss vegetables with Italian dressing; heat, covered, 6 to 7 minutes or until vegetables are crisp-tender, stirring once. Chill before serving.

Hint: *Choose a variety of vegetables that heat in about the same time (see Vegetable chart, page 97). If using vegetables with different heating times, cut vegetable with shorter heating time into larger pieces.*

MEATBALL MORSELS

Power Select: MEDIUM
Approx. Cooking Time: 7 minutes
Yield: about 36 meatballs

1 pound ground beef
1 egg
½ cup soft bread crumbs
¼ cup catsup
1 tablespoon parsley flakes
1 teaspoon onion powder
1 teaspoon salt
⅛ teaspoon pepper

Set Power Select at MEDIUM. Thoroughly combine all ingredients; shape into 1-inch meatballs (about 36). In oblong baking dish, arrange meatballs; heat 6 to 7 minutes, stirring once and draining liquid when necessary.
Serve with favorite sauce or gravy. See Sauces and Toppings chapter (page 25) for easy microwave accompaniments.

MEXICALI FIESTA DIP

Power Select: MEDIUM-LOW
Approx. Cooking Time: 10 minutes
Yield: about 3 cups

1 pound pasteurized process cheese spread, cubed
1 can (16 oz.) whole tomatoes, drained and chopped
1 can (4 oz.) green chilies, drained and chopped
Dash hot pepper sauce
Taco chips

Set Power Select at MEDIUM-LOW. In large glass bowl, combine cheese, tomatoes, chilies and pepper sauce. Heat 9 to 10 minutes or until cheese is melted, stirring occasionally. Serve warm with taco chips.

NEPTUNE'S CHEESE CANAPES

Power Select: LOW
                  MEDIUM
Approx. Cooking Time: 6 minutes
Yield: 48 hors d'oeuvres

1 package (10 oz.) sharp Cheddar cold pack cheese food
⅓ cup butter or margarine

1 can (6 oz.) crabmeat, drained and flaked*
1 tablespoon flour
Dash hot pepper sauce
6 English muffins, split and toasted

Set Power Select at LOW. In medium glass bowl, heat cheese and butter 1½ to 2 minutes or until softened. Stir in crab, flour and pepper sauce; spread on muffins. Cut each muffin into quarters and garnish, if desired, with pimento or paprika.
Set Power Select at MEDIUM. On paper plate or glass serving tray, arrange 12 canapes and heat ½ to 1 minute or until crab mixture begins to melt; repeat procedure.

*Substitution: *Use 1 can (7 oz.) tuna, drained and flaked.*

NUTS AND BOLTS PARTY MIX

Power Select: MEDIUM-HIGH
Approx. Cooking Time: 9 minutes
Yield: about 2 quarts

½ cup butter or margarine
2 tablespoons Worcestershire sauce
½ teaspoon garlic salt
½ teaspoon salt
2 cups bite-size crispy corn squares
2 cups bite-size crispy rice squares
2 cups bite-size crispy wheat squares
1 cup salted peanuts
1 cup thin pretzel sticks

Set Power Select at MEDIUM-HIGH. In oblong baking dish, heat butter 1 to 1½ minutes or until melted; stir in Worcestershire, garlic and salt. Add remaining ingredients, stirring well.
Heat 6 to 7 minutes or until butter is absorbed and mixture is crispy, stirring occasionally.
Let cool before serving or storing.

PARTY BLUE CHEESE SPREAD

Power Select: HIGH
Approx. Cooking Time: 3 minutes
Yield: about 3 cups

1 envelope unflavored gelatin
¾ cup water
1 tablespoon lemon juice
1 package (3 oz.) cream cheese, softened*
⅓ cup milk
¼ pound blue cheese, crumbled
½ cup sour cream
¼ cup diced green pepper or finely chopped walnuts
2 teaspoons Worcestershire sauce

Set Power Select at HIGH. In small glass bowl, sprinkle unflavored gelatin over water. Heat 2½ to 3 minutes or until gelatin is dissolved, stirring twice. Add lemon juice; cool slightly.
In medium bowl, blend cream cheese and milk until smooth; stir in blue cheese, sour cream, green pepper, Worcestershire and gelatin mixture.
Turn into 3-cup mold or bowl and chill until firm. Unmold and serve with crackers as a spread.

*Hint: *To soften cream cheese in your microwave, see Quick Tips, page 140.*

SESAME CHEESE WAFERS

Power Select: MEDIUM-LOW→STAND
Approx. Cooking Time: 14 minutes
Yield: 48 wafers

1 jar (8 oz.) processed cheese spread
6 tablespoons butter or margarine, softened*
1 to 1¼ cups flour
Dash hot pepper sauce
3 tablespoons sesame seeds, toasted

Blend cheese, butter, flour and pepper sauce until smooth. On lightly floured board, roll mixture into two logs (6 in. ea.); roll in sesame seeds. Wrap in wax paper and chill until firm.
Set Power Select at MEDIUM-LOW. Cut each cheese log into ¼-inch slices. On paper plate, arrange 12 in circular pattern. Heat 3 to 3½ minutes. Let STAND 1 minute before removing to serving platter with spatula.

Hint: *To soften butter in your microwave oven, see Quick Tips, page 140.*

SPICED NUTS

Power Select: HIGH
Approx. Cooking Time: 6 minutes
Yield: about 2 cups

2 tablespoons butter or margarine
1 to 2 tablespoons curry powder
1 tablespoon Worcestershire sauce
2 cups blanched almonds

Set Power Select at HIGH. In oblong baking dish, heat butter 1 minute or until melted; stir in curry and Worcestershire. Add almonds and coat thoroughly. Heat 4 to 5 minutes, stirring twice; cool.

Variations:
For CHILI CASHEWS, *stir 1 to 2 tablespoons chili powder and 2 cups salted cashews into melted butter.*
For GINGER WALNUTS, *stir 1 to 2 tablespoons ground ginger, 1 tablespoon soy sauce and 2 cups walnuts into melted butter.*

STUFFED MUSHROOMS

Power Select: HIGH
                HIGH→STAND
Approx. Cooking Time: 18 minutes
Yield: about 24 mushrooms

1 pound medium fresh mushrooms (about 24), cleaned
4 slices bacon, chopped
¼ cup finely chopped onion
1 cup soft bread crumbs
¼ cup grated Parmesan cheese
¼ teaspoon pepper

Set Power Select at HIGH. Remove mushroom stems and finely chop 1 cup; reserve.
In medium glass bowl, heat bacon and onion 3 to 3½ minutes or until bacon is crisp, stirring once; drain.
Stir in reserved mushroom stems, bread crumbs, cheese and pepper.
Stuff mushroom caps with bread crumb mixture and on glass platter, arrange 12 in circular pattern. Heat, covered, 6 to 7 minutes at HIGH, turning dish once. Let STAND uncovered, 2 minutes before serving; repeat procedure.

Variation:
For SPINACH stuffed mushrooms, *partially thaw 1 package (12 oz.) frozen spinach souffle. Cut into squares and place in mushroom caps; sprinkle, if desired, with onion salt. Heat as directed above.*

SWISS MELTS

Power Select: MEDIUM
Approx. Cooking Time: 6 minutes
Yield: about 40 hors d'oeuvres

1 cup (8 oz.) sour cream*
2 envelopes (¼ oz. ea.) instant onion soup*
Whole wheat crackers (about 40)
5 slices (rectangular) Swiss cheese, each cut into 8 squares

Set Power Select at MEDIUM. Thoroughly combine sour cream and instant soup; spread ½ tablespoon on each cracker and top with cheese. On paper plate or glass serving tray, arrange ⅓ crackers in circular pattern; heat 1 to 2 minutes or until cheese begins to melt, turning plate once. Repeat procedure with remaining crackers.

Substitution: *Use 1 container (8 oz.) ready-to-serve onion dip.*

TANGY SAUCY SHRIMP

Power Select: HIGH→MEDIUM
                MEDIUM→STAND
Approx. Cooking Time: 18 minutes
Yield: about 4 servings

½ cup chili sauce
½ cup pickle relish
½ cup beer
½ pound medium shrimp, shelled and cleaned

Set Power Select at HIGH. In medium glass bowl, combine chili sauce, pickle relish and beer; heat 3 to 4 minutes, stirring once.
Set Power Select at MEDIUM. Heat 10 minutes or until sauce is thickened, stirring occasionally. Stir in shrimp and heat 3 to 4 minutes at MEDIUM or until shrimp is tender, stirring once. Let STAND, covered, 2 minutes. To serve, arrange on small plates or skewer with picks.

Cranberry Glazed Fantail Franks, page 19

BEVERAGES ᵜᵜᵜᵜᵜᵜᵜᵜᵜᵜᵜᵜᵜᵜᵜᵜᵜᵜᵜᵜᵜᵜᵜᵜᵜᵜᵜᵜᵜᵜᵜᵜᵜᵜᵜᵜᵜᵜᵜ

HEATING LIQUIDS CHART For tea, instant coffee, hot chocolate mix, instant soups, hot cereal, recipes, etc.

DESIRED TEMPERATURE	LIQUID	AMOUNT	POWER SELECT	APPROXIMATE HEATING TIME (in minutes)
Boiling (212°F)	Water	1 cup (8 oz.)	HIGH	2 to 3
		2 cups (16 oz.)	HIGH	4 to 5
		4 cups (32 oz.)	HIGH	8 to 9
Scalding (about 150°F)	Milk	1 cup (8 oz.)	MEDIUM	2½ to 3½
		2 cups (16 oz.)	MEDIUM	4 to 5
Steaming (for beverages) (140°F to 150°F)	Water	1 mug (8 oz.)	HIGH	1 to 1½
		2 mugs (8 oz. ea.)	HIGH	2 to 2½
		4 mugs (8 oz. ea.)	HIGH	3½ to 4
		1 coffee cup (5 oz.)	HIGH	¾ to 1¼
		2 coffee cups (5 oz. ea.)	HIGH	1½ to 2
		4 coffee cups (5 oz. ea.)	HIGH	3 to 3½
	Milk	1 mug (8 oz.)	MEDIUM	2 to 3
		2 mugs (8 oz. ea.)	MEDIUM	3½ to 6
		4 mugs (8 oz. ea.)	MEDIUM	6 to 7½
		1 coffee cup (5 oz.)	MEDIUM	1½ to 2
		2 coffee cups (5 oz. ea.)	MEDIUM	2 to 3
		4 coffee cups (5 oz. ea.)	MEDIUM	4 to 5

BRAZILIAN COFFEE

Power Select: HIGH
Approx. Cooking Time: 4 minutes
Yield: 4 servings (8 oz. ea.)

4 cups strong coffee*
8 tablespoons instant cocoa mix
Sugar to taste
8 tablespoons vanilla, chocolate or coffee ice cream
Ground cinnamon

Set Power Select at HIGH. Into each of 4 mugs, pour 1 cup coffee; heat 3½ to 4 minutes. For each drink, stir in 2 tablespoons cocoa mix and sugar. Top with 2 tablespoons ice cream and a dash cinnamon.

***Hint:** If using instant or freeze-dried coffee, stir in coffee after heating water.*

Note: **For TWO servings,** *follow above procedure. Halve all ingredients and heat coffee 2 to 2½ minutes.*
For ONE serving, *heat coffee 1 to 1½ minutes.*

CAFE BRÛLOT

Power Select: HIGH
Approx. Cooking Time: 1 minute
Yield: about 6 demitasse servings

⅓ to ½ cup brandy
1 tablespoon sugar
3 whole cloves
1 stick cinnamon, broken
Peel of 1 lemon or orange
2 cups hot strong coffee

Set Power Select at HIGH. In 1-cup glass measure, combine brandy, sugar, cloves, cinnamon and lemon peel. Heat ¾ to 1 minute; stir.
Carefully flame and strain brandy into coffee. Serve in demitasse cups.

Variation: *If desired, pour coffee into cups. Top with heated brandy; flame.*

CAPE COD WARMER

Power Select: HIGH→MEDIUM-LOW
Approx. Cooking Time: 16 minutes
Yield: about 4 servings (6 oz. ea.)

3 cups cranapple or cranberry juice
8 whole allspices
8 whole cloves
4 cinnamon sticks, broken

Set Power Select at HIGH. In 4-cup glass measure, combine all ingredients; Heat 5 to 6 minutes.
Set Power Select at MEDIUM-LOW. Heat 9 to 10 minutes. To serve, cool slightly; strain into mugs.

Note: **For TWO servings,** *follow above procedure. Halve all ingredients and heat juice at HIGH 3 to 3½ minutes; at MEDIUM-LOW 5 minutes.*
For ONE serving, *heat juice at HIGH 1½ to 2½ minutes; at MEDIUM-LOW 3 minutes.*

ENGLISH WASSAIL CHEER

Power Select: HIGH→MEDIUM-LOW
Approx. Cooking Time: 17 minutes
Yield: about 6 servings (6 oz. ea.)

4 cups apple cider
¼ cup lemon juice
¼ cup brown sugar
½ teaspoon whole allspice
½ teaspoon whole cloves
⅛ teaspoon ground nutmeg

Set Power Select at HIGH. In medium glass bowl, combine all ingredients; heat 8 to 9 minutes. Set Power Select at MEDIUM-LOW. Heat 7 to 8 minutes. To serve, cool slightly; strain into mugs.

HOT BUTTERED RUM

Power Select: HIGH
Approx. Cooking Time: 4 minutes
Yield: 4 servings (about 6 oz. ea.)

2⅔ cups apple cider or water
4 cinnamon sticks
4 tablespoons brown sugar
6 ounces rum
4 teaspoons butter or margarine
Ground nutmeg

Set Power Select at HIGH. Into each of 4 mugs, combine ⅔ cup cider, 1 cinnamon stick and 1 tablespoon sugar; heat 3½ to 4 minutes. For each drink, stir in 1½ ounces rum; top with 1 teaspoon butter and dash nutmeg.

Note: **For TWO servings,** *follow above procedure. Halve all ingredients; heat cider 1½ to 2 minutes.* **For ONE serving,** *heat cider 1 to 1½ minutes.*

HOT SCOTCHIE

Power Select: HIGH
           MEDIUM
Approx. Cooking Time: 11 minutes
Yield: 4 servings (8 oz. ea.)

8 tablespoons butterscotch flavored pieces
4 cups milk
Ground cinnamon
8 tablespoons mini-marshmallows

Set Power Select at HIGH. Into each of 4 mugs, add 2 tablespoons butterscotch pieces; heat 2 to 2½ minutes. For each drink, stir in 1 cup milk and dash ground cinnamon. Set Power Select at MEDIUM. Heat 6 to 7 minutes; stir in marshmallows. Heat ¾ to 1 minute.

Note: **For TWO servings,** *follow above procedure; halve all ingredients. Heat butterscotch 1¼ to 1¾ minutes, milk 3½ to 4 minutes and marshmallows ½ to ¾ minute.* **For ONE serving,** *heat butterscotch ¾ to 1 minute, milk 2 to 2½ minutes and marshmallows ½ minute.*

IRISH COFFEE

Power Select: HIGH
Approx. Cooking Time: 4 minutes
Yield: 4 servings (about 6 oz. ea.)

2 to 3 cups strong coffee
4 teaspoons sugar
6 ounces Irish whiskey
Sweetened whipped cream

Set Power Select at HIGH. Into each of 4 cups, pour ½ to ¾ cup coffee; heat 3 to 3½ minutes. For each drink, stir in 1 teaspoon sugar and 1½ ounces Irish whiskey; top with whipped cream.

Note: **For TWO servings,** *follow above procedure. Halve all ingredients; heat coffee 1½ to 2 minutes.* **For ONE serving,** *heat coffee 1 to 1½ minutes.*

MULLED WINE

Power Select: MEDIUM
Approx. Cooking Time: 6 minutes
Yield: 4 servings (6 oz. ea.)

3 cups dry red wine
8 teaspoons brown sugar or to taste
2 cinnamon sticks, broken
Ground nutmeg

Set Power Select at MEDIUM. Into each of 4 mugs, combine ¾ cup wine, 2 teaspoons brown sugar, ½ cinnamon stick and dash nutmeg. Heat 4½ to 6 minutes.

Note: **For TWO servings,** *follow above procedure. Halve all ingredients; heat wine 3½ to 4½ minutes.* **For ONE serving,** *heat wine 1½ to 2½ minutes.*

ORANGE GLOW

Power Select: HIGH→MEDIUM-LOW
Approx. Cooking Time: 14 minutes
Yield: about 4 servings (8 oz. ea.)

3 cups apricot nectar
1 cup orange juice
2 cinnamon sticks, broken
1 teaspoon whole cloves

Set Power Select at HIGH. In 4-cup glass measure, combine all ingredients and heat 7 to 8 minutes. Set Power Select at MEDIUM-LOW. Heat 5 to 6 minutes. To serve, strain into mugs and garnish, if desired, with orange slices.

Variation: *Into each mug, stir in ½ tablespoon rum.*

TEA JAMMER

Power Select: HIGH
Approx. Cooking Time: 4 minutes
Yield: 4 servings (8 oz. ea.)

3 cups water
4 tea bags
4 tablespoons apricot preserves*
4 tablespoons apricot brandy (optional)*
Sugar to taste
Sweetened whipped cream or whipped topping
Ground nutmeg or cinnamon

Set Power Select at HIGH. Into each of 4 mugs, pour ¾ cup water; heat 3 to 3½ minutes. For each drink, add one tea bag; brew 3 to 5 minutes. Stir in 1 tablespoon preserves, 1 tablespoon brandy and sugar. Top with whipped cream and dash nutmeg.

***Variation:** *Try a variety of jelly, jam or preserves and fruit-flavored brandies.*

Note: **For TWO servings,** *follow above procedure. Halve all ingredients; heat water 2 to 2½ minutes.* **For ONE serving,** *heat water 1 to 1½ minutes.*

NOTES

Do not skip over this chapter because you think sauces are difficult to make and only for the gourmet cook. With the speedy assistance of your microwave oven, savory sauces and delicious dessert toppings are a snap. Make a zesty Creole Sauce to liven-up leftovers. Once you have served homemade Hot Fudge Sauce or Banana Split Topping—your family will always want homemade sundaes!

Sauces and toppings can disguise Sunday's pork roast as Sweet and Sour Pork, add a gourmet flair to company fare, or add a special touch to your favorite dessert. Whatever your reason, the recipes in this chapter are sure to fit into your daily meal planning.

SAUCES

BARBECUE SAUCE

Power Select: HIGH→MEDIUM-LOW
Approx. Cooking Time: 15 minutes
Yield: about 2 cups

1 cup chili sauce
¾ cup water
¼ cup lemon juice
1 envelope (1⅜ oz.) onion soup mix
½ cup brown sugar
1 teaspoon dry mustard
⅛ teaspoon garlic powder

Set Power Select at HIGH. In medium glass bowl, combine all ingredients; heat 5 minutes, stirring once. Set Power Select at MEDIUM-LOW. Heat 8 to 10 minutes or until sauce is slightly thickened, stirring twice. Use as a basting sauce on chicken, ribs, hamburgers, etc.

BASIC WHITE SAUCE

Power Select: MEDIUM
Approx. Cooking Time: 7 minutes
Yield: about 1 cup

2 tablespoons butter or margarine
2 tablespoons flour
½ teaspoon salt (optional)
1 cup milk

Set Power Select at MEDIUM. In small glass bowl, heat butter ½ to ¾ minute or until melted; stir in flour and salt. Gradually add milk, stirring until smooth. Heat 5 to 6 minutes or until sauce is thickened, stirring occasionally.

Variations:
For CHEESE Sauce, *stir in ½ to ¾ cup shredded cheese. Heat 1 minute, if necessary, to completely melt cheese.*
For CURRY Sauce, *stir in 1 to 2 teaspoons curry powder.*
For HORSERADISH Sauce, *add 1 tablespoon prepared horseradish.*
For MUSTARD Sauce, *add 2 tablespoons prepared mustard and dash Worcestershire sauce.*

BEARNAISE SAUCE

Power Select: HIGH
              MEDIUM-LOW
Approx. Cooking Time: 4 minutes
Yield: about ½ cup

¼ cup finely chopped onion
2 tablespoons wine vinegar
4 egg yolks
¼ cup butter or margarine
1 teaspoon parsley flakes

Set Power Select at HIGH. In small glass bowl, heat onion and vinegar 1 to 1½ minutes. Stir in egg yolks until well blended.
Set Power Select at MEDIUM-LOW. Heat 1 to 1½ minutes or until sauce is thickened, stirring twice; stir in butter until melted. Heat ¼ to ½ minute, stirring once. Strain and sprinkle with parsley.

BORDELAISE SAUCE

Power Select: HIGH
Approx. Cooking Time: 8 minutes
Yield: about 1 cup

2 tablespoons finely chopped onion
1 tablespoon butter or margarine
½ cup red wine
1 bay leaf
2 teaspoons cornstarch
½ cup beef broth
1 teaspoon butter
1 teaspoon parsley flakes

Set Power Select at HIGH. In 2-cup glass measure, heat onion and butter 1 to 1½ minutes; add wine and bay leaf. Heat 3½ to 4 minutes or until mixture is reduced to ⅓ cup. Strain and reserve wine. Into wine, add cornstarch blended with broth and heat 2 to 2½ minutes or until sauce is thickened, stirring once. Stir in butter and parsley.

Variation: *With broth, add 1 can (2 oz.) sliced mushrooms, drained.*

CRANBERRY SAUCE

Power Select: HIGH
Approx. Cooking Time: 10 minutes
Yield: about 3½ cups

2 cups sugar
¼ cup water
1 pound fresh cranberries
1 medium orange

Set Power Select at HIGH. In large glass bowl, combine sugar and water; heat 3 to 4 minutes or until sugar is dissolved, stirring once. Add cranberries and heat, covered, 5 to 6 minutes or until berries are soft.
Meanwhile, grate peel from orange and squeeze juice. Add peel and juice to cranberries. Mash berries with masher or stir well to crush; cool slightly. If desired, add additional sugar to taste; chill before serving.

Pictured on the preceding page: Custard Sauce, Hot Fudge Sauce, Brandied Cherry Sauce, Creole Sauce, Homemade Gravy.

CREAMY SALAD DRESSING

Power Select: MEDIUM
Approx. Cooking Time: 5 minutes
Yield: about 1 cup

½ cup water
⅓ cup vinegar
¼ to ⅓ cup sugar
1 egg
1 tablespoon flour
1 teaspoon salt
½ teaspoon dry mustard
1 tablespoon butter or margarine

Set Power Select at MEDIUM. In medium glass bowl, with wire whip or rotary beater, thoroughly combine water, vinegar, sugar, egg, flour, salt and mustard. Heat 4 to 5 minutes or until mixture is thickened, stirring twice; stir in butter. Use in place of mayonnaise when making coleslaw or potato salad.

CREOLE SAUCE

Power Select: HIGH
                HIGH→MEDIUM-LOW
Approx. Cooking Time: 10 minutes
Yield: about 2½ cups

¼ cup finely chopped green pepper
¼ cup finely chopped onion
¼ cup thinly sliced celery
2 tablespoons butter or margarine
1 teaspoon finely chopped garlic
¼ to ½ teaspoon chili powder
1 can (15 oz.) tomato sauce

Set Power Select at HIGH. In medium glass bowl, combine green pepper, onion, celery, butter, garlic and chili powder; heat, covered, 2 to 3 minutes. Stir in tomato sauce; heat, covered, 1½ to 2 minutes at HIGH.
Set Power Select at MEDIUM-LOW. Heat, covered, 4 to 5 minutes, stirring once.

EASY HOLLANDAISE SAUCE

Power Select: HIGH
                MEDIUM-LOW
Approx. Cooking Time: 5 minutes
Yield: about 1½ cups

3 tablespoons butter or margarine
2 tablespoons flour
1 cup hot water
1 to 2 tablespoons lemon juice
2 egg yolks
Salt and pepper to taste

Set Power Select at HIGH. In small glass bowl, heat butter ¾ to 1 minute or until melted; stir in flour; gradually add water and lemon juice. Heat 1½ to 2 minutes or until sauce is slightly thickened, stirring once. Quickly add egg yolks, stirring constantly with wire whip.
Set Power Select at MEDIUM-LOW. Heat 1½ to 2 minutes or until sauce is thickened, stirring once. Season with salt and pepper.

HOMEMADE GRAVY

Power Select: HIGH
Approx. Cooking Time: 5 minutes
Yield: about 1 cup

1 to 2 tablespoons butter or margarine
2 tablespoons flour
Salt and pepper to taste
Few drops browning sauce (optional)
1 cup roast drippings*

Set Power Select at HIGH. In small glass bowl, heat butter ½ to ¾ minute or until melted; stir in flour, salt, pepper and browning sauce. Gradually add drippings, stirring until smooth; heat 2½ to 3½ minutes or until gravy is thickened, stirring twice.

If necessary, add broth, milk or water to roast drippings to equal 1 cup. If using milk, set Power Select at MEDIUM and heat 3 to 4 minutes.

HOMEMADE SPECIAL SPAGHETTI SAUCE

Power Select: HIGH
                HIGH→LOW
Approx. Cooking Time: 1¼ hours
Yield: 1½ quarts

2 tablespoons oil
¾ cup chopped onion
2 cloves garlic, finely chopped
1 can (28 oz.) whole tomatoes, chopped
1 can (6 oz.) tomato paste
½ cup water
1 bay leaf, crushed
½ teaspoon salt
¼ teaspoon basil
¼ teaspoon oregano

Set Power Select at HIGH. In 3-quart glass bowl, heat oil, onion and garlic 1½ to 2 minutes. Add remaining ingredients. Heat, covered with wax paper, 6 to 7 minutes at HIGH.
Set Power Select at LOW. Heat, covered with wax paper, 1 hour, stirring occasionally.

Variation: *Add ½ pound browned ground beef or sausage, drained with tomatoes.*

Homemade Special Spaghetti Sauce, page 27

JIFFY SPAGHETTI SAUCE

Power Select: HIGH
               HIGH→MEDIUM-LOW
Approx. Cooking Time: 10 minutes
Yield: about 2½ cups

½ **cup finely chopped onion**
2 **tablespoons oil**
2 **teaspoons finely chopped garlic**
1 **teaspoon oregano**
⅛ **teaspoon basil**
2 **cans (8 oz. ea.) tomato sauce**
2 **teaspoons sugar (optional)**

Set Power Select at HIGH. In medium glass bowl, combine onion, oil, garlic, oregano and basil. Heat, covered, 2 to 2½ minutes or until onion is tender, stirring once. Stir in remaining ingredients and heat 2 to 2½ minutes at HIGH.
Set Power Select at MEDIUM-LOW. Heat, covered, 4 to 5 minutes, stirring once.

MORNAY SAUCE

Power Select: MEDIUM
               MEDIUM→STAND
Approx. Cooking Time: 10 minutes
Yield: about 1½ cups

2 **tablespoons butter or margarine**
2 **tablespoons flour**
1 **cup chicken broth**
⅓ **cup light cream or milk**
¼ **cup shredded Swiss cheese (about 1 oz.)**
¼ **cup grated Parmesan cheese**
2 **tablespoons parsley flakes**

Set Power Select at MEDIUM. In small glass bowl, heat butter ¾ to 1 minute or until melted; stir in flour. Gradually add broth and cream, stirring until smooth. Heat 5 to 5½ minutes or until sauce is slightly thickened, stirring twice. Stir in cheeses and parsley. Heat 2 to 3 minutes at MEDIUM or until cheese is almost melted, stirring twice. Let STAND 2 minutes for cheese to completely melt.

NEWBURG SAUCE

Power Select: MEDIUM
               MEDIUM-LOW
Approx. Cooking Time: 8 minutes
Yield: about 2½ cups

1 **cup half 'n half**
1 **cup milk**
3 **to 4 tablespoons sherry**
3 **tablespoons flour**
3 **egg yolks**
Salt and pepper to taste

Set Power Select at MEDIUM. In medium glass bowl, combine cream, milk, sherry and flour. Heat 5 to 6 minutes or until sauce is slightly thickened, stirring twice. With wire whip, quickly stir in egg yolks; season with salt and pepper.
Set Power Select at MEDIUM-LOW. Heat 1½ to 2 minutes or until sauce is thickened, stirring twice.

RAISIN SAUCE FOR HAM

Power Select: HIGH
Approx. Cooking Time: 5 minutes
Yield: about 1½ cups

½ **cup raisins**
½ **cup orange juice**
⅓ **cup currant jelly***
Dash ground allspice
1 **tablespoon rum (optional)**
1 **tablespoon cornstarch**
½ **cup water**

Set Power Select at HIGH. In small glass bowl, heat raisins, orange juice, jelly and allspice 1½ to 2 minutes, stirring once. Add rum and cornstarch blended with water. Heat 2½ to 3 minutes or until sauce is thickened, stirring occasionally.

***Substitution:** Use pineapple or apricot preserves for currant jelly.*

SWEET AND SOUR SAUCE

Power Select: HIGH
Approx. Cooking Time: 5 minutes
Yield: about 2 cups

Water
1 **can (8¼ oz.) crushed pineapple in heavy syrup, drained (reserve syrup)**
¼ **cup brown sugar**
1 **tablespoon soy sauce (optional)**
1 **tablespoon cornstarch**
⅓ **to ½ cup cider vinegar**

Set Power Select at HIGH. In 2-cup glass measure, add enough water to reserved syrup to equal ¾ cup; stir in pineapple, brown sugar and soy sauce. Heat 2 to 2½ minutes, stirring once. Stir in cornstarch blended with vinegar; heat 2 to 2½ minutes or until sauce is slightly thickened, stirring once.

Variation: *Add ½ cup finely chopped green pepper with pineapple.*

TURKEY GIBLET GRAVY

Power Select: HIGH→LOW
               HIGH
Approx. Cooking Time: 38 minutes
Yield: about 1¼ cups

Turkey giblets
1 **rib celery, cut up**
1 **small onion, quartered**
1½ **cups water**
2 **tablespoons flour**
½ **teaspoon salt**
Dash pepper
Few drops browning sauce (optional)

Set Power Select at HIGH. Trim giblets and cut into 1-inch pieces. In 4-cup glass measure, combine giblets, celery, onion and water. Heat, covered, 3½ to 4 minutes.
Set Power Select at LOW. Heat, covered, 25 to 30 minutes or until giblets are tender, stirring once; cool. Strain broth and reserve; finely chop giblets.

Into broth, add giblets, flour, salt, pepper and browning sauce.
Set Power Select at HIGH. Heat 3 to 3½ minutes or until gravy is thickened, stirring once.

PREPARING CONVENIENCE SAUCES

- Use a glass container twice the volume of the sauce.
- Prepare sauce ingredients according to package directions.
- Stir twice during heating.

ITEM	POWER SELECT	APPROXIMATE HEATING TIME (in minutes)
Packaged Sauce and Gravy Mixes (¾ to 1½ oz.) prepared with water prepared with milk	HIGH MEDIUM	2½ to 3½ 3½ to 4½
Sauces from condensed cream-style soups	MEDIUM	5 to 6
Spaghetti Sauce Mix (2 cup yield)	MEDIUM	5 to 6

TOPPINGS ❦❦❦❦❦❦❦❦❦❦❦❦❦❦❦❦

BANANA SPLIT TOPPING

Power Select: HIGH
Approx. Cooking Time: 7 minutes
Yield: about 3 cups

1 can (8¼ oz.) chunk pineapple, drained (reserve syrup)
1 can (17 oz.) dark sweet pitted cherries in heavy syrup, drained (reserve syrup)
1½ tablespoons cornstarch
2 bananas, cut into 1-inch pieces
Favorite flavors ice cream

Set Power Select at HIGH. Reserve ¼ cup syrup.
In medium glass bowl, combine remaining syrups, pineapple and cherries; heat 3 to 4 minutes, stirring once. Stir in cornstarch blended with reserved syrup and heat 2 to 2½ minutes or until sauce is thickened, stirring once.
Cool slightly; slice bananas over ice cream and add topping.

BRANDIED CHERRY SAUCE

Power Select: HIGH
Approx. Cooking Time: 8 minutes
Yield: about 6 servings

1 can (17 oz.) dark sweet pitted cherries in heavy syrup, drained (reserve syrup)
Water
½ cup sugar
1½ tablespoons cornstarch
¼ cup brandy

Set Power Select at HIGH. Reserve ¼ cup syrup. To remaining syrup, add enough water to equal 1¼ cups. In medium glass bowl, combine syrup-water mixture, cherries and sugar; heat 3 to 4 minutes, stirring once. Stir in cornstarch blended with reserved syrup and heat 2 to 2½ minutes or until sauce is thickened, stirring once. Transfer to serving dish.
In 1-cup glass measure, heat brandy ½ to ¾ minute. Pour over cherries and carefully flame. Serve, as desired, over vanilla ice cream, angel food cake or chocolate souffle.

CARAMEL SAUCE

Power Select: HIGH
Approx. Cooking Time: 4 minutes
Yield: 1¼ cups

1 package (14 oz.) caramels
2 tablespoons rum (optional)
1 tablespoon water
¼ teaspoon ground cinnamon

Set Power Select at HIGH. In small glass bowl, combine all ingredients; heat 3 to 4 minutes, stirring twice until smooth.

CUSTARD SAUCE

Power Select: MEDIUM
                         MEDIUM-LOW
Approx. Cooking Time: 6 minutes
Yield: about 2 cups

1½ cups milk
3 tablespoons sugar
2 tablespoons flour
2 egg yolks
1 teaspoon vanilla extract

Set Power Select at MEDIUM. In medium glass bowl, combine milk, sugar and flour; heat 4 to 4½ minutes or until sauce is slightly thickened, stirring twice. With wire whip, quickly stir in egg yolks.
Set Power Select at MEDIUM-LOW. Heat 1 to 1½ minutes or until sauce is thickened, stirring twice; stir in vanilla. Chill slightly before serving.

Brandied Cherry Sauce, page 29

HOT FUDGE SAUCE

Power Select: MEDIUM-LOW
Approx. Cooking Time: 5 minutes
Yield: 1½ cups

1 cup semi-sweet chocolate pieces (6 oz.)
½ cup light corn syrup
¼ cup half 'n half or milk
1 tablespoon butter or margarine
1 teaspoon vanilla extract*

Set Power Select at MEDIUM-LOW. In small glass bowl, heat chocolate and syrup 4 to 4½ minutes, stirring once. Gradually add half 'n half, stirring until smooth; stir in butter and vanilla.

Variation:
For CHOCOLATE MINT SAUCE, *use ½ to ¾ teaspoon mint extract for vanilla extract.*

LEMON SAUCE

Power Select: HIGH
Approx. Cooking Time: 5 minutes
Yield: about 1 cup

1 cup water
⅓ cup sugar
1 tablespoon cornstarch
1 tablespoon lemon juice
1 tablespoon butter or margarine
1 drop yellow food coloring

Set Power Select at HIGH. In medium glass bowl, heat ¾ cup water and sugar 2 to 2½ minutes or until sugar is dissolved, stirring once. Stir in cornstarch blended with remaining water and lemon juice; heat 2 to 2½ minutes or until sauce is thickened, stirring once. Stir in butter and food coloring; cool slightly before serving.

MELBA SAUCE

Power Select: HIGH
Approx. Cooking Time: 5 minutes
Yield: about 2 cups

1 package (10 oz.) frozen raspberries in heavy syrup, thawed*
1 can (8¼ oz.) sliced peaches, drained (reserve syrup)
¼ cup water
1½ tablespoons cornstarch

Set Power Select at HIGH. In small glass bowl, combine raspberries, reserved syrup, water and cornstarch. Heat 4 to 4½ minutes or until sauce is thickened, stirring once. Chill; just before serving, add peaches. Serve, as desired, over pound cake, ice cream or shortcake.

To quickly thaw frozen fruit, see page 139.

ORANGE LIQUEUR SAUCE

Power Select: HIGH
Approx. Cooking Time: 2 minutes
Yield: about 1 cup

½ cup water
¼ cup orange juice
3 to 4 tablespoons sugar
1 tablespoon cornstarch
1 to 2 tablespoons orange flavored liqueur

Set Power Select at HIGH. In small glass bowl, combine water, orange juice, sugar and cornstarch. Heat 1½ to 2 minutes or until sauce is thickened, stirring once; stir in liqueur; cool. Serve, as desired, over rice pudding, chocolate mousse or plain cake.

VANILLA SAUCE

Power Select: MEDIUM
Approx. Cooking Time: 7 minutes
Yield: about 1½ cups

1 cup milk
⅓ cup sugar
1½ tablespoons cornstarch
1 tablespoon butter or margarine
1 teaspoon vanilla extract

Set Power Select at MEDIUM. In medium glass bowl, heat ¾ cup milk and sugar 3½ to 4 minutes or until sugar is dissolved, stirring once. Stir in cornstarch blended with remaining milk and heat 2 to 2½ minutes or until sauce is thickened, stirring once. Stir in butter and vanilla; chill. Serve, as desired, in place of whipped cream—delicious on fresh berries.

Satisfy the heartiest appetites with savory stews and soups easily prepared in your microwave oven. Whether you like traditional <u>Beef Stew</u> or are in an adventurous mood for <u>Apple Cider Stew</u>, the lower power settings make this choice possible. Using MEDIUM, MEDIUM-LOW, and LOW allows less tender cuts of meat to heat gently while blending the flavors into something good and tasty.

Homemade soup does not mean long hours of careful cooking. Has your family ever tasted fresh vegetable soup? They can in about half an hour.
The following recipes are a mixture of basic from-scratch recipes as well as directions for convenient canned soups and dry soup mixes. You will no longer have to sacrifice flavor due to lack of time. Everyone will like that!

SOUPS

CHEESY VEGETABLE CHOWDER

Power Select: HIGH→MEDIUM-LOW
MEDIUM-LOW
Approx. Cooking Time: 18 minutes
Yield: about 4 servings

1 envelope (2 oz.) vegetable soup mix
2 cups water
6 tablespoons flour
2 cups milk
1 to 2 cups shredded Cheddar cheese

Set Power Select at HIGH. In 2-quart casserole dish, combine soup mix and water. Heat, covered, 5 to 6 minutes.
Set Power Select at MEDIUM-LOW. Heat, covered, 5 minutes, stirring once. Stir in flour blended with milk and cheese and heat, covered, 5 to 7 minutes at MEDIUM-LOW, or until soup is thickened and cheese is melted, stirring once.

CHICKEN GUMBO

Power Select: HIGH
HIGH→MEDIUM
MEDIUM→STAND
Approx. Cooking Time: 34 minutes
Yield: about 6 servings

1 pound chicken parts
¾ cup sliced onion
1 tablespoon flour
1 can (16 oz.) stewed tomatoes, chopped
1 package (10 oz.) frozen sliced okra, thawed
1 can (8 oz.) whole kernel corn
2 cups chicken broth
2 teaspoons salt
2 dashes hot pepper sauce
⅛ teaspoon garlic powder
Pepper to taste

Set Power Select at HIGH. In 3-quart casserole dish, arrange chicken. Heat, covered, 6 to 8 minutes or until tender; remove chicken and cool. Into casserole, add onion and heat 3 minutes; stir in flour, tomatoes, okra, corn, broth, salt, hot pepper sauce, garlic and pepper. Heat, covered, 5 to 7 minutes, stirring twice at HIGH.
Set Power Select at MEDIUM. Heat, covered 8 to 10 minutes, stirring twice.
Meanwhile, remove chicken from bones. Add to soup and heat, covered, 4 to 6 minutes at MEDIUM. Let STAND, covered, 5 minutes before serving.

CREAMY CORN CHOWDER

Power Select: MEDIUM
MEDIUM→STAND
Approx. Cooking Time: 16 minutes
Yield: about 4 servings

3 tablespoons butter or margarine
¼ cup finely chopped celery or green pepper
3 tablespoons flour
1 teaspoon dried chives or dried onion flakes
1 teaspoon salt
⅛ teaspoon pepper
2 cups milk
1 can (17 oz.) cream-style corn

Set Power Select at MEDIUM. In 2-quart casserole dish, heat butter and celery 2 to 3 minutes. Stir in flour, chives, salt and pepper; gradually add milk stirring until smooth. Heat 5½ to 7½ minutes at MEDIUM or until soup is slightly thickened, stirring twice. Add corn and heat 4 to 5 minutes or until heated through, stirring twice. Let STAND, covered, 3 minutes before serving.

CHUNKY HAM CHOWDER

Power Select: HIGH
MEDIUM→STAND
Approx. Cooking Time: 15 minutes
Yield: about 6 servings

1 cup cut-up cooked ham (about 6 oz.)
½ cup sliced celery
3 tablespoons butter or margarine
2 cans (10¾ oz. ea.) condensed cream of celery or cream of onion soup
2½ cups milk
1 package (10 oz.) frozen succotash, thawed

Set Power Select at HIGH. In 2-quart casserole dish, combine ham, celery and butter; heat, covered, 3 to 4 minutes, stirring once. Add remaining ingredients.
Set Power Select at MEDIUM. Heat, covered, 10 to 11 minutes or until heated through, stirring twice. Let STAND, covered, 5 minutes, before serving.

Pictured on the preceding page: Chicken Gumbo, Mom's Homemade Chicken Soup, Beef Stew, Manhattan Clam Chowder, French Onion Soup.

CREAM OF BROCCOLI SOUP

Power Select: HIGH
                        MEDIUM
Approx. Cooking Time: 15 minutes
Yield: about 4 servings

6 tablespoons butter or margarine
1 tablespoon finely chopped onion
5 tablespoons flour
1 cup chicken broth
2 cups milk
¾ teaspoon salt
Dash pepper
Dash ground nutmeg (optional)
1 package (10 oz.) frozen chopped broccoli, thawed

Set Power Select at HIGH. In large glass bowl, heat butter and onion 1½ to 2 minutes; blend in flour. Gradually add broth, milk, salt, pepper and nutmeg, stirring until smooth.
Set Power Select at MEDIUM. Heat 7 to 9 minutes or until soup is slightly thickened, stirring occasionally. Add broccoli and puree in food processor or blender. Return to bowl and heat 3 to 4 minutes, stirring once.

Variations:
For Cream of MUSHROOM Soup, *follow above procedure. Substitute 2 cans (4 oz. ea.) sliced mushrooms, drained, for broccoli.*
For Cream of SPINACH Soup, *follow above procedure. Substitute 1 package (10 oz.) frozen spinach, thawed, for broccoli.*
For Cream of CHICKEN Soup, *follow above procedure. With butter and onion, heat ¼ pound chicken meat, diced 2½ to 3 minutes, stirring once. Use 2 cups chicken broth and 1 cup milk; omit broccoli.*

FRENCH ONION SOUP

Power Select: HIGH
                        HIGH→MEDIUM→STAND
Approx. Cooking Time: 28 minutes
Yield: about 4 servings

3 tablespoons butter or margarine
3 cups sliced onions (about 3 medium)
3 cups beef broth
1 cup water*
1 teaspoon Worcestershire sauce
Salt and pepper to taste
Croutons
Grated Parmesan cheese

Set Power Select at HIGH. In 3-quart casserole dish, heat butter and onions, covered, 7 to 8 minutes. Stir in broth, water, Worcestershire, salt and pepper. Heat, covered, 9 to 10 minutes at HIGH.
Set Power Select at MEDIUM. Heat, covered, 10 minutes or until onions are tender. Let STAND, covered, 4 minutes before serving. Serve with croutons and cheese.

***Variation;** *Use ½ cup water and ½ cup white wine.*

GARDEN VEGETABLE SOUP

Power Select: HIGH→MEDIUM→STAND
Approx. Cooking Time: 17 minutes
Yield: about 4 servings

2 cups beef broth
1 cup water
1 can (16 oz.) whole tomatoes, chopped
1 medium carrot, shredded (about ¾ cup)
¾ cup thinly sliced celery
¼ cup finely chopped onion
1 bay leaf
1 teaspoon salt
⅛ teaspoon pepper
Dash ground marjoram
Dash thyme

Set Power Select at HIGH. In 2-quart casserole dish, combine all ingredients; heat, covered, 6 to 7 minutes. Set Power Select at MEDIUM. Heat, covered, 10 minutes or until vegetables are tender. Let STAND, covered, 3 minutes before serving.

Variation:
For Beefy Vegetable Soup, *add ½ pound browned ground beef with other ingredients.*

MANHATTAN CLAM CHOWDER

Power Select: HIGH→STAND
Approx. Cooking Time: 10 minutes
Yield: about 4 servings

1 can (10½ oz.) condensed vegetable soup
1½ cups tomato juice
1 can (7½ oz.) minced clams
Dash thyme

Set Power Select at HIGH. In 1-quart casserole dish, combine all ingredients; heat, covered, 8 to 10 minutes or until heated through, stirring occasionally. Let STAND, covered, 3 minutes; serve, if desired, with oysterette crackers.

Creamy Corn Chowder, page 32

MEATBALL RATATOUILLE SOUP

Power Select: HIGH
HIGH→MEDIUM→STAND
Approx. Cooking Time: 30 minutes
Yield: about 4 servings

½ pound ground beef
1 large onion, sliced
1 medium green pepper, cut into chunks
½ tablespoon finely chopped garlic
1 can (16 oz.) stewed tomatoes, chopped
1 cup beef broth
1 zucchini, thinly sliced
½ small eggplant, diced
1 teaspoon salt
½ teaspoon basil

Set Power Select at HIGH. Shape ground beef into small meatballs. In 2½-quart casserole dish, heat meatballs 3 to 3½ minutes, stirring once; remove. To drippings, add onion, green pepper and garlic; heat 6 to 7 minutes. Add meatballs and remaining ingredients and heat, covered, 5 minutes at HIGH. Set Power Select at MEDIUM. Heat, covered, 13 to 14 minutes or until vegetables are tender, stirring occasionally. Let STAND, covered, 3 minutes before serving.

MINESTRONE

Power Select: HIGH
MEDIUM-LOW→STAND
Approx. Cooking Time: 25 minutes
Yield: about 4 servings

2 tablespoons butter or margarine
½ cup thinly sliced carrots
½ cup chopped onion
2 cups chicken broth
1 can (16 oz.) stewed tomatoes, chopped
1 cup shredded cabbage or zucchini
1 teaspoon basil
1 teaspoon parsley flakes
1 teaspoon salt
1 can (16 oz.) kidney beans, drained
¼ to ⅓ cup broken spaghetti (about 2-inch pieces)

Set Power Select at HIGH. In 3-quart casserole dish, heat butter, carrots and onions, covered, 5 to 6 minutes. Add broth, tomatoes, cabbage, basil, parsley and salt. Heat, covered, 7 to 8 minutes, stirring once. Set Power Select at MEDIUM-LOW. Add kidney beans and spaghetti and heat, covered, 9 to 11 minutes or until vegetables are tender, stirring once. Let STAND, covered, 10 minutes or until spaghetti is tender, before serving.

MOM'S HOMEMADE CHICKEN SOUP

Power Select: HIGH→MEDIUM-LOW
MEDIUM-LOW
Approx. Cooking Time: 55 minutes
Yield: about 8 servings

2 to 2½ pounds chicken parts
3 ribs celery, cut up
2 bay leaves, crushed
1½ to 2 teaspoons peppercorns or pepper to taste
1 onion, sliced
8 cups hot water
2 carrots, shredded (about 1 cup)
1 to 1½ cups fine egg noodles
2 teaspoons salt

Set Power Select at HIGH. In 5-quart casserole dish, combine chicken, celery, bay leaves, pepper, onion and water. Heat, covered, 10 minutes. Set Power Select at MEDIUM-LOW. Heat 35 to 37 minutes or until chicken is tender. Strain broth into 3-quart casserole dish; add carrots, noodles and salt. Heat, covered, 7 to 8 minutes at MEDIUM-LOW. Meanwhile, remove chicken from bone. Add chicken to soup and let stand, covered, 7 to 8 minutes or until noodles are tender.

NEW ENGLAND CHOWDER

Power Select: HIGH
HIGH→MEDIUM-LOW
MEDIUM-LOW→STAND
Approx. Cooking Time: 24 minutes
Yield: about 4 servings

4 slices bacon
¼ cup finely chopped onion
2 tablespoons flour
Milk
1 can (7½ oz.) minced clams, drained (reserve liquid)
2 small potatoes (about 4 oz. ea.), partially baked*, peeled and diced
1 teaspoon salt
⅛ teaspoon thyme
Dash pepper

Set Power Select at HIGH. In 3-quart casserole dish, arrange bacon; heat, covered with paper towel, 3 to 4 minutes. Remove and crumble. Into bacon drippings, add onion and heat 2 minutes; stir in flour. Add enough milk to reserved liquid to equal 2½ cups; gradually stir into dish. Add potatoes, salt, thyme and pepper. Heat; covered, 3 to 4 minutes, stirring once, at HIGH. Set Power Select at MEDIUM-LOW. Heat, covered, 5 minutes; stir in clams. Heat, covered, 5 minutes at MEDIUM-LOW. Let STAND, covered, 3 minutes; top with bacon.
*To partially bake potatoes, follow basic information for baking potatoes (page 104) except reduce heating time to 3 to 4 minutes. Let stand 5 minutes before peeling.

QUICK CURRY SOUP

Power Select: MEDIUM→STAND
Approx. Cooking Time: 13 minutes
Yield: about 6 servings

1 can (11 oz.) condensed tomato bisque soup
1 can (10¾ oz.) condensed cream of chicken soup
3 cups milk
½ cup chopped apple*
¼ cup flaked coconut or unsalted peanuts
1 to 2 teaspoons curry powder

Set Power Select at MEDIUM. In 2-quart casserole dish, combine all ingredients. Heat, covered, 12 to 13 minutes or until heated through, stirring once. Let STAND, covered, 3 minutes before serving.

*Variation: Use 2 tablespoons sliced green onion for apple.

SAVORY SPLIT PEA SOUP

Power Select: HIGH→MEDIUM-LOW
Approx. Cooking Time: 1 hour
Yield: about 6 servings

6 cups hot water
1 package (16 oz.) dried split peas
½ pound bacon, diced*
1 cup chopped celery
½ cup chopped onion
½ cup sliced carrots
1 teaspoon salt
⅛ teaspoon thyme or basil (optional)

Set Power Select at HIGH. In 4-quart casserole dish, combine all ingredients; heat, covered, 8 to 9 minutes. Set Power Select at MEDIUM-LOW. Heat, covered, 45 to 50 minutes or until peas are tender, stirring occasionally. Put mixture through food mill or puree in food processor or blender. Reheat, adding additional water, if necessary.

Substitution: Use ham bone in place of bacon. Before putting soup through food mill, remove bone from soup and cut off any ham; blend into soup before reheating.

SUNDAY SUPPER SOUPS

Power Select: MEDIUM-HIGH→STAND
Approx. Cooking Time: 11 minutes
Yield: about 6 servings each

Cheesy Tomato Soup:

1 can (10¾ oz.) condensed tomato soup
1 can (11 oz.) condensed cheddar cheese soup
2 cans water
¼ teaspoon basil

Set Power Select at MEDIUM-HIGH. In large glass bowl, combine all ingredients; heat 9 to 11 minutes or until heated through, stirring occasionally. Let STAND, covered, 3 minutes before serving. Garnish, if desired, with seasoned croutons or small pretzel rings.

Creamy Noodle Soup:

1 can (10¾ oz.) condensed cream of mushroom soup
1 can (10¾ oz.) condensed turkey noodle soup
1½ cans water
⅛ teaspoon sage

Follow above procedure for Cheesy Tomato Soup. Garnish, if desired, with toasted slivered almonds.

Want to Make Your Soup Something Special?
Just before serving, add any one, or even two, of the following:

- chopped hard-cooked egg
- chopped or sliced olives
- corn chips
- crisp, bite-size cereal
- dried chives or dill weed
- french fried onion pieces
- grated cheese
- lemon slices
- popcorn
- seasoned croutons
- sliced frankfurters
- sliced mushrooms
- slivered almonds
- small pretzel rings
- sour cream
- thin strips of cheese

VICHYSSOISE

Power Select: HIGH
                       HIGH→MEDIUM
Approx. Cooking Time: 17 minutes
Yield: about 4 servings

3 tablespoons butter or margarine
3 medium leeks, white part sliced
1½ cups chicken broth
¾ teaspoon salt
⅛ teaspoon pepper
2 medium potatoes, baked (see page 104)
1½ cups milk
½ cup whipping cream
1 tablespoon sherry (optional)

Set Power Select at HIGH. In 2-quart casserole dish, heat butter and leeks 3 to 4 minutes; stir in broth, salt and pepper. Heat, covered, 3 to 4 minutes. at HIGH. Set Power Select at MEDIUM. Heat, covered, 5 minutes. Meanwhile, peel and dice potatoes. With electric mixer, blender or food processor, puree potatoes, broth mixture and milk. Return to dish and heat, covered, 3 to 4 minutes; stir in cream and sherry. Chill thoroughly and garnish, if desired, with chopped chives before serving.

Note: *This soup is also delicious piping hot!*

PREPARING CONVENIENCE SOUPS

Canned Soups
- Empty contents into casserole dish or soup bowl
- Dilute according to label directions
- Set Power Select at MEDIUM-HIGH*
- Heat, covered, stirring once
- Let STAND, covered, 3 minutes before serving

If heating soup diluted with milk, set Power Select at MEDIUM. Increase heating time by 1 minute.

SOUP	APPROXIMATE HEATING TIME (in minutes)
Condensed (10½ to 11½ oz.)	4 to 6
Semi-condensed, single serving (7½ to 7¾ oz.)	2 to 3
Ready-to-heat (19 oz.)	6 to 7
(10¾ oz.)	3 to 4

Dry Soup Mixes
- Add soup mix to given amount of water specified by package directions (or add mix to boiling water) in casserole dish or glass bowl.
- Set Power Select at HIGH.
- Bring to a boil*
- Set Power Select at MEDIUM-LOW
- Heat, covered, 3 to 4 minutes**, stirring once.
- Let STAND, covered, 5 minutes or until noodles or vegetables are tender.

See Heating Liquids Chart, page 22, for time to bring water to a boil.
**Heat soup mixes with broad noodles 7 to 8 minutes.*

STEWS ꙮꙮꙮꙮꙮꙮꙮꙮꙮꙮꙮꙮꙮꙮꙮꙮ

APPLE CIDER STEW 🍴

Power Select: HIGH
                 HIGH→LOW
                 LOW
                 HIGH
Approx. Cooking Time: 1¾ hours
Yield: about 8 servings

½ small turnip, diced (about 3 cups)*
½ pound fresh green beans, cut into 1½-inch pieces*
¼ cup water
2 tablespoons oil
1 cup sliced onion
2 pounds beef cubes, cut into 1-inch pieces
2 cups apple cider
2 tablespoons catsup
2 teaspoons salt
1 bay leaf
¼ teaspoon pepper
⅛ teaspoon thyme
¼ cup flour

Set Power Select at HIGH. In medium glass bowl, combine turnips, beans and water; heat, covered, 8 to 9 minutes, stirring once. Drain; reserve vegetables. In 3-quart casserole dish, heat oil and onion 3 to 4 minutes or until onion is tender. Add beef, 1½ cups cider, catsup, salt, bay leaf, pepper and thyme; heat, covered, 5 to 6 minutes at HIGH.
Set Power Select at LOW. Heat, covered, 60 minutes, stirring occasionally. Add reserved vegetables and heat, covered, 15 minutes, or until beef and vegetables are tender at LOW. Stir in flour blended with remaining cider.
Set Power Select at HIGH. Heat 3 to 4 minutes or until stew is slightly thickened, stirring once.

*Substitutions: *Use 1 can (16 oz.) sliced potatoes, drained and 1 can (16 oz.) sliced green beans, drained. Do not precook; add to stew as directed omitting water.*

BAVARIAN STEW 🍴

Power Select: HIGH→LOW
                 LOW
                 HIGH
Approx. Cooking Time: 1¼hours
Yield: about 6 servings

1½ pounds beef cubes, cut into strips
2 cups water
2 medium onions, sliced
¼ cup cider vinegar
1 tablespoon sugar
1 bay leaf
1 teaspoon salt
½ teaspoon caraway seeds
1 small head (about 1 lb.) red cabbage, shredded*
¼ cup flour

Set Power Select at HIGH. In 4-quart casserole dish, combine beef, 1½ cups water, onions, vinegar, sugar, bay leaf, salt and caraway. Heat, covered, 6 to 7 minutes.
Set Power Select at LOW. Heat, covered, 30 to 35 minutes, stirring occasionally. Add red cabbage and heat, covered, 20 to 25 minutes or until beef and cabbage are tender, stirring occasionally at LOW. Set Power Select at HIGH. Stir in flour blended with remaining water and heat 4 to 5 minutes or until stew is thickened, stirring once.

*Substitution: *Use 1 jar (16 oz.) red cabbage, drained for fresh red cabbage.*

BEEF STEW 🍴

Power Select: HIGH→LOW
                 LOW
Approx. Cooking Time: 1¼ hours
Yield: about 8 servings

2 pounds boneless beef, cut into 1-inch cubes
2 cups water
1 envelope (1⅜ oz.) onion soup mix
1 bay leaf
4 medium carrots, thinly sliced
1 can (8 oz.) green peas, drained
2 baking potatoes (about 8 oz. ea.) partially baked*, peeled and cubed
¼ cup flour

Set Power Select at HIGH. In 4-quart casserole dish, combine beef, 1½ cups water, soup mix, bay leaf and carrot. Heat, covered, 7 to 8 minutes.
Set Power Select at LOW. Heat, covered, 55 to 60 minutes or until beef and carrots are tender, stirring occasionally.
Add peas, potatoes and flour blended with remaining water. Heat 7 to 8 minutes at LOW or until stew is thickened, stirring occasionally.

*Hint: *To partially bake potatoes, follow basic information for baking potatoes (page 104). Reduce heating time to 3 to 4 minutes. Let stand 5 minutes before peeling.*

BRUNSWICK STEW 🍴 ▦

Power Select: HIGH→MEDIUM
                 MEDIUM
Approx. Cooking Time: 42 minutes
Yield: about 4 servings

2½ to 3 pound chicken, cut into serving pieces
2 cups water
5 whole peppercorns
2 bay leaves, crushed
1 can (16 oz.) whole tomatoes, chopped
1 medium onion, thinly sliced
1 package (10 oz.) frozen succotash, thawed*
1 package (10 oz.) frozen sliced okra, thawed*
2 teaspoons salt

Set Power Select at HIGH. In 3-quart casserole dish, combine chicken, water, peppercorns and bay leaves. Heat, covered, 6 to 7 minutes.
Set Power Select at MEDIUM. Heat, covered, 12 to 15 minutes or until chicken is tender. Strain broth and return broth to dish; add tomatoes, onion, succotash, okra and salt. Heat, covered, 12 to 15 minutes, stirring once at MEDIUM.
Meanwhile, remove chicken from bone. Add to stew and heat, covered, 3 to 5 minutes.

Hint: To quickly thaw packaged frozen vegetables, see page 139.

CHILI STEW

Power Select: HIGH
                HIGH→MEDIUM-LOW
Approx. Cooking Time: 54 minutes
Yield: about 4 servings

1 pound ground beef
2 medium onions, chopped
¼ teaspoon dried garlic pieces
1 can (16 oz.) pinto or red kidney beans
1 can (15 oz.) stewed tomatoes, chopped
1 can (15 oz.) tomato sauce
1 teaspoon salt
2 to 3 tablespoons chili powder

Set Power Select at HIGH. In 3-quart casserole dish, crumble ground beef; stir in onion and garlic. Heat 6 to 7 minutes, stirring once; drain. Stir in remaining ingredients. Heat, covered, 6 to 7 minutes at HIGH. Set Power Select at MEDIUM-LOW. Heat, covered, 35 to 40 minutes, stirring occasionally.

DUMPLINGS FOR STEW

Power Select: HIGH
Approx. Cooking Time: 6 minutes
Yield: 4 to 6 servings

2 cups buttermilk biscuit mix
⅔ cup milk
4 to 6 servings cooked stew

Set Power Select at HIGH. Bring stew ingredients to a boil (make sure meat, vegetables, etc. are already tender). Combine biscuit mix and milk until smooth; drop by tablespoonsful around edge of stew, forming about 10 dumplings. Heat, covered, 4½ to 6 minutes or until dumplings are cooked.

FISHERMAN'S POT

Power Select: HIGH→MEDIUM
                MEDIUM
Approx. Cooking Time: 25 minutes
Yield: about 4 servings

1 can (28 oz.) whole tomatoes, chopped
1 cup chicken broth
½ cup thinly sliced celery
½ cup sliced onion
1 tablespoon sugar (optional)
½ teaspoon finely chopped garlic
1 teaspoon parsley flakes
1 teaspoon salt
Dash thyme
1 pound fish fillets, chopped*
¼ cup white wine (optional)

Set Power Select at HIGH. In 3-quart casserole dish, combine tomatoes, broth, celery, onion, sugar, garlic, parsley, salt and thyme. Heat, covered, 5 minutes.
Set Power Select at MEDIUM. Heat, covered, 9 to 10 minutes, stirring once. Add fish and wine and heat, covered, at MEDIUM 10 minutes or until fish is tender, stirring once.

***Variation:**   *Use a combination of your favorite fish.*

IRISH STEW

Power Select: HIGH→LOW
                LOW
                HIGH
Approx. Cooking Time: 1½ hours
Yield: about 8 servings

2 pounds boneless lamb, cut into 1-inch cubes
2 cups water
1 envelope (1 oz.) onion-mushroom soup mix
1 bay leaf
2 medium carrots, thinly sliced
2 potatoes (about 6 oz. ea.), baked (see page 104)
¼ cup flour

Set Power Select at HIGH. In 4-quart casserole dish, combine lamb, 1¼ cups water, soup mix and bay leaf. Heat, covered, 7 to 8 minutes.
Set Power Select at LOW. Heat covered, 40 to 45 minutes, stirring occasionally. Add carrots and heat, covered, 15 to 20 minutes at LOW or until lamb and vegetables are tender, stirring once. Meanwhile, peel and cube potatoes; add to stew with flour blended with remaining water.
Set Power Select at HIGH. Heat 4 to 5 minutes or until stew is thickened, stirring twice.

Variation: *Add 1 package (10 oz.) frozen peas with the carrots.*

SOCRATES STEW

Power Select: HIGH
                HIGH→LOW
                HIGH
Approx. Cooking Time: 1 hour
Yield: about 8 servings

1 small eggplant (about ¾ lb.)
2 pounds boneless lamb, cut into 1-inch cubes
1 can (28 oz.) whole tomatoes, chopped
½ cup white wine
2 cloves garlic, finely chopped
2 tablespoons lemon juice
1½ to 2 tablespoons sugar
1 teaspoon salt
¼ teaspoon oregano
1 medium green pepper, chopped
¼ cup flour
½ cup water

Set Power Select at HIGH. Pierce eggplant several times; heat on paper towel lined glass oven tray 3 to 4 minutes or until eggplant is tender. Let stand 5 minutes; chop. In 3-quart casserole dish, combine eggplant, lamb, tomatoes, wine, garlic, lemon juice, sugar, salt, oregano and green pepper. Heat, covered, 7 to 8 minutes at HIGH.
Set Power Select at LOW. Heat, covered, 40 to 45 minutes or until lamb is tender, stirring occasionally.
Set Power Select at HIGH. Stir in flour blended with water; heat 3 to 4 minutes or until stew is thickened, stirring once.

SPICY SAUSAGE STEW

Power Select: HIGH
                    HIGH→LOW
Approx. Cooking Time: 1¼ hours
Yiled: about 6 servings

1 pound Italian sausage links, cut into 1½-inch pieces
1 pound boneless pork, cut into 1½-inch cubes
1 can (28 oz.) whole tomatoes, chopped
1 can (8 oz.) tomato sauce
1 green pepper, cut into chunks
1 teaspoon basil
1 teaspoon oregano
½ teaspoon garlic powder

Set Power Select at HIGH. In 3-quart casserole dish, heat sausage 5 to 6 minutes, stirring once; drain. Add remaining ingredients and heat, covered, 5 to 6 minutes at HIGH.
Set Power Select at LOW. Heat, covered, 55 to 58 minutes or until pork is tender, stirring occasionally. Serve, if desired, with rice or pasta.

TERRIFIC BEER STEW

Power Select: HIGH→LOW
                    LOW
Approx. Cooking Time: 65 minutes
Yield: about 6 servings

1½ pounds boneless beef, cut into 1-inch cubes
1 cup beef broth
½ cup beer
1 tablespoon brown sugar
1½ teaspoons salt
½ teaspoon pepper
½ teaspoon caraway seeds
1 cup sliced onions (about 3 small)
1 package (10 oz.) frozen green peas
3 tablespoons flour
¼ cup water
1 regular size (10" × 16") cooking bag

Set Power Select at HIGH. Place cooking bag in 2-quart casserole dish. Combine beef, broth, beer, sugar, salt, pepper and caraway in bag, turning bag several times to mix. Pull bag up around beef and close (3-in. from top) with twist tie, wrapping ends around closure; make six half-inch slits in top of bag. Heat 5 to 7 minutes.
Set Power Select at LOW. Heat 20 to 25 minutes. Add onions and peas; reclose. Heat an additional 30 minutes at LOW or until beef and vegetables are tender. Carefully open bag and turn down sides. Stir in flour blended with water* and heat 2 to 2½ minutes or until slightly thickened.

If desired, add ½ teaspoon browning sauce.

Irish Stew, page 37

If you are excited about microwave cooking saving time, effort and energy, you are about to experience the easiest dinner planning ever.

Most roasts can be cooked to perfection in less than one hour. But do not forget about the thrifty cuts of meat that help stretch your food dollar. With the lower power settings on your microwave oven, these less tender cuts can be simmered fork-tender in a delicious sauce or gravy to satisfy the fussiest eater. In this chapter, there are a variety of recipes to please everyone—everyday favorites, entertaining specials and calorie savers. Use these times and procedures as well as the information from the charts as a guideline when microwaving a favorite recipe for the first time.

SPECIAL HINTS FOR ROASTING MEATS

- Place roast, cleaned and wiped dry, on microwave oven safe roasting rack in a shallow baking dish. If this specially designed rack is unavailable, an inverted saucer or casserole lid works well in holding the roast out of its juices.
- Loosely cover the baking dish with wax paper to prevent splattering.
- Drain juices as they accumulate in baking dish. If desired, reserve for making gravy.
- Cover thin points of meat (less meaty portions) with aluminum foil half way through heating to prevent overcooking of these areas. Wooden toothpicks can be used to hold the foil in place.
- Let stand, covered, 10 to 15 minutes after heating. This time allows the temperature to equalize throughout. The internal temperature will rise 5°F to 10°F...a good time to prepare gravy or a vegetable.
- Use a cooking bag or covered casserole when cooking less tender cuts of meat (pot roast, etc.) These should be surrounded by liquid (soup, broth, etc.) to help foods retain moisture, producing a tender, juicy roast.
- Prepare cooking bag as package directs. The enclosed twist-tie may be used to seal the cooking bag; be sure to wrap ends tightly around the closure (and do not allow the ends to stick up). Make six half-inch slits near the top to allow excess steam to escape.

MEAT ROASTING CHART

MEAT	POWER SELECT	TEMPERATURE SELECT	APPROXIMATE HEATING TIME (minutes per pound)
Beef Roasts			
Rare	MEDIUM	130°F	8 to 9
Medium	MEDIUM	145°F	9½ to 10½
Well	MEDIUM	160°F	11 to 12
*Chuck, Rump	LOW		25 to 30
Flank, Brisket			
Pork Leg of Pork (Fresh Ham)	MEDIUM	160°F	11 to 12
Loin of Pork	MEDIUM	160°F	12 to 13
Ham			
Canned (Fully Cooked)	MEDIUM	130°F	9 to 11
Cured or Smoked	MEDIUM	160°F	10 to 13
Picnic Shoulder	MEDIUM	160°F	14 to 16
Lamb Medium	MEDIUM	145°F	9 to 11
Well	MEDIUM	160°F	11 to 13

These meats should be heated in a cooking bag or covered casserole surrounded with liquid.

With Temperature Select
Insert probe into meat as horizontally as possible.
Do not let tip of probe touch bone or fatty area.
Set Temperature Select and Power Select as indicated in chart or recipe.

Without Temperature Select
If your microwave oven does not have this feature, simply set Power Select and Time (according to MINUTES PER POUND) as indicated in chart or recipe. A microwave oven safe thermometer may be used during cooking. A conventional meat thermometer may be used after cooking is complete to check the internal temperature of foods.
DO NOT USE A CONVENTIONAL THERMOMETER IN MEAT WHILE OPERATING THE MICROWAVE OVEN.

Pictured on the preceding page: Fruited Glazed Ham, Crown Roast of Lamb, Roast Beef.

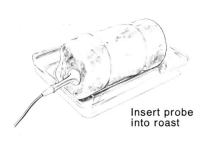

Insert probe
into roast

Using foil
on roast

Using twist-tie on
cooking bag

DEFROSTING MEATS

- Defrost meat in original wrapper, set in a shallow baking dish to catch any liquid.
- Set Power Select at DEFROST and heat for the time recommended in the chart.
- Turn roasts (weighing over 4 pounds) over two or three times during defrosting cycle.
- Let meat stand equal time before preparing.
- Estimate 5 minutes per pound defrosting time for beef and 6 minutes per pound for pork and lamb not listed below.

MEAT		APPROXIMATE DEFROSTING TIME (minutes per pound) at Power Select DEFROST	STANDING TIME (minutes per pound)
Beef	Roasts		
	Beef tenderloin	5 to 6	5 to 6
	Chuck or rump	5 to 6	5 to 6
	Sirloin, rolled	5 to 6	5 to 6
	Steak		
	Boneless sirloin	6 to 7	6 to 7
	Flank	4 to 5	4 to 5
	Miscellaneous		
	Frankfurters	5 to 6	5 to 6
	Ground beef*	5 to 6	5 to 6
	Liver	5 to 6	5 to 6
Pork	Chops	6 to 7	6 to 7
	Ribs	6 to 7	6 to 7
	Roasts	6 to 7	6 to 7

*Note: When defrosting ground beef, half way through heating remove outer portions of beef (thawed) to prevent cooking of edges before center is completely thawed.

BEEF

BEEF BOURGUIGNON

Power Select: HIGH
                HIGH→LOW
                LOW
                HIGH
Approx. Cooking Time: 1 hour
Yield: about 6 servings

¼ cup butter or margarine
1½ pounds boneless beef, cut into 1½-inch cubes
3 tablespoons brandy
1 cup beef broth
½ cup red Burgundy wine
2 bay leaves
⅛ teaspoon pepper
1 jar (16 oz.) whole boiled onions, drained and rinsed
¼ pound fresh mushrooms, halved or 1 jar (4½ oz.) sliced mushrooms, drained
¼ cup flour

Set Power Select at HIGH. In 4-quart casserole dish, heat butter 1½ minutes or until melted. Add beef and heat 4 to 5 minutes, stirring once.
In small glass bowl, heat brandy ¼ to ½ minute; carefully flame. Stir into beef with ½ cup broth, wine, bay leaves and pepper. Heat, covered, 4 to 5 minutes at HIGH.
Set Power Select at LOW. Heat, covered, 25 to 30 minutes, stirring once. Add onions and mushrooms and heat, covered, 15 minutes at LOW or until beef and vegetables are tender. Stir in flour blended with remaining broth.
Set Power Select at HIGH. Heat 2½ to 3 minutes or until sauce is thickened.

Hint: For more wine flavor, increase wine to ¾ cup and use only ¾ cup broth.

BEEF STROGANOFF

Power Select: HIGH
                 MEDIUM-HIGH
                 MEDIUM
Approx. Cooking Time: 15 minutes
Yield: about 4 servings

3 tablespoons butter or margarine
1 large onion, thinly sliced
1 pound boneless steak, cut into thin strips
¼ pound fresh mushrooms, sliced
Beef broth
½ teaspoon salt
¼ teaspoon pepper
2 tablespoons flour
½ to 1 cup sour cream or plain yogurt
⅛ teaspoon browning sauce (optional)

Set Power Select at HIGH. In oblong baking dish, heat butter 1½ to 2 minutes; add onion and heat 2 to 2½ minutes, stirring once.
Set Power Select at MEDIUM-HIGH. Add beef and mushrooms and heat 6½ to 7 minutes, stirring twice. Drain and reserve liquid; add enough broth to reserved liquid to equal ¾ cup. Sprinkle beef with salt and pepper. Into dish, blend in flour, then broth mixture; heat 2½ to 3 minutes at MEDIUM or until sauce is thickened. Blend in sour cream and browning sauce and heat, if necessary, 2 to 3 minutes at Power Select MEDIUM.

Note: For TWO servings, *following above procedure; halve all ingredients. Heat butter 1 minute, onion 1 to 1¼ minutes, beef 3 to 3½ minutes and sauce 1 to 1½ minutes.*

BEEF WITH BROCCOLI

Power Select: HIGH
Approx. Cooking Time: 17 minutes
Yield: about 4 servings

1 tablespoon oil
1 pound boneless steak, cut into thin strips
1 clove garlic, finely chopped
⅛ teaspoon ground ginger
3 to 4 cups broccoli flowerets
1 tablespoon cornstarch
½ cup beef broth
1 tablespoon sherry
1 tablespoon soy sauce
Toasted sesame seeds

Set Power Select at HIGH. In oblong baking dish, heat oil 2 minutes. Stir in beef, garlic and ginger; heat 3½ to 4½ minutes, stirring twice. Add broccoli and heat, covered, 5 to 6 minutes or until broccoli is crisp tender, stirring once. Stir in cornstarch blended with broth, sherry and soy sauce; heat 3 to 4 minutes or until sauce is thickened, stirring once. Top with sesame seeds.

Hint: *If desired, combine beef with garlic, ginger, broth, sherry and soy sauce; marinate 30 minutes. Drain and reserve marinade to thicken. Proceed as directed above.*

BEST BEEF GOULASH

Power Select: HIGH→LOW
                 LOW
Approx. Cooking Time: 1¼ hours
Yield: 6 to 8 servings

2 pounds boneless beef, cut into 1-inch cubes
1¼ cups water
1 envelope (1⅜ oz.) onion soup mix
1 can (3 oz.) whole mushrooms, drained
2 tablespoons paprika
¼ teaspoon caraway seeds
3 tablespoons cornstarch

Set Power Select at HIGH. In 3-quart casserole dish, combine beef, 1 cup water, onion soup mix, mushrooms, paprika and caraway. Heat, covered, 6 to 7 minutes.
Set Power Select at LOW. Heat, covered, 55 to 60 minutes or until beef is tender, stirring twice. Stir in cornstarch blended with remaining water. Heat, uncovered, 3 minutes at LOW or until thickened.

BRAISED BRISKET

Power Select: HIGH→LOW→STAND
Approx. Cooking Time: 1½ hours
Yield: about 8 servings

3 to 3¼ pound beef brisket
1 cup water
1 envelope (1⅜ oz.) onion soup mix
1 regular size (10" × 16") cooking bag*

Set Power Select at HIGH. Prepare cooking bag according to package directions; place brisket, water and soup mix in bag. Set in oblong baking dish; close bag with twist-tie, wrap ends around closure and make 6 (½-in.) slits in top of bag. Heat 5 minutes.
Set Power Select at LOW. Heat 90 minutes or until beef is tender. Let STAND 10 minutes before serving.

*Note: *Brisket may also be heated in covered casserole dish.*

CHILI BEEF LIVER

Power Select: HIGH
                 HIGH→MEDIUM
Approx. Cooking Time: 25 minutes
Yield: about 4 servings

6 slices bacon
1 pound beef liver, thinly sliced
2 tablespoons flour
1 can (10½ oz.) condensed onion soup
1 can (4 oz.) sliced mushrooms, drained
¼ cup chili sauce or catsup

Set Power Select at HIGH. In oblong baking dish, arrange bacon; heat, covered with paper towel, 4½ to 5½ minutes. Remove bacon; crumble and reserve. In dish, arrange liver lightly coated with flour; heat 1 to 2 minutes. Turn liver over; add soup, mushrooms and chili sauce. Heat, covered, 5 minutes at HIGH.
Set Power Select at MEDIUM. Heat, covered, 10 to 12 minutes or until liver is tender; top with reserved bacon. Serve, if desired, over rice.

CITRUS SIMMERED STEAK 📻

Power Select: HIGH→LOW
                          HIGH
Approx. Cooking Time: 1¼ hours
Yield: 6 to 8 servings

**2 to 2½ pounds boneless chuck steak (about 2-in.
   thick)**
½ cup orange juice
2 tablespoons barbecue sauce or catsup
2 tablespoons dried onion flakes
1 teaspoon grated orange peel
1 can (4 oz.) sliced mushrooms, drained
1 orange, sliced
2 tablespoons cornstarch
¼ cup water

Set Power Select at HIGH. In 3-quart casserole dish,
combine steak, juice, barbecue sauce, onion and
orange peel. Heat, covered, 5 minutes.
Set Power Select at LOW. Heat, covered, 60 minutes
or until steak is tender, turning steak over once.
Remove steak to serving platter; let stand, covered, 10
minutes.
Meanwhile, into casserole, stir in mushrooms, orange
and cornstarch blended with water.
Set Power Select at HIGH. Heat 2 to 3 minutes or until
sauce is thickened; serve over steak.

CORNED BEEF DINNER 📻

Power Select: HIGH
                          HIGH→LOW
                          HIGH
Approx. Cooking Time: 2 hours
Yield: 6 servings

6 medium potatoes (about 6 oz. ea.)
3 to 3½ pound corned beef brisket
2 onions, quartered
1½ cups water
1 small head cabbage (about 1½ lb.), cut into 6 wedges
1 regular size (10"×16") cooking bag

Set Power Select at HIGH. Following method for
baking potatoes (page 104), heat potatoes 11 to 12
minutes. Cool, then peel.
Meanwhile, prepare cooking bag according to package
directions; place corned beef, onion and water in bag.
Set bag in medium glass bowl; pull bag up around
beef: Close bag with twist-tie, wrap ends around
closure and make 6 (½-in.) slits in top of bag. Heat 6
to 7 minutes at HIGH.
Set Power Select at LOW. Heat 90 minutes or until
beef is tender. Remove to serving platter; let stand,
covered, 15 minutes.
Meanwhile, in oblong baking dish, arrange cabbage
(thick sides toward edge of dish) and potatoes; add ½
cup cooking liquid.
Set Power Select at HIGH. Heat, covered, 9 to 11
minutes or until cabbage and potatoes are tender.
Serve with sliced corned beef.

FILET AU JUS 📻🍳▨

Power Select: MEDIUM→STAND
Approx. Cooking Time: 7 minutes
Yield: 4 servings

4 tenderloin steaks, 1-inch thick (about ¼ lb. ea.)
½ teaspoon pepper
4 slices bacon
Browning sauce

Set Power Select at MEDIUM. Rub steaks with pepper;
wrap bacon around steaks and secure bacon with
wooden toothpicks. In baking dish, arrange steaks;
brush with browning sauce. Heat 6 to 7 minutes*,
turning steaks over halfway through heating. Let
STAND, covered, 2 to 4 minutes before serving.

*Heating time given is for beef-Rare. For Medium,
  heat 8 to 9 minutes and for Well, heat to 11 minutes.

Note: **For TWO servings,** *follow above procedure;
          halve all ingredients, heat 3½ to 4½ minutes (for
          Rare), 4½ to 5½ (for Medium) or 5½ to 6½ (for
          Well).*

FLANK STEAK FLORENTINE 📻

Power Select: HIGH
                          HIGH→LOW→STAND
Approx. Cooking Time: 37 minutes
Yield: about 4 servings

¼ pound fresh mushrooms
½ cup finely chopped onion
1 clove garlic, finely chopped
3 tablespoons butter or margarine
**1 package (10 oz.) frozen chopped spinach, thawed
   and well drained***
1 beef flank steak (1½ to 1¾ lb.)
2 beef bouillon cubes
1 cup hot water
1 can (10¾ oz.) condensed cream of mushroom soup
2 tablespoons dry vermouth (optional)

Set Power Select at HIGH. Chop ½ cup mushrooms; in
glass bowl, combine with onion, garlic and butter.
Heat 2 to 3 minutes or until onion and mushrooms
are tender; stir in spinach.
Pound flank steak with a mallet; spread spinach
mixture on steak in a lengthwise strip. Roll steak
lengthwise around filling; tie with string or secure
with wooden toothpicks. Place steak roll in an oblong
baking dish.
Combine bouillon, water, soup and vermouth; add
remaining mushrooms, sliced. Pour sauce over steak
roll. Heat, covered, 8 to 9 minutes at HIGH.
Set Power Select at LOW and heat, covered, 20 to 25
minutes or until beef is tender. Let STAND, covered,
10 minutes before serving.

*Hint: *To quickly thaw packaged frozen vegetables, see
          page 139.*

FRUITED POT ROAST

Power Select: HIGH→LOW
                HIGH
Approx. Cooking Time: 1¼ hours
Yield: about 6 servings

2 to 2½ pound boneless chuck roast (about 2-in. thick)
1 cup apple cider
2 tablespoons brown sugar
3 whole cloves
1 stick cinnamon, broken
½ teaspoon salt
⅛ teaspoon pepper
12 pitted prunes
12 dried apricot halves
3 to 4 tablespoons flour
½ cup water

Set Power Select at HIGH. In 3-quart casserole dish, combine roast, cider, sugar, cloves, cinnamon, salt and pepper. Heat, covered, 5 minutes.
Set Power Select at LOW. Heat, covered, 60 minutes or until roast is tender, turning roast over once. Add prunes and apricots and heat, covered, 5 minutes at HIGH.
Remove roast to serving platter; let stand, covered, 10 minutes. Meanwhile, remove whole spices; into dish, stir flour blended with water. Heat at HIGH 2 to 3 minutes or until gravy is thickened, stirring once.

MUSHROOM STUFFED STEAK ROLLS

Power Select: HIGH
                HIGH→MEDIUM→STAND
Approx. Cooking Time: 15 minutes
Yield: 4 servings

¼ pound fresh mushrooms, finely chopped
¼ cup finely chopped onion
2 tablespoons butter or margarine
2 cups soft bread crumbs
1 tablespoon parsley flakes
1 to 1½ pounds top round steak, cut into 4 pieces
Salt and pepper to taste
1 can (10¼ oz.) beef gravy

Set Power Select at HIGH. In medium glass bowl, combine mushrooms, onion and butter; heat 2 to 3 minutes. Stir in bread crumbs and parsley.
Butterfly steak and pound thin for rolling*. Season one side with salt and pepper. Place mushroom mixture on seasoned side of each steak and roll up jelly-roll style. Tie with string or secure with wooden toothpicks. In square baking dish, arrange rolls; top with gravy. Heat, covered, 5 minutes at HIGH.
Set Power Select at MEDIUM. Heat, covered, 6 to 7 minutes, rearranging rolls once. Let STAND, covered, 5 minutes before serving.

***Hint:** In some markets, steaks may be purchased ready for rolling.*

PEPPER STEAK

Power Select: MEDIUM-HIGH
                HIGH
Approx. Cooking Time: 15 minutes
Yield: about 4 servings

2 tablespoons oil
1 pound boneless steak, cut into thin strips
2 tablespoons soy sauce
Dash ground ginger
Salt to taste
2 medium green peppers, cut into chunks
2 medium onions, sliced
1 tablespoon cornstarch
½ cup beef broth

Set Power Select at MEDIUM-HIGH. In oblong baking dish, heat oil 2 minutes; add steak, soy sauce and ginger. Heat 5 to 6 minutes, stirring once; season with salt and stir in peppers and onions.
Set Power Select at HIGH. Heat, covered, 3 to 3½ minutes or until vegetables are crisp-tender. Stir in cornstarch blended with broth and heat 3 to 3½ minutes or until sauce is thickened, stirring once.

Note: **For TWO servings,** *follow above procedure; halve all ingredients. Heat oil 1 minute, steak 2 to 2½ minutes, vegetables 1½ to 2 minutes and broth 1½ to 2 minutes.*

RANCHERO POT ROAST

Power Select: HIGH→LOW→STAND
Approx. Cooking Time: 1½ hours
Yield: about 8 servings

1 teaspoon garlic salt
½ to 1 teaspoon pepper
¼ teaspoon paprika
3 to 3¼ pound bottom round roast
1 cup beef broth
½ cup chili sauce
2 tablespoons dried onion flakes
1 regular size (10"×16") cooking bag

Set Power Select at HIGH. Prepare cooking bag according to package directions. Combine garlic, pepper and paprika; rub over roast. Place in cooking bag and add broth, chili sauce and onion. Set bag in medium glass bowl; pull bag up around roast. Close with twist-tie, wrap ends around closure and make 6 (½-in.) slits in top of bag. Heat 5 minutes.
Set Power Select at LOW. Heat 90 minutes or until beef is tender. Let STAND, 10 minutes before serving.

Hint: *If thicker gravy is desired, remove roast to serving platter; let stand, covered. Pour gravy into glass bowl and add 3 to 4 tablespoons flour blended with ½ cup water. Set Power Select at HIGH. Heat 3 to 4 minutes, stirring once.*

SAUERBRATEN

Power Select: HIGH→LOW→STAND
Approx. Cooking Time: 1½ hours
Yield: 6 to 8 servings

3 to 3½ pound bottom round or rump roast
1 medium onion, sliced
1 carrot, sliced
Celery tops (optional)
1 cup cider vinegar
1 cup water
½ cup red wine
2 tablespoons pickling spices
12 gingersnap cookies, crushed
1 cup brown sugar
1 large size (14" × 20") cooking bag

In large glass bowl, combine roast, onion, carrot, celery, vinegar, water, wine and spices. Marinate, covered, in refrigerator 3 days*, turning roast occasionally.
Set Power Select at HIGH. Prepare cooking bag according to package directions; place roast, marinade, gingersnaps and sugar in bag. Set in large glass bowl; pull bag up around roast. Close with twist-tie, wrap ends around closure and make 6 (½-in.) slits in top of bag. Heat 7 to 8 minutes.
Set Power Select at LOW. Heat 90 minutes or until roast is tender. Let STAND 15 minutes before serving. Strain gravy and serve with roast.

This recipe can also be prepared without marinating for a flavorful pot roast.

SHORT RIBS WITH BARBECUE SAUCE

Power Select: MEDIUM
            HIGH→LOW
Approx. Cooking Time: 1¼ hours
Yield: about 4 servings

4 pounds beef short ribs
1 medium onion, sliced
½ cup sliced celery
1¼ cups catsup
¼ cup brown sugar
¼ cup cider vinegar
¼ cup flour
1 tablespoon Worcestershire sauce
½ teaspoon salt
¼ teaspoon dried mustard powder

Set Power Select at MEDIUM. In oblong baking dish, arrange ribs*, onion and celery. Heat, covered, 10 minutes.
Meanwhile, combine remaining ingredients; pour over ribs.
Set Power Select at HIGH. Heat, covered, 5 minutes.
Set Power Select at LOW. Heat, covered, 60 minutes or until ribs are tender, rearranging ribs once and basting with sauce occasionally.

*Hint: *Arrange ribs with meatiest portions toward edge of dish.*

Note: *If desired, recipe may be prepared in oven cooking bag.*

SWISS STEAK SPECIAL

Power Select: HIGH→LOW
Approx. Cooking Time: 50 minutes
Yield: about 6 servings

1½ pounds boneless round steak, cut into individual servings and pounded ¼-inch thin
1 can (16 oz.) whole tomatoes, chopped
1 can (8 oz.) tomato sauce
1 envelope (1⅜ oz.) onion or onion-mushroom soup mix
1 teaspoon basil
¼ teaspoon garlic powder
6 slices Mozzarella cheese (about 6 oz.)

Set Power Select at HIGH. In oblong baking dish, combine steak, tomatoes, sauce, soup mix, basil and garlic. Heat, covered, 4 to 5 minutes.
Set Power Select at LOW. Heat, covered, 40 to 45 minutes or until steak is tender. Top with cheese and let stand, covered, 10 minutes before serving.

TERIYAKI BEEF KABOBS

Power Select: MEDIUM
Approx. Cooking Time: 9 minutes
Yield: 4 servings

2 tablespoons brown sugar
2 tablespoons soy sauce
1 tablespoon lemon juice
1 tablespoon oil
1 pound boneless steak, cut into 1½-inch cubes
½ pint cherry tomatoes
1 medium green pepper, cut into chunks

In glass bowl, combine sugar, soy sauce, lemon juice and oil; add steak. If desired, cover and marinate in refrigerator at least 3 hours, stirring occasionally.
Set Power Select at MEDIUM. On four 9 or 10-inch wooden skewers, alternately thread steak, tomatoes and green pepper. Arrange skewers on 8-inch square baking dish and heat 7 to 9* minutes, rearranging skewers once and turning dish occasionally.

Heating time given is for beef Medium-Rare. Adjust time accordingly for desired doneness.

Note: *If wooden skewers are unavailable, metal skewers may be used. Refer to Introduction (page 7) for special instructions.*

GROUND BEEF ❦❦❦❦❦❦❦❦❦❦❦❦❦

CHEESEBURGER PIE

Power Select: MEDIUM-HIGH
Approx. Cooking Time: 17 minutes
Yield: about 4 servings

1 pound ground beef
1 package (5 oz.) instant mashed potato flakes
  (2¼ cups)
1¼ cups milk
1 egg
¼ cup catsup
1 tablespoon dried onion flakes
1½ teaspoons salt
¼ teaspoon pepper
6 slices American cheese
1 cup hot water
2 tablespoons butter or margarine

Set Power Select at MEDIUM-HIGH. Combine ground beef, 1⅓ cups instant mashed potato flakes, 1 cup milk, egg, catsup, onion, 1 teaspoon salt and ⅛ teaspoon pepper. Spread into 9-inch glass pie plate. Heat 6½ to 7½ minutes; drain. Arrange 2 slices cheese on top. Let stand, loosely covered, 7 minutes. Meanwhile, in medium glass bowl, heat water, butter, remaining milk, salt and pepper 5 to 6 minutes. Add remaining instant mashed potato flakes and cheese, diced and stir until potatoes are fluffy. Spread over "cheeseburger". Heat 2 to 3 minutes or until heated through.

ITALIAN MEATBALLS

Power Select: MEDIUM-HIGH
Approx. Cooking Time: 9 minutes
Yield: about 4 servings

1 pound ground beef
1 egg
1½ cups soft bread crumbs
¼ cup water or milk
2 to 3 tablespoons grated Parmesan cheese
¾ teaspoon oregano
1 teaspoon parsley
1 teaspoon onion salt

Set Power Select at MEDIUM-HIGH. Combine all ingredients and shape into 1½-inch meatballs (about 20). Arrange in oblong baking dish and heat 7½ to 8½ minutes, draining liquid and rearranging meatballs once.

MARVELOUS MEAT LOAF

Power Select: MEDIUM-HIGH→STAND
Temperature Select: 145°F
Approx. Cooking Time: 25 minutes
Yield: about 6 servings

1½ pounds ground beef
1 egg
½ cup dry bread crumbs
⅓ cup catsup
⅓ cup finely chopped onion
2 tablespoons milk or water
1 teaspoon Worcestershire sauce
½ teaspoon salt
¼ teaspoon pepper

Set Power Select at MEDIUM-HIGH. Combine all ingredients. In oblong baking dish, shape beef mixture into loaf (about 8" × 4")

TO HEAT BY TEMPERATURE: Insert probe into center of loaf. Set Temperature Select at 145°F.

TO HEAT BY TIME: Set time for 22 to 25 minutes.

Heat, covered with wax paper; drain liquid occasionally. If necessary, shield ends of loaf with aluminum foil halfway through heating. Let STAND, covered, 5 minutes before serving.

Hint: *While meat loaf is standing, heat 1 cup gravy or seasoned tomato sauce; pour over loaf.*

MIDGET MEAT LOAF

Power Select: MEDIUM-HIGH→STAND
Temperature Select: 145°F
Approx. Cooking Time: 16 minutes
Yield: about 4 servings

1 pound ground beef
1 egg
⅓ cup dry bread crumbs
⅓ cup catsup
2 tablespoons milk or water
2 envelopes (¼ oz. ea.) instant onion soup

Set Power Select at MEDIUM-HIGH. Combine all ingredients. In shallow baking dish, shape beef mixture into loaf.

TO HEAT BY TEMPERATURE: Insert probe into center of loaf; set Temperature Select at 145°F.

TO HEAT BY TIME: Set time for 14 to 16 minutes.

Heat, covered with wax paper; drain liquid occasionally. If necessary, shield ends of loaf with aluminum foil halfway through heating. Let STAND, covered, 5 minutes before serving.

Hint: *For even quicker heating, shape meat into ring shape in 9-inch pie plate. Set time for 9 to 10 minutes.*

Note: **For TWO servings,** *follow above procedure using ½ pound ground beef, 1 egg, ¼ cup bread crumbs, 2 tablespoons catsup and 1 envelope instant onion soup. Shape into two loaves. Heat by TIME only, 7 to 8 minutes.*

ORIENTAL PEPPER BURGERS

Power Select: MEDIUM-HIGH
                MEDIUM-HIGH→STAND
Approx. Cooking Time: 12 minutes
Yield: 4 servings

1 pound ground beef
¼ teaspoon salt
⅛ teaspoon pepper
1 large onion, sliced
1 medium green pepper, cut into chunks
1 can (8 oz.) tomato sauce
¼ teaspoon ground ginger
4 teaspoons soy sauce

Set Power Select at MEDIUM-HIGH. Combine beef, salt and pepper; shape into 4 patties and arrange in baking dish. Heat 4½ to 5½ minutes; drain. Add onion, green pepper and tomato sauce blended with ginger and soy sauce. Heat, covered, 5½ to 6½ minutes at MEDIUM-HIGH or until vegetables are tender. Let STAND, covered, 5 minutes before serving.

PIZZA WHEELS

Power Select: MEDIUM-HIGH
Approx. Cooking Time: 6 minutes
Yield: 4 servings

1 pound ground beef
2 tablespoons finely chopped onion
½ teaspoon salt
Oregano
¼ cup spaghetti sauce
4 slices Mozzarella cheese, cut into strips

Set Power Select at MEDIUM-HIGH. Combine ground beef, onion, salt and ¼ teaspoon oregano; shape into 4 patties raising the edge ¼ inch to form a center well. In baking dish, arrange patties; heat 3 to 4 minutes, then drain. Fill center well with spaghetti sauce and sprinkle with oregano; Heat 1 to 1½ minutes. Top with cheese and let stand, covered, 3 minutes before serving.

Note: **For TWO servings,** *follow above procedure; halve all ingredients. Heat patties 1½ to 2 minutes and with sauce ½ to 1 minute.*

SALISBURY STEAK

Power Select: MEDIUM-HIGH
Approx. Cooking Time: 17 minutes
Yield: 6 servings

1½ pounds ground beef
1 can (10¾ oz.) condensed cream of mushroom soup
1 can (4 oz.) sliced mushrooms, drained
1 egg
¾ cup milk
½ cup dry bread crumbs
¼ cup finely chopped onion
⅛ teaspoon pepper

Set Power Select at MEDIUM-HIGH. Combine ground beef, ¼ soup, ½ mushrooms, chopped, egg, ¼ cup milk, bread crumbs, onion and pepper. Shape into 6 patties and arrange in oblong baking dish. Heat, covered with wax paper, 13 to 14 minutes, turning patties over* and rearranging once. Drain and let stand, covered, 5 minutes.
Meanwhile, in small glass bowl, combine remaining soup, mushrooms and milk; heat 2 to 3 minutes, stirring once. Pour sauce over patties and garnish, if desired, with parsley.

If desired, brush top of patties with browning sauce blended with water.

SAVORY CABBAGE ROLLS

Power Select: HIGH
                            HIGH→STAND
Approx. Cooking Time: 17 minutes
Yield: 4 servings

1 small head cabbage (about 1½ lb.)
1 pound ground beef
¾ cup chopped onion
1 can (15 oz.) tomato sauce
½ cup cooked rice (see chart, page 108)
1 teaspoon salt
⅛ teaspoon pepper
2 tablespoons brown sugar
2 tablespoons cider vinegar

Set Power Select at HIGH. Cut core from cabbage; rinse. In medium glass bowl, heat, covered, 4 to 5 minutes. Remove 8 leaves; reserve (use remaining cabbage in other recipes).
Into glass bowl, crumble ground beef; stir in onions. Heat 3½ to 4½ minutes or until beef is browned, stirring once; drain. Stir in ½ tomato sauce, rice, salt and pepper. To stuff cabbage, place beef-rice filling in cabbage leaf; roll up, folding edges in.
Arrange seam-side down in square baking dish. Pour in remaining tomato sauce blended with brown sugar and vinegar. Heat, covered, 6 to 7 minutes at HIGH. Let STAND, covered, 5 minutes before serving.

Marinated Lamb Kabobs, page 53

STUFFED GREEN PEPPERS

Power Select: HIGH
                HIGH→STAND
Approx. Cooking Time: 20 minutes
Yield: 4 servings

1 pound ground beef
⅓ cup finely chopped onion
2 cans (8 oz. ea.) tomato sauce
¼ cup water
3 tablespoons grated Parmesan cheese
1 teaspoon salt
⅛ teaspoon pepper
½ cup packaged precooked rice
4 medium green peppers (about 1 lb.)

Set Power Select at HIGH. In medium glass bowl, crumble ground beef; stir in onion. Heat 3½ to 4½ minutes or until beef is brown, stirring once; drain. Stir in 1 can tomato sauce, water, 1 tablespoon cheese, salt and pepper. Heat, covered, 2½ to 3½ minutes. Stir in rice; let stand, covered, 5 minutes. Meanwhile, cut peppers in half lengthwise; remove seeds and rinse. Spoon beef-rice filling into each half; place in oblong baking dish. Top with remaining sauce and cheese. Heat, covered, 10 to 12 minutes at HIGH or until peppers are tender. Let STAND, covered, 5 minutes before serving.

Note: **For TWO servings,** *follow above procedure; halve all ingredients. Heat ground beef 2 to 2½ minutes, tomato sauce 2 to 2½ minutes and peppers 5½ to 6½ minutes.*

SWEDISH MEATBALLS

Power Select: MEDIUM-HIGH
Approx. Cooking Time: 11 minutes
Yield: 4 to 6 servings

1 pound ground beef
1 egg
½ cup dry bread crumbs
½ cup milk
¼ cup finely chopped onion
2 teaspoons parsley flakes
½ teaspoon salt
⅛ teaspoon ground allspice
⅛ teaspoon pepper
1 can (10¾ oz.) condensed cream of mushroom soup

Set Power Select at MEDIUM-HIGH. Combine ground beef, egg, bread crumbs, ¼ cup milk, onion, parsley, salt, allspice and pepper. Shape into 1¼-inch meatballs (about 30) and arrange in oblong baking dish. Heat 5½ to 6½ minutes, rearranging meatballs once; push meatballs to one side of dish. Blend in soup and remaining milk; combine with meatballs. Heat, covered, 3 to 4 minutes or until heated through. Serve, if desired, over buttered noodles, sprinkled with additional parsley.

VEAL

VEAL CUTLETS CORDON BLEU

Power Select: MEDIUM-HIGH→STAND
Approx. Cooking Time: 8 minutes
Yield: 4 servings

4 veal cutlets (about 1 lb.), pounded thin*
2 thin slices cooked ham, halved
2 slices (rectangular) Swiss cheese, halved
1 cup seasoned dry bread crumbs
½ teaspoon salt
⅛ teaspoon pepper
Ground allspice
1 egg, beaten with ¼ cup water
3 tablespoons oil

Set Power Select at MEDIUM-HIGH. On one side of each cutlet, place ham and cheese; fold cutlet in half. Pound edges together to seal or secure with wooden toothpicks. Dip cutlets in bread crumbs mixed with salt, pepper and allspice; dip in egg, then again in bread crumbs. Coat bottom of oblong baking dish with ½ oil; place cutlets in dish. Sprinkle remaining oil on cutlets; heat 7 to 8 minutes, turning cutlets over once. Let STAND, covered with wax paper, 5 minutes before serving.

***Variation:**   *Use chicken cutlets for veal.*

VEAL CUTLETS WITH CAPER SAUCE

Power Select: MEDIUM-HIGH
                MEDIUM
Approx. Cooking Time: 13 minutes
Yield: 4 servings

4 veal cutlets (about 1 lb.), pounded thin
1 egg, beaten with ¼ cup water
½ cup seasoned dry bread crumbs
½ tablespoon parsley flakes
½ teaspoon paprika
2 tablespoons oil
1 tablespoon butter or margarine
1 tablespoon flour
½ cup milk
½ cup sour cream
1 to 2 tablespoons capers

Set Power Select at MEDIUM-HIGH. Dip cutlets in egg, then in bread crumbs mixed with parsley and paprika. Coat bottom of oblong baking dish with oil; place cutlets in dish. Heat 5 to 7 minutes, turning cutlets over once; drain on paper towel. Remove to serving platter and let stand, covered, 5 minutes. Meanwhile, in small glass bowl, heat butter ½ minute or until melted; stir in flour, then milk. Heat 3 minutes or until thickened, stirring once. Stir in sour cream and capers; if necessary, heat at Power Select MEDIUM 1 to 2 minutes. Serve over cutlets.

Note: **For TWO servings,** *follow above procedure; halve all ingredients. Heat cutlets 1 to 1½ minutes each side and heat milk 1¼ to 1¾ minutes.*

VEAL PAPRIKA 🔳

Power Select: HIGH→LOW
                          HIGH
Approx. Cooking Time: 38 minutes
Yield: about 4 servings

1 pound boneless veal, cut into 1½-inch cubes
½ pound fresh mushrooms, sliced
1 cup chicken broth
½ cup finely chopped onions
½ to 1 teaspoon paprika
½ teaspoon salt
⅛ to ¼ teaspoon pepper
Dash caraway seeds
2 to 3 tablespoons flour
½ cup sour cream

Set Power Select at HIGH. In 2-quart casserole dish,
combine veal, mushrooms, ½ cup broth, onion,
paprika, salt, pepper and caraway. Heat, covered,
5 minutes.
Set Power Select at LOW. Heat, covered, 25 to 30
minutes or until veal is tender, stirring occasionally.
Drain liquid and reserve ½ cup. Into dish, add flour
blended with remaining broth and reserved liquid.
Set Power Select at HIGH. Heat 2 to 3 minutes or until
sauce is thickened; blend in sour cream.

WURST MIT KRAUT

Power Select: HIGH
Approx. Cooking Time: 17 minutes
Yield: 6 servings

6 tablespoons butter or margarine
1½ cups chopped onion (about 2 medium)
2 cups sliced apples (about 2 medium)
2 cans (16 oz. ea.) sauerkraut, drained and rinsed
½ cup beef broth
¼ teaspoon caraway seeds
¼ teaspoon pepper
6 knockwurst sausages (about 3 oz. ea.)

Set Power Select at HIGH. In oblong baking dish,
heat butter and onion 3 to 3½ minutes. Stir in apples
and heat 3 to 4½ minutes. Stir in sauerkraut, broth,
caraway and pepper.
Score knockwurst diagonally and arrange on sauerkraut mixture. Heat 8 to 9 minutes, rearranging
knockwurst once. Let stand, covered, 5 minutes.
Garnish, if desired, with additional apple slices and
parsley.

PORK AND HAM   ♧♧♧♧♧♧♧♧♧♧♧♧♧

AUTUMN STUFFED PORK CHOPS

Power Select: MEDIUM
Approx. Cooking Time: 18 minutes
Yield: 4 servings

4 rib-cut pork chops (¾-in. thick)
Pepper
½ cup finely chopped apple
¼ cup thinly sliced celery
3 tablespoons raisins
⅛ teaspoon ground cinnamon
¾ cup apple juice
Browning sauce
2 tablespoons flour
½ teaspoon salt

Set Power Select at MEDIUM. Cut pocket in each
chop; sprinkle inside with pepper. Combine apple,
celery, raisins and cinnamon. Stuff each chop with
apple mixture and secure opening with wooden toothpicks. In square baking dish, arrange chops, ribs
toward center, add ¼ cup apple juice. Brush chops
with browning sauce.
Heat, covered, 14 to 16 minutes, basting chops once.
Remove chops to serving platter; let stand, covered
5 minutes.
Meanwhile, into baking dish, stir in flour blended with
remaining apple juice and salt. Heat 2 minutes or
until thickened, stirring once. Serve over chops.

CHINESE PORK AND GREEN VEGETABLES

Power Select: MEDIUM-HIGH
Approx. Cooking Time: 14 minutes
Yield: about 4 servings

2 tablespoons oil
1 pound boneless pork, cut into thin strips
2 tablespoons soy sauce
⅛ teaspoon garlic powder
1 package (6 oz.) frozen pea pods, thawed*
2 bunches green onions, cut into ¾-inch pieces
** (about ⅔ cup)**
1½ to 2 tablespoons cornstarch
1 cup beef broth

Set Power Select at MEDIUM-HIGH. In oblong baking
dish, heat oil 2 minutes; stir in pork, soy sauce and
garlic. Heat 4 to 5 minutes, stirring occasionally.
Add pea pods and green onions; heat, covered, 3
minutes, stirring once. Stir in cornstarch blended with
broth and heat 3 to 4 minutes or until sauce is slightly
thickened, stirring occasionally. Serve, if desired, over
rice.

***Hint:** *To quickly thaw packaged frozen vegetables, see*
page 139.

CRANBERRY GLAZED HAM

Power Select: HIGH
                 MEDIUM→STAND
Temperature Select: 130°F
Approx. Cooking Time: 11 minutes per pound
Yield: 12 to 20 servings

¾ cup cranberry juice
¼ cup orange juice
¼ cup brown sugar
¼ cup raisins
1 tablespoon cornstarch
Dash ground cloves
3 to 5 pound canned ham
Whole cloves

Set Power Select at HIGH. In small glass bowl, combine juices, sugar, raisins, cornstarch and ground cloves. Heat 2½ to 3½ minutes or until glaze is thickened, stirring once. Decorate ham with whole cloves. Place ham on microwave oven safe roasting rack set in oblong baking dish.
Set Power Select at MEDIUM.

TO HEAT BY TEMPERATURE: Insert probe into ham. Set Temperature Select at 130°F.

TO HEAT BY TIME: Set time 9 to 11 minutes per pound.

Heat; halfway through heating, spoon on ½ glaze; baste occasionally with remaining glaze. Let STAND, covered, 10 minutes before serving.

FRUITED GLAZED HAM

Power Select: MEDIUM→STAND
Temperature Select: 145°F
Approx. Cooking Time: about 2 hours
Yield: about 12 to 14 servings

1 cup light brown sugar
¾ cup light corn syrup
⅓ cup prepared mustard
10 to 12 pound cooked ham (bone-in)
1 can (20 oz.) sliced pineapple, drained
1 can (20 oz.) pear halves, drained
8 to 10 preserved kumquats
8 to 10 maraschino cherries

Set Power Select at MEDIUM. In small glass bowl, combine sugar, syrup and mustard; heat 3 to 4 minutes or until sugar is dissolved and mixture boils, stirring once. Place ham (fat side up) on microwave oven safe roasting rack set in oblong baking dish; heat, covered with wax paper, 30 minutes, turning dish once. Remove skin from ham (if necessary) and score fat; brush with ¼ cup glaze.

TO HEAT BY TEMPERATURE: Insert probe into ham. Set Temperature Select at 130°F; heat. Arrange fruit on ham; secure with wooden toothpicks and brush with glaze. Set Temperature Select at 145°F; heat.

TO HEAT BY TIME: Set time for additional 60 minutes; heat. Arrange fruit on ham as instructed above. Heat 30 minutes or until ham registers 145°F when tested with conventional meat thermometer. (Remove ham from microwave oven before reading temperature.)

Drain liquid from dish occasionally. Let STAND, covered, 15 minutes before serving.

HAM STEAK WITH RAISIN SAUCE

Power Select: HIGH
                 MEDIUM-HIGH→STAND
Approx. Cooking Time: 13 minutes
Yield: about 4 servings

½ cup water
⅓ cup raisins
⅓ cup currant jelly
½ teaspoon grated orange peel
Dash ground allspice
1 tablespoon cornstarch
⅓ cup orange juice
1 pound ham steak (1-in. thick)

Set Power Select at HIGH. In glass bowl, combine water, raisins, jelly, orange peel and allspice; heat 3 to 4 minutes; stirring once.
Set Power Select at MEDIUM-HIGH. Stir in cornstarch blended with orange juice and heat 1 minute or until sauce is thickened, stirring once.
In oblong baking dish, heat ham 6 to 7 minutes, turning ham over and rotating dish once. Pour raisin sauce over ham; heat 1 minute at MEDIUM-HIGH. Let STAND, covered, 4 minutes before serving.

LOIN OF PORK WITH APRICOT GLAZE

Power Select: HIGH→MEDIUM
                 MEDIUM
                 MEDIUM→STAND
Temperature Select: 160°F
Approx. Cooking Time: about 1½ hours
Yield: about 8 servings

1 package (12 oz.) dried apricots, chopped
1 cup apricot nectar or apple juice
½ cup water
2 tablespoons honey
1 tablespoon lemon juice
1 stick cinnamon, broken
2 tablespoons cornstarch
2 tablespoons orange juice
5 to 6 pound pork rib roast*
Pepper

Set Power Select at HIGH. In small glass bowl, combine apricots, nectar, water, honey, lemon juice and cinnamon. Heat 4 to 5 minutes or until mixture boils.
Set Power Select at MEDIUM. Heat 5 minutes; stir in cornstarch blended with orange juice. Heat 2 to 3 minutes at MEDIUM or until glaze is thickened, stirring twice; remove cinnamon.
Season roast with pepper; arrange on microwave oven safe roasting rack in oblong baking dish.

TO HEAT BY TEMPERATURE: Insert probe into roast. Set Temperature Select at 160°F.

TO HEAT BY TIME: Set time 11 to 13 minutes per pound or until roast registers 160°F when tested with conventional meat thermometer. (Remove roast from oven before testing doneness).

Heat at MEDIUM, basting every 10 minutes with glaze and draining liquid occasionally. Let STAND, covered, 15 minutes before serving.

*Hint: For easy carving, when buying roast have backbone (chinbone) cracked.

OVEN-FRIED PORK CHOPS

Power Select: MEDIUM→STAND
Approx. Cooking Time: 17 minutes
Yield: 6 servings (1 chop ea.)

6 rib pork chops, ½-inch thick
1 package (1⅜ oz.) seasoned coating mix for pork

Set Power Select at MEDIUM. Coat chops according to package directions. In paper towel lined oblong baking dish, arrange chops, ribs toward center. Heat 15 to 16½ minutes, turning chops over once and rotating dish once. Let STAND, covered, 5 minutes before serving.

Note: **For FOUR pork chops,** *follow above procedure. Heat 11½ to 13 minutes.*
For TWO pork chops, *heat 6½ to 8 minutes.*
For ONE pork chop, *heat 3 to 4½ minutes.*

PEACHY PORK ROAST

Power Select: HIGH
MEDIUM→STAND
Temperature Select: 160°F
Approx. Cooking Time: 45 minutes
Yield: about 6 servings

Water
1 can (8½ oz.) sliced peaches, drained and chopped (reserve syrup)
1 package (6 oz.) stuffing mix for pork with seasoning packet
1 egg
⅓ cup chopped walnuts
¼ cup butter or margarine
3 to 3¼ pound pork rib roast (about 6 ribs)*
¼ cup peach preserves

Set Power Select at HIGH. In 2-cup glass measure, add enough water to reserved syrup to equal 1½ to 1¾ cups. Heat 2 to 3 minutes or until hot. In medium glass bowl, combine liquid with peaches, stuffing mix (and included seasoning packet), egg, walnuts and butter; stir until liquid is absorbed and butter is melted.
Cut pockets in pork roast, one opposite each bone. Stuff each pocket with 2 tablespoons stuffing; secure with string or wooden toothpicks. In oblong baking dish, arrange roast on microwave oven safe roasting rack.
Set Power Select at MEDIUM.

TO HEAT BY TEMPERATURE: Insert probe into roast (make sure tip of probe is touching meat—not stuffing). Set Temperature Select at 160°F.

TO HEAT BY TIME: Set time for 11 to 13 minutes per pound.

Heat; halfway during heating, brush on peach preserves. Let STAND, covered, 10 minutes before serving. Meanwhile, set Power Select at MEDIUM-LOW. Heat remaining stuffing 6 to 7 minutes, stirring twice. Serve with roast.
To carve roast, remove string; cut in between each bone.

*Hint: *For easy carving, when buying roast, have the backbone (chinbone) cracked.*

POLISH SAUSAGE (KIELBASA) WITH RED CABBAGE

Power Select: HIGH
HIGH→STAND
Approx. Cooking Time: 21 minutes
Yield: about 6 servings

1 small head (about 2 lb.) red cabbage, shredded*
1 small apple, chopped
¼ cup sugar
¼ cup cider vinegar
1 tablespoon dried onion flakes
½ teaspoon caraway seeds
½ teaspoon salt
1 ring (1¾ to 2 lb.) Kielbasa sausage

Set Power Select at HIGH. In oblong baking dish, combine cabbage, apple, sugar, vinegar, onion, caraway and salt. Heat, covered, 7 to 8 minutes, stirring twice.
Meanwhile, make ¼-inch slits every few inches in Kielbasa; arrange on red cabbage. Heat, covered, 12 to 13 minutes at HIGH or until heated through. Let STAND, covered, 5 minutes before serving.

*Substitution: *Use 2 jars (16 oz. ea.) red cabbage, drained for fresh cabbage. Do not heat cabbage separately. Arrange Kielbasa on red cabbage blended with remaining ingredients. Heat, covered, 15 to 17 minutes or until heated through.*

SOUTHERN BARBECUED RIBS

Power Select: HIGH→LOW
Approx. Cooking Time: 35 minutes
Yield: about 4 servings

1 cup barbecue sauce
2 tablespoons honey or dark corn syrup
2 tablespoons flour
1 tablespoon soy sauce
2 pounds pork spareribs, cut into individual ribs

Set Power Select at HIGH. In oblong baking dish, combine all ingredients. Heat, covered, 10 minutes. Set Power Select at LOW. Heat, covered, 20 to 25 minutes or until ribs are tender, stirring once.

Loin of Pork with Apricot Glaze, page 50

STUFFED PORK CHOPS

Power Select: HIGH
               MEDIUM→STAND
Approx. Cooking Time: 14 minutes
Yield: 4 servings

¼ cup thinly sliced celery
¼ cup finely chopped onion
2 tablespoons butter or margarine
1½ cups seasoned croutons
10 tablespoons beef broth or water
4 rib pork chops, ¾-inch thick (about 1¾ lb.)
Pepper
Browning sauce

Set Power Select at HIGH. In small glass bowl, heat celery, onion and butter 3 to 4 minutes or until vegetables are tender. Add croutons and 6 tablespoons broth, stirring until broth is absorbed.
Cut pocket in each chop for stuffing; season with pepper. Stuff chops with crouton mixture; secure with wooden toothpicks.
Set Power Select at MEDIUM. In oblong baking dish, arrange chops, ribs toward center; add remaining broth. Brush chops with browning sauce mixed with a little water and heat, covered, 9 to 10 minutes or until chops are tender, turning chops over once. Let STAND, covered, 5 minutes before serving.

Note: For TWO pork chops, *follow above procedure. Halve all ingredients; heat, celery, onion and butter 2 to 3 minutes and chops 6 to 8 minutes.*

SWEET 'N SOUR PORK

Power Select: MEDIUM-HIGH
               MEDIUM-HIGH→STAND
Approx. Cooking Time: 14 minutes
Yield: about 4 servings

1 can (8¼ oz.) chunk pineapple in heavy syrup,
   drained (reserve ⅓ cup syrup)
¼ cup cider vinegar
1 tablespoon cornstarch
2 tablespoons oil
1 pound boneless pork, cut into ¾-inch cubes
¼ cup soy sauce
1 bunch green onions, thinly sliced (about 3 tbsp.)
1 green pepper, cut into small chunks

Set Power Select at MEDIUM-HIGH. In small glass bowl, combine reserved syrup, vinegar and cornstarch; heat ¾ to 1 minute or until thickened, stirring once.
In square baking dish, heat oil 2 minutes; stir in pork, soy sauce and onion. Heat 7 to 8 minutes, stirring twice. Add green pepper and pineapple; heat, covered, 2 to 3 minutes at MEDIUM-HIGH or until pork is tender. Stir in sauce and let STAND, covered, 5 minutes before serving.

LAMB

CROWN ROAST OF LAMB

Power Select: MEDIUM
               MEDIUM→STAND
Temperature Select: 145°F for Medium
                      160°F for Well
Approx. Cooking Time: 37 minutes
Yield: about 6 servings

¼ cup orange marmalade
2 racks of lamb (about 2¾ lb.), cut and tied into
   crown roast
¼ cup thinly sliced celery
¼ cup finely chopped onion
2 tablespoons butter or margarine
2 to 3 cups cooked rice (see page 108)
1 small orange, peeled, sectioned and chopped
1 small grapefruit, peeled, sectioned and chopped
½ teaspoon salt
⅛ teaspoon ground sage
⅛ teaspoon pepper
Browning sauce

Set Power Select at MEDIUM. In small glass bowl, heat marmalade 1 minute or until marmalade is melted; set aside.
In oblong baking dish, set roast on microwave oven safe roasting rack. Heat 10 to 12 minutes. Let stand, covered, 5 minutes.
Meanwhile, in medium glass bowl, heat celery, onion and butter 2½ to 3 minutes or until celery is tender. Stir in rice, orange, grapefruit, salt, sage and pepper; heat 2 to 3 minutes.
Transfer roast to microwave oven safe serving platter; gently fill center with stuffing mixture. Brush outside of roast with browning sauce, then marmalade.

TO HEAT BY TEMPERATURE: Insert probe into meaty portion of roast. Set Temperature Select at 145°F for Medium, 160°F for Well.

TO HEAT BY TIME: Set time for 10 minutes for Medium, 18 minutes for Well at MEDIUM or until roast registers 145°F or 160°F when tested with conventional meat thermometer. (Remove roast from microwave oven before reading temperature).

Heat; let STAND, covered, 10 minutes before serving.

Note: *If desired, add ½ pound browned ground lamb, drained, to stuffing mixture; reduce rice to 1½ to 2 cups.*

CURRY LAMB

Power Select: HIGH
                HIGH→LOW
Approx. Cooking Time: 31 minutes
Yield: about 4 servings

1 pound boneless lamb, cut into 1½-inch cubes
¾ cup finely chopped onion
¼ cup butter or margarine
3 tablespoons flour
1 cup chicken broth
⅓ cup flaked coconut
⅓ cup raisins or peanuts
3 tablespoons lemon juice
1 to 1½ tablespoons curry powder
½ teaspoon ground ginger
½ teaspoon salt

Set Power Select at HIGH. In 2½-quart casserole dish, heat lamb, onion and butter 5 to 6 minutes, stirring once. Stir in flour, then remaining ingredients. Heat, covered, 5 minutes at HIGH.
Set Power Select at LOW. Heat, covered, 20 to 25 minutes or until lamb is tender, stirring twice. Serve, if desired, over rice.

MARINATED LAMB KABOBS

Power Select: HIGH
                MEDIUM-HIGH
                HIGH
Approx. Cooking Time: 21 minutes
Yield: 4 servings

2 cups water
¾ cup finely chopped onion
½ cup lemon juice
3 tablespoons bacon drippings or oil
2 tablespoons brown sugar
½ teaspoon curry powder
1 teaspoon coriander (optional)
½ teaspoon tumeric (optional)
2 bay leaves
1 pound boneless lamb, cut into 1½-inch cubes
8 small onions, peeled
1 large yam, cut into 1½-inch chunks
1 large green pepper, cut into chunks
1 tablespoon cornstarch

Set Power Select at HIGH. In medium glass bowl, combine water, chopped onion, lemon juice, bacon drippings, sugar, curry, coriander, tumeric and bay leaves; heat 9 to 10 minutes, stirring once. Add lamb and marinate, if desired, in refrigerator at least 3 hours, stirring occasionally.

On four 9 or 10-inch wooden skewers*, alternately thread lamb, onion, yam and green pepper; arrange kabobs on 8-inch square baking dish.
Set Power Select at MEDIUM-HIGH. Heat 6 to 8 minutes rearranging kabobs and basting with drippings once. Let stand, covered, 5 minutes before serving. Meanwhile, strain marinade into small glass bowl and blend in cornstarch.
Set Power Select at HIGH. Heat 2 to 3 minutes, stirring twice; serve with kabobs.

*Note: *If wooden skewers are unavailable, metal skewers may be used. (See Introduction page 7) for special instructions.*

MINT GLAZED LAMB

Power Select: MEDIUM
                MEDIUM→STAND
Temperature Select: 145°F for Medium
                      160°F for Well
Approx. Cooking Time: 9 to 11 minutes per pound
Yield: about 8 servings

4 to 5 pound leg of lamb
3 cloves garlic
1 teaspoon crushed rosemary
¼ teaspoon pepper
½ cup mint jelly
1 can (8½ oz.) pear slices, drained and mashed (reserve 1 tablespoon syrup)

Set Power Select at MEDIUM. Make 6 slits in lamb, insert ⅓ clove garlic in each. Mix rosemary and pepper; rub over lamb. In oblong baking dish, place lamb on microwave oven safe roasting rack.
In small glass bowl, combine remaining garlic, finely chopped, jelly and reserved syrup. Heat 2 to 3 minutes or until melted; stir in pears. Spoon ⅓ mint glaze over lamb.

TO HEAT BY TEMPERATURE: Insert probe into lamb. Set Temperature Select at 145°F for Medium, 160°F for Well.

TO HEAT BY TIME: Set time 9 to 11 minutes per pound for Medium, 11 to 13 minutes per pound for Well at MEDIUM.

Heat, brushing with mint glaze and draining liquid occasionally. Let STAND, covered, 15 minutes before serving.

PERSIAN LAMB WITH PEACHES

Power Select: HIGH→LOW
                HIGH
Approx. Cooking Time: 42 minutes
Yield: about 6 servings

Water
1 can (16 oz.) peach slices, drained (reserve syrup)
1½ pounds boneless lamb, cut into 1½-inch cubes*
1 envelope (1 oz.) onion-mushroom soup mix
1 tablespoon lemon juice
¼ teaspoon ground cinnamon
⅛ teaspoon ground cloves
¼ cup raisins
2 tablespoons cornstarch

Set Power Select at HIGH. Add enough water to reserved syrup to equal 1 cup. In 2-quart casserole dish, combine with lamb, soup mix, lemon juice, cinnamon and cloves. Heat, covered, 6 to 7 minutes.
Set Power Select at LOW. Heat, covered, 30 minutes or until lamb is tender. Stir in peaches, raisins and cornstarch blended with ¼ cup water.
Set Power Select at HIGH. Heat 4 to 5 minutes or until sauce is thickened, stirring once.

*Substitution: *Use beef cubes for lamb.*

PREPARING CONVENIENCE MEATS 🔥

- Arrange meats on microwave oven roasting rack set in shallow baking dish. Cover loosely with wax paper to prevent splatter.
- Meat (especially bacon*) can also be prepared between layers of paper towel on a paper plate.

ITEM	AMOUNT	POWER SELECT	APPROXIMATE HEATING TIME (in minutes)	STANDING TIME (in minutes)
Beef Patties, frozen (3½ oz. ea.)	1 2 4	MED-HIGH	2½ to 3 3½ to 4½ 5½ to 6½	2 3 3
Bacon, slices	2 3 4 8	HIGH	1 to 1½ 1½ to 2 2 to 3 4½ to 5½	1 1 1 1
Canadian bacon, slices (2 oz. ea.)	2 4 8	HIGH	1 to 1½ 2 to 3 3 to 4	3 3 3
Frankfurters, scored	2 4	HIGH	1½ to 2 2½ to 3½	3 3
Ham, slices (about 2 oz. ea.)	2 4	HIGH	1½ to 2½ 2½ to 3½	3 3
Hamburgers (4 oz. ea.)	1 2 4	MED-HIGH	¾ to 1¼ 1½ to 2 3½ to 4	2 2 2
Sausage Links, frozen (precooked, brown and serve)	2 4 8	HIGH	1 to 1½ 1½ to 2 3 to 4	2 2 2
**Sausage Links, fresh (1 to 2 oz. ea.)	2 4 8	HIGH	2 to 3 4 to 5 6 ½ to 7½	3 3 3
Sausage Patties, fresh (1 to 2 oz. ea.)	2 4	HIGH	1 to 2½ 2 to 4	2 2

*Note: *Cooking more than 8 pieces bacon on paper utensils at one time is not recommended.*

**Special Hint: *Pierce with fork and brush with browning sauce before heating.*

Roast turkey is not only for special holidays! The long preparation once associated with cooking poultry vanishes when you microwave this family favorite. All types of poultry can be easily cooked in microwave minutes. You will please everyone with delicious moist meals while saving yourself lots of time and effort.

Whether you are cooking a whole bird or preparing poultry parts, following "Hints for Preparing Poultry" will put you on the road to sensational, quick poultry dishes.

DEFROSTING POULTRY AND GAME

- Defrost poultry and game in original wrapper (not foil), set in a shallow baking dish to catch liquid.
- Set Power Select at DEFROST and heat for the time recommended in the chart.
- Turn poultry or game over every 15 minutes.
- Let poultry or game stand equal time before preparing.
- Rinse under cold water to remove remaining ice crystals.
- Estimate 5 minutes per pound defrosting time for poultry and game not listed below.

POULTRY	APPROXIMATE DEFROSTING TIME (minutes per pound) at Power Select DEFROST	STANDING TIME (minutes per pound)
Chicken		
whole	6 to 7	6 to 7
cut-up	4 to 5	4 to 5
boneless breasts	6 to 7	6 to 7
Cornish Hens		
whole	6 to 8	6 to 7
Duck		
whole	8 to 9	8 to 9
Goose		
whole	5 to 6	5 to 6
Pheasant		
whole	8 to 9	8 to 9
Turkey		
whole	5 to 7	5 to 7
half	8 to 9	8 to 9

Insert probe into thigh joint

Using foil when cooking chicken

Arrange chicken pieces meatier portions toward edge of dish

Pictured on the preceding page: Roast Whole Turkey with Apple Sausage Stuffing, Roast Chicken with Corn Bread Stuffing, Stuffed Cornish Hens with Orange Honey Sauc

SPECIAL HINTS FOR POULTRY 🔲

For Whole Birds—Fresh or thawed

- Stuff bird, if desired; close cavity with string or wooden toothpicks.
- Tie wings and legs tightly to body of bird.
- Place poultry, cleaned and wiped dry, on microwave oven safe roasting rack in a shallow baking dish. If this specially designed rack is unavailable, an inverted saucer or casserole lid works well in holding the bird out of its juices.
- Brush bird with browning sauce before heating to enhance appearance.
- Heat poultry (over 5 lb.) breast-side down during first half of cooking.
- Loosely cover baking dish with wax paper to prevent splattering.
- Drain juices as they accumulate in baking dish. If desired, reserve for making gravy.
- Cover thin points (wings and legs) with strips of aluminum foil halfway through heating to prevent overcooking in these areas. Wooden toothpicks can be used to hold foil in place.
- Let STAND, covered, 10 to 15 minutes before serving. This time allows the temperature to equalize throughout. The internal temperature will rise 5° to 10°F...a good time to prepare gravy or a vegetable.
- Use a cooking bag or covered casserole when cooking less tender hens. These should be surrounded by liquid (soup, broth, etc.) to help retain moisture, producing a tender, juicy bird.
- Prepare cooking bag as package directs. The enclosed twist-tie may be used to seal the cooking bag: be sure to wrap ends tightly around the closure (and do not allow the ends to stick up). Make six half-inch slits near the top to allow excess steam to escape.

With Temperature Select:

- Insert probe into thigh joint. With birds over 5 pounds, reinsert probe into other thigh joint after turning the bird breast-side up. Set Temperature Select and Power Select as indicated in chart or recipe.

Without Temperature Select:

- If your microwave oven does not have this feature, simply set Power Select and Time (according to MINUTES PER POUND) as indicated in chart or recipe.
- A microwave oven safe thermometer may be used during cooking.
- A conventional meat thermometer may be used after cooking is complete to check the internal temperature of foods.
- Do NOT use a conventional meat thermometer in poultry while operating the microwave oven.

For Poultry Parts

- Arrange pieces in shallow baking dish, meatier portions toward edge of dish.
- When cooking poultry in a sauce, rearrange pieces once during heating.
- Cover with wax paper or as recipe indicates to prevent splatter.
- Let stand 7 minutes before serving or as recipe indicates.

POULTRY ROASTING CHART

POULTRY	POWER SELECT	TEMPERATURE SELECT	APPROXIMATE HEATING TIME (minutes per pound)
Cornish Hens	HIGH	*	6½ to 8
Chickens (up to 3 lb.)	HIGH	175°	5½ to 7
Hens	MEDIUM	175°	10 to 11½
Turkey (see recipe page 64 for specific directions)	MEDIUM-HIGH and MEDIUM	—— 175°	2½ to 3½ and 4½ to 5½
Turkey Parts	MEDIUM	175°	9½ to 11½
Goose	MEDIUM	*	5½ to 7½
Duck	MEDIUM	*	10½ to 12
Pheasant	MEDIUM	*	8 to 9½

Not suitable for cooking with Temperature Probe.

CHICKEN ✿✿

APRICOT GLAZED CHICKEN

Power Select: HIGH
               MEDIUM→STAND
Approx. Cooking Time: 16 minutes
Yield: about 4 servings

2½ to 3 pound chicken, cut into serving pieces
¾ cup apricot preserves
½ cup bottled red Russian dressing
2 envelopes (¼ oz. ea.) instant onion soup

Set Power Select at HIGH. In oblong baking dish, arrange chicken, meatier portions toward edge of dish. Heat, covered with wax paper, 9 to 10 minutes or until chicken is almost tender; drain. Combine remaining ingredients and spoon over chicken.
Set Power Select at MEDIUM. Heat chicken, uncovered, 5 to 5½ minutes or until chicken is glazed.
Let STAND 7 minutes before serving.

BAKED CHICKEN WITH CORN BREAD STUFFING

Power Select: HIGH
               HIGH→STAND
Approx. Cooking Time: 21 minutes
Yield: 6 servings

1¼ to 1½ cups hot water
½ cup butter or margarine
1 package (6 oz.) corn bread stuffing mix with seasoning packet
3 chicken breasts, split (about 2½ lb.)
1 tablespoon butter or margarine, melted
¼ teaspoon browning sauce
1 can (10½ oz.) chicken gravy

Set Power Select at HIGH. In 3-quart oblong baking dish, heat water, ½ cup butter and seasoning packet 3½ to 4 minutes; stir in stuffing crumbs. Arrange chicken on stuffing; brush with melted butter mixed with browning sauce. Heat, covered with wax paper, 12 to 13 minutes at HIGH or until chicken is tender. Let STAND, covered 5 minutes.
Meanwhile, in small glass bowl, heat gravy 3 to 3½ minutes stirring once; serve over chicken.

BARBECUED CHICKEN

Power Select: HIGH
Approx. Cooking Time: 15 minutes
Yield: about 4 servings

2½ to 3 pound chicken, cut into serving pieces
1 cup barbecue sauce*

Set Power Select at HIGH. In oblong baking dish, arrange chicken, meatier portions toward edge of dish; evenly spread sauce over chicken. Heat, covered with wax paper, 10 to 11 minutes, basting chicken with sauce once. Heat, uncovered, 3 to 4 minutes or until chicken is tender. Let stand, covered, 7 minutes before serving.

***Hint:** *Use bottled barbecue sauce or see page 26 for a tangy homemade sauce.*

Note: **For TWO servings,** *follow above procedure; halve all ingredients. Heat chicken, covered with wax paper, 5½ to 6½ minutes. Heat, uncovered, 1½ to 2 minutes.*
        For ONE serving, *heat chicken, covered with wax paper, 3½ to 4½ minutes. Heat, uncovered, 1 to 1½ minutes.*

BUTTER BAKED CHICKEN

Power Select: HIGH→STAND
Approx. Cooking Time: 13 minutes
Yield: about 4 servings

2½ to 3 pound chicken, cut into serving pieces
3 tablespoons butter or margarine, melted*
1 teaspoon browning sauce

Set Power Select at HIGH. In oblong baking dish, arrange chicken, meatier portions toward edge of dish. Combine butter and browning sauce and brush ½ mixture over chicken. Heat, covered with wax paper, 11 to 13 minutes or until chicken is tender; half way through heating, brush remaining butter mixture on chicken. Let STAND, covered, 7 minutes before serving.

***Hint:** *To melt butter in your microwave oven, see Quick Tips, page 140.*

Note: **For TWO servings,** *follow above procedure. Halve all ingredients and heat 5½ to 6½ minutes.*
        For ONE serving, *heat chicken 3½ to 4½ minutes.*

CALIFORNIA CHICKEN

Power Select: HIGH
               HIGH→STAND
Approx. Cooking Time: 13 minutes
Yield: 4 servings

2 chicken breasts, split (1¾ to 2 lb.)
2 teaspoons lemon juice
1 teaspoon dried onion flakes
Basil
Pepper
⅔ cup shredded Cheddar cheese
½ small avocado, thinly sliced
4 thin slices tomato

Set Power Select at HIGH. In square baking dish, arrange chicken; sprinkle with lemon juice and onion and season with basil and pepper. Heat, covered with wax paper, 8½ to 9½ minutes or until chicken is tender. Top chicken with ½ cheese, avocado and tomato; top with remaining cheese. Heat, covered, 2½ to 3 minutes at HIGH. Let STAND 5 minutes before serving.

Note: **For TWO servings,** *follow above procedure; halve all ingredients. Heat chicken 6 to 6½ minutes and vegetables 1½ to 2 minutes.*
        For ONE serving, *heat chicken 4 to 4½ minutes and vegetables ¾ to 1¼ minutes.*

CHICKEN CACCIATORE

Power Select: HIGH→STAND
Approx. Cooking Time: 20 minutes
Yield: about 4 servings

2½ to 3 pound chicken, cut into serving pieces
1 can (15 oz.) tomato sauce
1 jar (4½ oz.) sliced mushroom, drained
½ cup chopped onion
1 tablespoon sugar (optional)
1 teaspoon oregano
1 teaspoon salt
½ teaspoon finely chopped garlic
¼ teaspoon pepper

Set Power Select at HIGH. In oblong baking dish, arrange chicken. Combine remaining ingredients and spoon over chicken. Heat, covered with wax paper, 18 to 20 minutes or until chicken is tender, rearranging chicken once. Let STAND, covered, 7 minutes; serve, if desired, with spaghetti.

CHICKEN IN WINE SAUCE

Power Select: HIGH
Approx. Cooking Time: 14 minutes
Yield: about 4 servings

1 medium onion, sliced
¼ cup butter or margarine
2 boneless chicken breasts, skinned and thinly sliced (about 1 lb.)
Salt and pepper to taste
1 medium green pepper, cut into thin strips
⅓ cup white wine
1 jar (4½ oz.) sliced mushrooms, drained
2 tablespoons flour
⅔ cup chicken broth

Set Power Select at HIGH. In oblong baking dish, heat onion and butter 3 to 3½ minutes or until onion is tender. Add chicken and heat 3 to 3½ minutes, stirring once. Season with salt and pepper; add green pepper and wine. Heat, covered, 2½ to 3 minutes; add mushrooms and flour blended with broth. Heat 3 to 4 minutes or until sauce is thickened, stirring twice.

CHICKEN LIVERS SUPREME

Power Select: HIGH
                HIGH→MEDIUM
Approx. Cooking Time: 12 minutes
Yield: about 4 servings

½ pound fresh mushrooms, sliced
⅓ cup chopped onion
¼ cup butter or margarine
1 pound chicken livers, halved
2 to 3 tablespoons flour
1 teaspoon salt
½ teaspoon pepper
½ teaspoon thyme

Set Power Select at HIGH. In 2½-quart casserole dish, heat, covered, mushrooms, onion and butter 3 to 4 minutes or until onion and mushrooms are tender, stirring once. Stir in livers tossed with flour, salt, pepper and thyme. Heat 2 minutes at HIGH. Set Power Select at MEDIUM. Heat, covered, 5 to 6 minutes or until livers are tender, stirring twice. Serve, if desired, with rice.

CHICKEN PARMESAN

Power Select: HIGH
Approx. Cooking Time: 10 minutes
Yield: 4 servings

2 boneless chicken breasts, skinned, split and pounded thin (about 1 to 1¼ lb.)
¾ cup seasoned dry bread crumbs
¼ cup grated Parmesan cheese
¼ teaspoon paprika
1 egg, beaten with ¼ cup water
2 tablespoons oil
1 can (8 oz.) tomato sauce or 1 cup spaghetti sauce
Oregano
1 cup shredded Mozzarella cheese (about 4 oz.)

Set Power Select at HIGH. Dip chicken in bread crumbs mixed with parmesan cheese and paprika, then in egg and again in bread crumb mixture. Coat bottom of oblong baking dish with 1 tablespoon oil. Place chicken in dish; sprinkle with remaining oil. Heat 2 to 2½ minutes; turn chicken over and heat an additional 2 to 2½ minutes. Top with tomato sauce and season with oregano; heat 3½ to 4½ minutes or until sauce is hot. Sprinkle with mozzarella cheese and let stand, covered, 5 minutes or until cheese is melted.

Note: **For TWO servings,** *follow above procedure; halve all ingredients. Heat chicken 1 to 1½ minutes each side and with tomato sauce 2 to 2½ minutes.*

CHICKEN VERONIQUE

Power Select: HIGH
                MEDIUM
Approx. Cooking Time: 18 minutes
Yield: about 4 servings

2½ to 3 pound chicken, cut into serving pieces
3 tablespoons butter or margarine
1 teaspoon browning sauce
3 tablespoons flour
½ cup light cream or milk
¼ cup white wine
1 cup halved green grapes
Toasted slivered almonds

Set Power Select at HIGH. Prepare Butter Baked Chicken, page 58 using chicken, butter and browning sauce.
Remove chicken to serving platter; drain liquid, reserving ¾ cup. Into baking dish, stir flour blended with cream, wine, reserved liquid and grapes.
Set Power Select at MEDIUM. Heat 3½ to 4½ minutes or until sauce is thickened, stirring twice. Pour sauce over chicken and garnish with almonds.

CHICKEN WITH SNOW PEAS

Power Select: HIGH
               HIGH→STAND
Approx. Cooking Time: 15 minutes
Yield: about 6 servings

6 chicken legs, thighs detached (about 2¾ lb.)
1 tablespoon butter or margarine, melted
1 tablespoon soy sauce
1½ teaspoons paprika
½ teaspoon crushed rosemary
¼ teaspoon salt
1 package (6 oz.) frozen pea pods, thawed*
1 jar (2½ oz.) sliced mushrooms, drained

Set Power Select at HIGH. In oblong baking dish, arrange chicken. Combine butter, soy sauce, paprika, rosemary and salt; brush over chicken. Heat, covered with wax paper, 8 to 9 minutes. Top with pea pods and mushrooms; heat, covered, 5 to 6 minutes at HIGH or until chicken and vegetables are tender. Let STAND covered, 5 minutes before serving.

*Hint: *To quickly thaw packaged frozen vegetables, see page 139.*

CHICKEN WITH CREAMY MUSHROOM SAUCE

Power Select: HIGH
              MEDIUM→STAND
Approx. Cooking Time: 21 minutes
Yield: about 4 servings

2½ to 3 pound chicken, cut into serving pieces
1 medium onion, sliced
Salt, pepper and garlic salt to taste
½ pound fresh mushrooms, sliced*
1 can (10¾ oz.) condensed cream of mushroom soup
1 cup sour cream

Set Power Select at HIGH. In oblong baking dish, arrange chicken, meatier portions toward edge of dish; top with onion. Heat, covered with wax paper, 10 to 12 minutes; season with salt, pepper and garlic salt. Add mushrooms and heat, covered 3 to 3½ minutes or until chicken and mushrooms are tender; drain liquid, reserving ⅓ cup. Blend reserved liquid, soup and sour cream until smooth; spoon over chicken.
Set Power Select at MEDIUM. Heat, covered, 4 to 5 minutes or until heated through; let STAND 5 minutes. Remove chicken to serving platter; stir sauce until smooth and serve over chicken.

*Substitution: *Use 1 jar (4½ oz.) sliced mushrooms, drained for fresh mushrooms.*

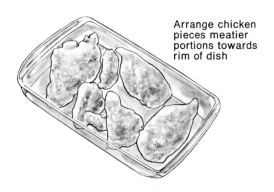

Arrange chicken pieces meatier portions towards rim of dish

FRUITED GLAZED CHICKEN

Power Select: HIGH
Approx. Cooking Time: 18 minutes
Yield: about 4 servings

¼ cup peach or apricot preserves
¼ teaspoon browning sauce
2½ to 3 pound chicken, cut into serving pieces
1 package (10 oz.) frozen mixed fruit, thawed*
1 tablespoon cornstarch
½ teaspoon lemon juice (optional)
Dash ground ginger or cinnamon

Set Power Select at HIGH. In small glass bowl, combine preserves and browning sauce; heat ½ to 1 minute. In oblong baking dish, arrange chicken, meatier portions toward edge of dish; brush with ½ preserves. Heat, covered with wax paper, 12 to 13 minutes, brushing with remaining preserves halfway through heating. Remove chicken to serving platter; let stand, covered, 7 minutes. Meanwhile, drain liquid, reserving ½ cup. In baking dish, combine reserved liquid and remaining ingredients. Heat 3 to 4 minutes or until sauce is slightly thickened, stirring twice; serve over chicken.

*Hint: *To quickly thaw frozen fruit, see page 139.*

FIESTA CHICKEN ROLL-UPS

Power Select: MEDIUM
              HIGH
Approx. Cooking Time: 11 minutes
Yield: 4 servings

2 boneless chicken breasts, skinned, split and pounded thin (about 1 to 1¼ lb.)
Chili powder
Pepper
½ cup shredded Cheddar or Monterey Jack cheese
4 teaspoons finely chopped jalapeno or green chili peppers
¼ cup butter or margarine, melted*
¾ cup crushed taco or corn chips
1 can (8 oz.) taco or seasoned tomato sauce

Set Power Select at MEDIUM. Season one side of each chicken with chili powder and pepper; sprinkle cheese and chopped peppers down center. Roll up jelly-roll style; secure with wooden toothpicks. Carefully roll in melted butter, then crushed chips. Arrange seam-side down in square baking dish. Heat, covered with wax paper, 7 to 8 minutes or until chicken is tender. Let stand, covered, 5 minutes.
Meanwhile, set Power Select at HIGH. In small glass bowl, heat taco sauce 2 to 3 minutes or until hot. Serve over chicken.

*Hint: *To melt butter in your microwave oven, see Quick Tips, page 140.*

Arrange food around edge of dish

HAWAIIAN ISLAND CHICKEN

Power Select: HIGH
Approx. Cooking Time: 21 minutes
Yield: about 4 servings

2½ to 3 pound chicken, cut into serving pieces
2 tablespoons soy sauce
¼ teaspoon ground ginger
1 green pepper, cut into chunks
1 can (11 oz.) mandarin oranges, drained (reserve syrup)
1 can (8¼ oz.) pineapple slices, drained and halved (reserve syrup)
1 tablespoon cornstarch

Set Power Select at HIGH. In oblong baking dish, arrange chicken, meatier portions toward edge of dish; brush with soy sauce blended with ginger. Add green pepper; heat, covered with wax paper, 13 to 15 minutes; drain. Let stand, covered, 7 minutes. Meanwhile, in 2-cup glass measure, blend cornstarch with 1 cup reserved syrups. Heat 2 minutes, stirring once. Add fruit and pour over chicken; if necessary, heat 3 to 4 minutes.

HERB BAKED CHICKEN

Power Select: HIGH→STAND
Approx. Cooking Time: 12 minutes
Yield: about 4 servings

1 teaspoon garlic salt
1 teaspoon paprika
½ teaspoon oregano
¼ teaspoon pepper
Juice and grated peel of 1 lemon
2½ to 3 pound chicken, cut into serving pieces
1 jar (4½ oz.) sliced mushrooms, drained

Set Power Select at HIGH. Combine garlic, paprika, oregano, pepper and lemon peel; rub over chicken. In oblong baking dish, arrange chicken, meatier portions toward edge of dish; drizzle with lemon juice and top with mushrooms. Heat, covered with wax paper, 10½ to 12 minutes or until chicken is tender. Let STAND, covered, 5 minutes before serving.

HURRY CURRY CHICKEN

Power Select: HIGH→STAND
Approx. Cooking Time: 15 minutes
Yield: about 4 servings

2½ to 3 pound chicken, cut into serving pieces
1 can (10¾ oz.) condensed cream of chicken soup
1 tomato, cut into wedges (optional)
½ cup raisins or peanuts
1 tablespoon curry powder
1 tablespoon dried onion flakes
⅛ teaspoon garlic powder

Set Power Select at HIGH. In oblong baking dish, arrange chicken. Thoroughly combine remaining ingredients and spoon over chicken. Heat, covered with wax paper, 13 to 15 minutes or until chicken is tender, rearranging chicken once. Let STAND, covered, 7 minutes. Remove chicken to serving platter; stir sauce until smooth and serve over chicken.

IN-A-JAM KABOBS

Power Select: HIGH
Approx. Cooking Time: 9 minutes
Yield: 4 servings

⅓ cup orange marmalade
2 tablespoons orange juice
2 tablespoons soy sauce
½ teaspoon lemon juice
Dash ground ginger
2 boneless chicken breasts, skinned and cut into 1½-inch pieces (about 1 to 1¼ lb.)
1 package (10 oz.) frozen brussel sprouts, thawed

Set Power Select at HIGH. In medium glass bowl, heat marmalade, orange juice, soy sauce, lemon juice and ginger 2½ to 3 minutes; add chicken and marinate, if desired, 30 minutes.
On four 9 or 10-inch wooden skewers*, alternately thread chicken and brussel sprouts. Arrange skewers on 8-inch square baking dish and heat 5 to 6 minutes or until chicken is tender, rearranging skewers once and brushing with marinade twice.

*Note: *If wooden skewers are unavailable, see Introduction page 7 for using metal skewers.*

MOROCCAN CHICKEN

Power Select: HIGH→MEDIUM-LOW
                       HIGH
Approx. Cooking Time: 36 minutes
Yield: about 4 servings

2 cups hot water
1 cup rice
1 envelope (1 oz.) onion-mushroom soup mix
½ cup raisins
½ teaspoon ground cinnamon
2½ to 3 pound chicken, cut into serving pieces
1 cup plain yogurt
2 tablespoons flour
1 to 2 tablespoons milk

Set Power Select at HIGH. In oblong baking dish, combine water, rice, ½ envelope soup mix, raisins and ¼ teaspoon cinnamon. Heat, covered, 4 to 5 minutes. Set Power Select at MEDIUM-LOW. Heat, covered, 13 to 15 minutes or until rice is almost tender, stirring once. Arrange chicken on rice; sprinkle with remaining cinnamon.
Set Power Select at HIGH. Heat, covered with wax paper, 12 to 14 minutes or until chicken is tender, rearranging chicken and stirring rice once. Meanwhile, combine yogurt, flour, milk and remaining soup mix. Spoon over chicken; let stand, covered, 7 minutes. If necessary, reheat at Power Select MEDIUM-LOW 1½ to 2 minutes before serving.

ORIENTAL CHICKEN AND CASHEWS

Power Select: HIGH
                HIGH→STAND
Approx. Cooking Time: 11 minutes
Yield: about 4 servings

3 tablespoons oil
2 boneless chicken breasts, skinned and thinly sliced
   (about 1 to 1¼ lb.)
2 cloves garlic, finely chopped
2 tablespoons soy sauce
1 tablespoon sherry
1 tablespoon cornstarch
¼ teaspoon ground ginger
1 medium green pepper, cut into small chunks
½ cup cashews halves or chopped walnuts

Set Power Select at HIGH. In oblong baking dish, heat
oil 2½ to 3 minutes. Meanwhile, combine chicken,
garlic, soy sauce, sherry, cornstarch and ginger.
Add to dish and heat 3 to 4 minutes, stirring twice.
Add green pepper and cashews and heat, covered,
2½ to 3½ minutes at HIGH or until chicken and green
pepper are tender, stirring once. Let STAND 3 minutes
before serving.

SPIRITED CHICKEN

Power Select: HIGH→STAND
Approx. Cooking Time: 16 minutes
Yield: about 6 servings

2¾ pounds chicken legs, thighs detached
½ cup dry sherry
¼ cup soy sauce
1 tablespoon Worcestershire sauce
½ teaspoon garlic powder

Set Power Select at HIGH. In oblong baking dish,
combine all ingredients; marinate, if desired, 30
minutes. Heat, covered with wax paper, 14 to 16
minutes or until chicken is tender, rearranging
chicken once. Let STAND, covered, 7 minutes before
serving.

TENDER CRISPY CHICKEN

Power Select: HIGH→STAND
Approx. Cooking Time: 11 minutes
Yield: about 4 servings

8 small chicken pieces (about 2 lb.)
1 package (2⅜ oz.) seasoned coating mix for chicken

Set Power Select at HIGH. Coat chicken according to
package directions; arrange in oblong baking dish.
Heat, covered with wax paper, 9 to 10½ minutes or
until chicken is tender. Let STAND, 5 minutes before
serving.

Note: **For TWO servings** (*4 pieces*), *follow above
procedure. Halve all ingredients and heat chicken
5½ to 6 minutes.*
   For ONE serving (*2 pieces*), *heat chicken 3½ to 4
minutes.*

Roast Goose with Apple Stuffing, page 64

TURKEY AND OTHER POULTRY ✿✿✿✿✿✿✿✿✿✿✿✿✿✿✿✿✿✿✿✿✿✿✿✿✿✿✿✿✿✿

CORNISH HENS WITH PEACH SAUCE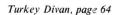

Power Select: HIGH→STAND
Approx. Cooking Time: 16 minutes
Yield: 4 servings

2 cornish hens (about 1 lb. ea.), split
Browning sauce
Paprika
Pepper
1 can (16 oz.) sliced peaches in heavy syrup, drained
  (reserve ⅓ cup syrup)
⅔ cup orange juice
1 tablespoon cornstarch
⅛ teaspoon ground ginger

Set Power Select at HIGH. In oblong baking dish, arrange hens; brush with browning sauce and season with paprika and pepper. Heat, covered with wax paper, 10 to 11 minutes or until hens are tender; drain. Let STAND covered, 7 minutes.
Meanwhile, in small glass bowl, combine reserved syrup, orange juice, cornstarch and ginger. Heat 1½ to 2½ minutes or until sauce is thickened, stirring once. Add peaches and spoon over hens. If necessary, heat 1½ to 2 minutes before serving. Garnish, if desired, with slivered almonds.

Note: **For TWO servings,** *follow above procedure. Halve all ingredients; heat hens 7 to 8 minutes. Add enough reserved syrup to orange juice to equal ½ cup; heat sauce 1 to 1½ minutes.*

PECAN STUFFED PHEASANT

Power Select: HIGH
  HIGH→MEDIUM-LOW
  HIGH
Approx. Cooking Time: 35 minutes
Yield: about 4 servings

½ cup thinly sliced celery
2 tablespoons butter or margarine
⅔ cup dry bread crumbs
⅓ cup chopped pecans
1 teaspoon salt
⅛ teaspoon pepper
2 pheasants (1 to 1½ lb. ea.)
1 cup water
2 to 3 tablespoons sherry
1½ teaspoons browning sauce
2 tablespoons cornstarch

Set Power Select at HIGH. In small glass bowl, heat celery and butter 1 to 2 minutes; stir in bread crumbs, pecans, ½ teaspoon salt and pepper. Stuff pheasant with pecan mixture; with string, tie wings and legs to body of pheasant. Arrange pheasant in square baking dish; add ¾ cup water, sherry and browning sauce. Heat, covered, 8 to 10 minutes at HIGH.
Set Power Select at MEDIUM-LOW. Heat, covered, 18 to 20 minutes or until pheasant is tender. Remove pheasant to serving platter; let stand, covered, 5 minutes. Meanwhile, into dish, stir in remaining salt and cornstarch blended with remaining water.
Set Power Select at HIGH. Heat 2 to 3 minutes or until thickened, stirring once; serve with pheasant.

STUFFED CORNISH HENS WITH ORANGE HONEY SAUCE

Power Select: HIGH
  MEDIUM-LOW
  HIGH→STAND
Approx. Cooking Time: 56 minutes
Yield: 4 servings

1½ cups hot water
1 cup orange juice
1 package (6 oz.) long grain and wild rice mix
4 slices bacon, cooked and crumbled (see page 54)
4 cornish hens (1 lb. ea.)
½ cup orange juice concentrate
⅓ cup honey
¼ to ½ teaspoon browning sauce

Set Power Select at HIGH. In 2-quart casserole dish, combine water, juice and rice. Heat, covered, 5 to 6 minutes.
Set Power Select at MEDIUM-LOW. Heat, covered, 20 minutes or until rice is tender; stir in bacon. Stuff hens with rice mixture; with string, tie wings to body of hen and legs together to cover stuffing. Place hens in oblong baking dish.
Set Power Select at HIGH. Heat, covered with wax paper, 28 to 30 minutes or until hens are tender, rearranging hens once. Meanwhile, combine remaining ingredients; brush hens every 10 minutes. Let STAND covered, 10 minutes before serving.

Turkey Divan, page 64

ROAST DUCK WITH ORANGE

Power Select: MEDIUM
                 MEDIUM→STAND
Approx. Cooking Time: 55 minutes
Yield: 4 to 6 servings

4 to 5 pound duck
¼ cup bottled fruit sauce (for poultry)
2 tablespoons orange liqueur or orange juice
¼ teaspoon browning sauce
1 can (11 oz.) mandarin oranges, drained (optional)

Set Power Select at MEDIUM. In oblong baking dish, arrange duck on microwave oven safe roasting rack; pierce skin several times. Heat 30 minutes; drain. Combine fruit sauce, liqueur and browning sauce; brush half on duck. Heat 20 to 25 minutes at MEDIUM or until duck is tender. Brush with remaining sauce. Let STAND, covered, 10 minutes before serving. Garnish with oranges.

ROAST GOOSE WITH APPLE STUFFING

Power Select: HIGH
                 MEDIUM
                 MEDIUM→STAND
Approx. Cooking Time: 1¼ hours
Yield: 6 to 8 servings

¼ cup butter, margarine or goose fat
1 cup thinly sliced celery
1 cup finely chopped onion
3 to 5 cups fresh bread cubes
2 cups chopped apples (2 medium)
1 egg, beaten
¼ cup brandy
1 tablespoon parsley flakes
1 teaspoon salt
¼ teaspoon pepper
9 to 10 pound goose
Browning sauce

Set Power Select at HIGH. In large glass bowl, heat butter, celery and onion 5 to 6 minutes or until celery and onion are tender. Add bread, apples, egg, brandy, parsley, salt and pepper; combine thoroughly. Stuff goose with apple mixture; secure opening with wooden toothpicks or string. Secure wings and legs to body of bird with string. Pierce skin several times and arrange bird, breast side down, on microwave oven safe roasting rack in oblong baking dish; brush with browning sauce.
Set Power Select at MEDIUM. Heat 30 minutes; turn bird over and drain fat. Heat 25 to 30 minutes at MEDIUM or until bird is tender. Let STAND covered, 15 minutes before serving

ROAST WHOLE TURKEY

Power Select: MEDIUM-HIGH
                 MEDIUM→STAND
Temperature Select: 175°F
Approx. Cooking Time: 2 hours
Yield: about 12 servings

12 pound turkey
Salt
Poultry seasoning
Browning sauce

Set Power Select at MEDIUM-HIGH. Season inside of turkey with salt and poultry seasoning. With string, tie legs and wings securely to body of bird. In oblong baking dish, arrange turkey, breast-side down on microwave oven safe roasting rack; brush with browning sauce. Heat, covered with wax paper, 35 minutes, draining liquid once. Arrange turkey breast-side up; brush with browning sauce. Set Power Select at MEDIUM.

TO HEAT BY TEMPERATURE: Insert probe into thigh joint. Set Temperature Select at 175°F. Heat, covered with wax paper, draining liquid when necessary. When oven shuts off; turn dish. Insert probe into other thigh joint; heat, covered with wax paper.

TO HEAT BY TIME: Set time for 1¼ hours. Heat, covered with wax paper, until turkey registers 175°F when tested with conventional meat thermometer (insert in both thigh joints as directed in Temperature heating). Do NOT use conventional meat thermometer in poultry while operating microwave oven. Drain liquid occasionally.

Let STAND, covered, 20 minutes before serving.

Note: Turkey may be stuffed before heating. Close cavity with string or wooden toothpicks. Halfway through heating at MEDIUM, shield legs and wings with aluminum foil to prevent over cooking.

TURKEY DIVAN

Power Select: MEDIUM-HIGH
Approx. Cooking Time: 15 minutes
Yield: about 4 servings

2 packages (10 oz. ea.) frozen broccoli spears,
** thawed**
2 to 3 cups cut-up cooked turkey or chicken*
Salt and pepper to taste
1 can (11 oz.) condensed cheddar cheese soup
½ cup milk
¼ cup buttered bread crumbs
½ teaspoon paprika

Set Power Select at MEDIUM-HIGH. In oblong baking dish, arrange broccoli; top with turkey. Heat, covered, 5 to 6 minutes; drain. Season with salt and pepper. In small glass bowl, combine soup and milk. Heat 2 to 3 minutes; stir until smooth. Pour sauce over turkey; heat, covered, 5 to 6 minutes or until heated through. Top with bread crumbs mixed with paprika; let stand, covered, 5 minutes before serving.

*If desired, turkey may be thinly sliced.

TURKEY ROAST

Power Select: MEDIUM
                 MEDIUM→STAND
Approx. Cooking Time: 32 minutes
Yield: 6 servings

2 pound frozen turkey roast

Set Power Select at MEDIUM. In glass loaf dish, place roast skin side down. Heat, covered with wax paper, 7 minutes; turn roast over. Heat, covered with wax paper 24 to 25 minutes at MEDIUM or until roast registers 175°F when tested with conventional meat thermometer. Let STAND, covered, 7 minutes before serving.

STUFFING Following other famous combinations, what is roast poultry without the STUFFING. We've collected a few favorite recipes for you to use to stuff a bird or to bake and serve with poultry.

APPLE SAUSAGE STUFFING

Power Select: HIGH
        HIGH →MEDIUM-LOW
Approx. Cooking Time: 16 minutes
Yield: about 8 servings (about 6 cups)

½ **pound bulk pork sausage**
1 **cup thinly sliced celery**
½ **cup finely chopped onion**
5 **cups fresh bread cubes**
3 **cups chopped apple (3 medium)**
2 **eggs, beaten**
1 **to 1½ teaspoons salt**
¼ **to ½ teaspoon poultry seasoning**

Set Power Select at HIGH. In oblong baking dish, crumble sausage; stir in celery and onion. Heat 4½ to 5½ minutes or until sausage is browned, stirring twice; drain. Add remaining ingredients; combine thoroughly.* Heat, covered, 3 to 4 minutes at HIGH. Set Power Select at MEDIUM-LOW. Heat, covered, 5 to 6 minutes or until heated through.

This makes enough to stuff a 7 to 9 lb. bird.

BASIC BREAD STUFFING

Power Select: HIGH
        MEDIUM-LOW
Approx. Cooking Time: 13 minutes
Yield: 6 to 8 servings (about 4 cups)

1½ **cups thinly sliced celery**
1 **cup chopped onion**
½ **cup butter or margarine**
8 **cups fresh bread cubes**
2 **eggs**
¼ **cup water (optional)**
3 **tablespoons parsley flakes**
1 **to 1½ teaspoons poultry seasoning**
1 **teaspoon salt**
½ **teaspoon pepper**

Set Power Select at HIGH. In 2-quart casserole dish, heat celery, onion and butter 6 to 7 minutes or until celery and onion are tender, stirring twice. Add remaining ingredients; combine thoroughly.* Set Power Select at MEDIUM-LOW. Heat, covered, 5 to 6 minutes or until heated through.

This makes enough to stuff 2 (2½ to 3 lb.) birds.

CONVENIENCE STUFFING MIXES

Power Select: HIGH
Approx. Cooking Time: 5 minutes
Yield: about 6 servings

1½ **to 1¾ cups hot water**
¼ **cup butter**
1 **package (6 to 6½ oz.) stuffing mix (chicken, cornbread, pork or rice varieties) with seasoning packet**

Set Power Select at HIGH. In 2-quart casserole dish, heat water, butter and seasoning packet 4½ to 5 minutes; stir in stuffing crumbs.*
Let stand, covered, 5 minutes before serving.

This makes enough to stuff a 2½ to 3 pound bird.

Variations: *Add one of the following with seasoning packet:*
  • *1 cup chopped fresh cranberries or apple*
  • *½ cup raisins, chopped nuts, or chopped apricots.*
  • *½ pound browned ground sausage, drained*
  • *1 can (8 oz.) whole kernel corn, drained*

CORN BREAD STUFFING

Power Select: HIGH
        MEDIUM-LOW→STAND
Approx. Cooking Time: 18 minutes
Yield: about 12 servings (about 9 cups)

1½ **cups thinly sliced celery**
1 **cup chopped onion**
½ **cup butter or margarine**
2 **packages (12 oz. ea.) corn bread or corn muffin mix, baked and crumbled (see page 112)**
2 **eggs**
1½ **cups orange juice or chicken broth**
1½ **teaspoons salt**
¾ **teaspoon sage**
¼ **teaspoon pepper**

Set Power Select at HIGH. In 2-quart oblong baking dish, heat celery, onion and butter 6 to 7 minutes or until celery and onion are tender, stirring twice. Add remaining ingredients; combine thoroughly.* Set Power Select at MEDIUM-LOW. Heat, covered, 10 to 11 minutes or until heated through. Let STAND, covered, 5 minutes before serving.

This makes enough to stuff a 9 to 12 pound bird.

MUSHROOM BARLEY STUFFING

Power Select: HIGH
        MEDIUM-LOW
Approx. Cooking Time: 19 minutes
Yield: about 6 servings (about 3 cups)

1½ **to 1¾ cups chicken broth**
1 **cup coarsely chopped fresh mushrooms**
½ **cup quick cooking barley**
3 **cups seasoned croutons**
1 **egg, beaten**
1 **tablespoon parsley**
½ **teaspoon salt**
¼ **teaspoon onion powder**

Set Power Select at HIGH. In 2-quart casserole dish, heat chicken broth, covered, 3 to 4 minutes; add mushrooms and barley. Set Power Select at MEDIUM-LOW. Heat, covered, 7½ to 8½ minutes. Add remaining ingredients; combine thoroughly.* Heat, covered, 5 to 6 minutes or until heated through.

This makes enough to stuff a 4 to 5 pound bird.

Fish for dinner is always a delightful surprise to daily meal planning. And how lucky you seafood lovers are—fish prepared in the microwave oven is moist and delicious (not to mention quick).

Whether you are experimenting with a new recipe or making an old favorite, you will marvel at the results. Just follow the simple instructions in the charts or one of these tasty recipes and your efforts are sure to be applauded.

DEFROSTING FISH AND SEAFOOD

- Defrost fish in original wrapper (not foil), set in a shallow dish to catch any liquid.
- Set Power Select at DEFROST and heat for the time recommended in the chart.
- Turn whole fish or blocks of fillets over halfway through defrosting cycle.
- Let fish stand equal time before preparing.
- Rinse under cold water to remove remaining ice crystals.
- Estimate 6 minutes per pound defrosting time for fish not listed below.

FISH	APPROXIMATE DEFROSTING TIME (minutes per pound) at Power Select at DEFROST	STANDING TIME (in minutes)
Crabmeat (6 oz. packages)	15 to 16	15 to 16
Fish Fillets	4 to 6	4 to 6
Fish Steaks (4 oz. ea.)	5 to 6	5 to 6
Lobster Tails (6 to 8 oz. ea.)	6 to 7	6 to 7
Scallops (sea)	8 to 10	8 to 10
Shrimp	6 to 7	6 to 7
Whole Fish (12 oz. ea.)	5 to 6	5 to 6

PREPARING FISH AND SEAFOOD

- Use only fresh or defrosted fish.
- Clean fish before starting recipe.
- Arrange fish in dish in single layer; do not overlap edges.
- Place thicker pieces toward outside edge of dish (i.e. tail section towards center)
- Heat fish covered.
- Rearrange or stir small pieces (scallop, shrimp etc.) halfway through heating.
- Test for doneness before adding extra heating time. Fish should be opaque in color and flake easily when tested with fork.
- Let fish stand, covered, before serving.

Arrangement of fish fillets

FISH OR SEAFOOD	AMOUNT	POWER SELECT	APPROXIMATE HEATING TIME (in minutes)
Fish Fillets	1 lb.	HIGH	4 to 6
Fish Steaks	4 (6 oz. ea.)	HIGH	6 to 8
Scallops (sea)	1 lb.	MEDIUM	6½ to 8½
Shrimp medium size (shelled and cleaned)	1 lb.	MEDIUM	4½ to 6½
Whole fish (stuffed or unstuffed)	1½ to 1¾ lb.	HIGH	9 to 11

Pictured on the preceding page: Bouillabaisse, Steamed Whole Lobster, Trout Amandine, Baked Stuffed Clams.

BAKED SNAPPER A LA ORANGE

Power Select: HIGH
                HIGH→STAND
Approx. Cooking Time: 20 minutes
Yield: about 4 servings

1 medium orange
6 tablespoons butter or margarine
1 small onion, finely chopped
1 tablespoon parsley flakes
½ teaspoon basil
⅛ teaspoon pepper
2 cups soft bread crumbs (about 4 slices bread)
2 whole red snappers (1¼ to 1½ lb. ea.), dressed and
**   heads removed**
Salt
1 can (6 oz.) frozen orange juice concentrate, thawed
**   (see page 139)**

Set Power Select at HIGH. Slice ½ orange; peel and chop remaining half.
In small glass bowl, heat butter, onion, parsley, basil and pepper 2½ to 3 minutes or until onion is tender; stir in bread crumbs and chopped orange.
In oblong baking dish, arrange fish; season inside with salt. Stuff cavity with bread crumb mixture. Heat, covered with wax paper, 13 to 15 minutes or until fish is tender. Pour orange juice over fish; add orange slices. Heat, covered with wax paper, 2 minutes at HIGH. Let STAND covered, 3 minutes before serving.

BAKED STUFFED CLAMS

Power Select: MEDIUM
Approx. Cooking Time: 6 minutes
Yield: 18 clams

18 small clams, scrubbed and opened (littleneck)
½ to ⅔ cup seasoned dry bread crumbs
2½ to 3 tablespoons olive oil
¼ teaspoon garlic powder
¼ teaspoon paprika
3 slices bacon, crisp-cooked and crumbled (see
**   page 54)**

Set Power Select at MEDIUM. Around the edge of a 12-inch glass pizza dish, arrange clams on half shell; with toothpick, pierce each clam several times. Heat, covered with wax paper, 3½ to 4 minutes or until clams are tender, turning dish once.
Meanwhile, combine bread crumbs, oil, garlic and paprika. Top each clam with bread crumb mixture, then bacon. Heat 1½ to 2 minutes.

BAKED STUFFED LOBSTER TAILS

Power Select: MEDIUM→STAND
Approx. Cooking Time: 10 minutes
Yield: 4 servings

4 lobster tails (about 8 oz. ea.)
3 tablespoons butter or margarine, melted
⅓ cup seasoned dry bread crumbs
⅛ teaspoon onion powder
⅛ teaspoon paprika
⅛ teaspoon salt

Set Power Select at MEDIUM. With kitchen shears, cut lobster through center of soft shell (underneath) to the tail. Lift lobster out of shell by loosening with fingers, leaving meat attached to tail section. (Lobster meat will rest on shell). Arrange on 12-inch glass pizza dish, tails toward center.
Combine remaining ingredients; sprinkle over lobster. Heat, covered with wax paper, 8½ to 9½ minutes or until lobster is done. Let STAND 5 minutes; serve, if desired, with Lemon Butter*.

*Lemon Butter:
In small glass bowl, heat ½ cup butter and 1 to 2 table-spoons lemon juice 1 to 1½ minutes or until butter is melted.

Note: **For TWO servings,** *follow above procedure. Halve all ingredients; heat lobster 5½ to 6½ minutes.*

BOUILLABAISSE

Power Select: HIGH
                HIGH→MEDIUM
                HIGH→STAND
Approx. Cooking Time: 35 minutes
Yield: about 6 servings

1 medium onion, sliced
2 tablespoons oil
2 cloves garlic, finely chopped
6 small clams, scrubbed (littleneck)
1 can (28 oz.) whole tomatoes, chopped
2 bottles (8 oz. ea.) clam juice
2 bay leaves
½ teaspoon salt
⅛ teaspoon pepper
Dash thyme
Pinch saffron (optional)
½ pound sea scallops
½ pound sole fillet, cut into 1½-inch pieces
2 lobster tails (8 oz. ea.) cut into 1½-inch pieces

Set Power Select at HIGH. In 4-quart casserole dish, combine onion, oil and garlic; heat, covered, 2 to 3 minutes. Add clams, tomatoes, clam juice, bay leaves, salt, pepper, thyme and saffron; heat, covered, 5 minutes at HIGH.
Set Power Select at MEDIUM. Heat, covered 15 to 20 minutes or until clams are open, stirring once.
Add scallops, fillet and lobster.
Set Power Select at HIGH. Heat, covered, 5 to 7 minutes or until fish is done. Let STAND, covered, 10 minutes before serving.

CLAMS—STEAMER STYLE

Power Select: HIGH→MEDIUM
Approx. Cooking Time: 7 minutes
Yield: 12 clams

12 small clams, scrubbed (littleneck)
¼ cup hot water

Set Power Select at HIGH. In shallow casserole dish, combine clams and water; heat, covered, 1 minute.
Set Power Select at MEDIUM. Heat, covered, 5 to 6 minutes or until clams are open. Serve, if desired, with melted butter and cocktail sauce.

COQUILLE ST. JACQUES

Power Select: MEDIUM
Approx. Cooking Time: 12 minutes
Yield: 4 servings

¼ cup white wine
1 pound sea scallops
2 tablespoons butter or margarine
1 tablespoon dried onion flakes
2 tablespoons flour
Dash white pepper
¾ cup light cream or milk
1 jar (2½ oz.) sliced mushrooms, drained
⅓ cup shredded Swiss cheese (about 1⅓ oz.)
¼ cup buttered bread crumbs
Parsley flakes

Set Power Select at MEDIUM. In round baking dish, pour wine over scallops; heat, covered, 5 to 6 minutes or until scallops are tender, stirring once. Drain liquid and reserve ¼ cup; let scallops stand, covered. In medium glass bowl, heat butter and onion ¾ to 1 minute; stir in flour and pepper. Gradually add cream and reserved liquid, stirring until smooth. Heat 3 to 3½ minutes or until mixture is thickened, stirring twice. Stir in mushrooms and cheese; add scallops. Spoon mixture into 4 individual glass ramekins or serving dishes, top with bread crumbs and parsley. Arrange ramekins on glass oven tray, heat 1 to 2 minutes or until heated through.

Note: **For TWO servings,** *follow above procedure; halve all ingredients. Heat scallops 2 to 3 minutes, butter ½ minute, cream mixture 1½ to 2 minutes and ramekin 1 minute.*

FILLET PROVENCALE

Power Select: HIGH
HIGH→MEDIUM
HIGH→STAND
Approx. Cooking Time: 17 minutes
Yield: 6 servings

2 small onions, sliced
2 tablespoons butter or margarine
1 clove garlic, finely chopped
1 can (16 oz.) stewed tomatoes, chopped
1 jar (4½ oz.) sliced mushrooms, drained
¼ cup white wine
⅛ teaspoon basil
6 flounder fillets (about ¼ lb. ea.)
Salt

Set Power Select at HIGH. In oblong baking dish, combine onion, butter and garlic; heat, covered, 3 to 3½ minutes. Stir in tomatoes, mushrooms, wine and basil. Heat, covered, 3 minutes at HIGH.
Set Power Select at MEDIUM. Heat, covered, 3 to 4 minutes.
Meanwhile, season fish with salt, skin side only. Roll up (skin-side in) and arrange seam-side down in sauce; spoon sauce over fish.
Set Power Select at HIGH. Heat, covered, 5 to 6 minutes or until fish is done. Let STAND, covered, 5 minutes before serving.

FLOUNDER WITH SHRIMP SAUCE

Power Select: HIGH→STAND
Approx. Cooking Time: 9 minutes
Yield: 4 servings

4 flounder fillets (about ¼ lb. ea.)
1 can (10¾ oz.) condensed cream of shrimp soup
¼ cup white wine or milk
½ cup shredded Swiss cheese (about 2 oz.)
Parsley or slivered almonds

Set Power Select at HIGH. Roll up fillets and arrange seam-side down in square baking dish. Combine soup, wine and cheese; spoon over fillets. Heat, covered, 7½ to 8½ minutes or until fish is done. Let STAND, covered, 3 minutes; sprinkle with parsley before serving.

Hint: *When rolling-up fillets, place a thin strip of Swiss cheese in center.*

Baked Snapper a la Orange, page 69

LANDLUBBER'S STUFFED CLAMS

Power Select: MEDIUM-HIGH
Approx. Cooking Time: 4 minutes
Yield: 4 servings

2 cups seasoned croutons, crushed*
1 can (7½ oz.) minced clams
2 tablespoons grated Parmesan cheese
½ teaspoon dried onion flakes
⅛ teaspoon garlic powder
Dash pepper
1 tablespoon butter or margarine, melted
½ tablespoon parsley flakes

Set Power Select at MEDIUM-HIGH. Reserve ¼ cup crouton crumbs. Combine remaining crouton crumbs, clams, cheese, onion, garlic and pepper. Spoon mixture into 4 individual glass baking shells or 6-ounce custard cups; top with reserved crumbs blended with butter and parsley. Heat 3 to 4 minutes or until heated through, rearranging dishes once.

Substitution: Use 1½ cups dry seasoned bread crumbs for crushed croutons.

MARYLAND CRAB BAKE

Power Select: HIGH
                MEDIUM→STAND
Approx. Cooking Time: 12 minutes
Yield: 4 to 6 servings

1 cup each chopped celery, green pepper and onion
3 tablespoons butter or margarine
1 cup mayonnaise
4 hard-cooked eggs, chopped (see page 85)
2 packages (6 oz. ea.) crabmeat, drained and flaked (canned or frozen, thawed)
1 teaspoon Worcestershire sauce
½ teaspoon pepper
½ teaspoon salt
1 cup buttery cracker crumbs
2 tablespoons butter or margarine, melted
Dash paprika

Set Power Select at HIGH. In 2-quart casserole dish, combine celery, green pepper, onion and 3 table-spoons butter. Heat, covered, 4 to 5 minutes or until vegetables are tender, stirring once. Stir in mayon-naise, eggs, crab, Worcestershire, pepper and salt. Set Power Select at MEDIUM. Heat, covered, 6 to 7 minutes or until heated through, stirring twice. Combine cracker crumbs, melted butter and paprika; sprinkle over casserole. Let STAND 5 minutes before serving.

OYSTERS ROCKEFELLER EN CASSEROLE

Power Select: HIGH
Approx. Cooking Time: 13 minutes
Yield: about 4 servings

1 can (10½ oz.) condensed oyster stew
3 tablespoons flour
⅔ cup shredded Cheddar cheese (about 2⅔ oz.)
1 tablespoon dried onion flakes
1 bay leaf, crushed

2 packages (10 oz. ea.) frozen chopped spinach, thawed (see page 139)
1 pint large oysters, drained
½ cup dry bread crumbs
¼ cup grated Parmesan cheese
2 tablespoons butter or margarine, melted
½ teaspoon paprika

Set Power Select at HIGH. In medium glass bowl, combine stew, flour, cheddar cheese, onion and bay leaf; heat 3 minutes or until sauce is thickened, stirring twice.
In 2½-quart casserole dish, spread spinach; pour on stew mixture. With toothpick, pierce each oyster several times and arrange on stew. Top with bread crumbs mixed with parmesan cheese, butter and paprika. Heat, uncovered, 5 minutes; turn dish and heat, covered, 5 minutes. Let stand, covered, 5 minutes before serving.

PARCHMENT SEAFOOD SPECTACULAR 🔲CALORIE

Power Select: HIGH
Approx. Cooking Time: 9 minutes
Yield: 4 servings

4 halibut or other seafood steaks (about 6 oz. ea.)
2 tablespoons brandy
1 tablespoon lemon juice
2 tablespoons butter or margarine
2 tablespoons dried chives
Salt and pepper to taste
1 cup sliced fresh mushrooms (about ¼ lb.)
1 small apple, thinly sliced

Set Power Select at HIGH. For each serving, place fish on 10 x 15-inch piece parchment paper. Combine brandy and lemon juice; brush on fish. Dot each with butter, chives and season with salt and pepper. Mound mushrooms and apple on top; bring paper up around fish. Fold edges over twice to seal top; fold side edges up. Place on glass oven tray, heat 7½ to 9 minutes. Serve packet directly on dinner plate.

Shrimp Scampi, page 73

SALMON ROMANOFF

Power Select: MEDIUM→STAND
Approx. Cooking Time: 12 minutes
Yield: 4 to 6 servings

1 package (8 oz.) medium egg noodles, cooked and
**   drained (see page 106)**
1½ cups cottage cheese
1½ cups sour cream
1 can (16 oz.) salmon, drained and flaked
1 can (4 oz.) sliced mushrooms, drained
½ cup shredded Cheddar cheese (about 2 oz.)
2 teaspoons dried onion flakes
2 teaspoons Worcestershire sauce
½ teaspoon salt
⅛ teaspoon dried garlic pieces
Shredded Cheddar cheese or buttered bread crumbs
Paprika

Set Power Select at MEDIUM. In 3-quart casserole dish,
thoroughly combine noodles, cottage cheese, sour
cream, salmon, mushrooms, ½ cup cheese, onion,
Worcestershire, salt and garlic. Heat, covered, 10 to
12 minutes or until heated through, stirring twice.
Top with shredded cheese and sprinkle with
paprika. Let STAND, covered, 5 minutes before serving.

SALMON STEAKS WITH DILL

Power Select: HIGH→STAND
Approx. Cooking Time: 10 minutes
Yield: 4 servings

½ cup thinly sliced celery
¼ cup butter or margarine
½ tablespoon parsley flakes
1 teaspoon salt
½ teaspoon dill weed
¼ teaspoon pepper
¼ cup white wine
4 salmon steaks (about 4 oz. ea.)

Set Power Select at HIGH. In oblong baking dish,
combine celery, butter, parsley, salt, dill and pepper.
Heat 3 to 4 minutes or until celery is tender; stir in
wine. Arrange salmon in dish; spoon wine and butter
mixture over salmon.
Heat, covered, with wax paper, 4½ to 5½ minutes or
until salmon is done. Let STAND, covered, 3 minutes
before serving.

SCALLOPS WITH HERB LEMON BUTTER

Power Select: HIGH
                     MEDIUM→STAND
Approx. Cooking Time: 10 minutes
Yield: about 4 servings

¼ cup butter or margarine
½ teaspoon basil
½ teaspoon crushed rosemary
¼ teaspoon salt
1 pound sea scallops
Juice from 1 lemon (about 2 tbsp.)
Paprika

Set Power Select at HIGH. In round baking dish, heat
butter, basil, rosemary and salt 1 to 1½ minutes or
until butter is melted. Stir in scallops and sprinkle
with lemon juice; spoon butter mixture over scallops.
Set Power Select at MEDIUM. Heat, covered with wax
paper, 7 to 8½ minutes or until scallops are tender,
stirring once; Let STAND, covered, 5 minutes,
sprinkle with paprika before serving.

Note: **For TWO servings,** *follow above procedure;*
halve all ingredients. Heat butter ½ to 1 minute
and scallops 4½ to 5½ minutes.

SCROD WITH GRAPE SAUCE

Power Select: HIGH
                     MEDIUM
Approx. Cooking Time: 16 minutes
Yield: 4 to 6 servings

2 tablespoons butter or margarine
1 tablespoon dried onion flakes
¾ cup chicken broth
Pepper to taste
1½ pounds scrod or sole fillets
1 cup halved green grapes
3 tablespoons flour
¾ cup light cream or milk
Parsley

Set Power Select at HIGH. In oblong baking dish,
heat butter, onion, broth and pepper 2 to 3 minutes.
Arrange fillets in single layer and heat, covered with
wax paper, 7 to 8 minutes or until fish is done. Arrange
fillets on serving platter; cover. Strain broth into small
glass bowl; stir in grapes and flour blended with cream.
Set Power Select at MEDIUM. Heat 3½ to 5 minutes or
until sauce is thickened, stirring twice. Pour some
sauce over fillets, sprinkle with parsley; serve
remaining sauce with fillets.

Variation: *Add 2 tablespoons white wine when heating fish.*

SHRIMP CREOLE

Power Select: HIGH
                     HIGH→MEDIUM→STAND
Approx. Cooking Time: 14 minutes
Yield: about 4 servings

½ cup each finely chopped celery, green pepper
**   and onion**
2 tablespoons oil
2 cloves garlic, finely chopped
1 can (15 oz.) tomato sauce
1 pound medium shrimp, shelled and cleaned
1 teaspoon salt
¼ teaspoon pepper
¼ to ½ teaspoon hot pepper sauce

Set Power Select at HIGH. In 2-quart casserole dish,
combine celery, green pepper, onion, oil and garlic.
Heat 4 to 5 minutes or until vegetables are tender.
Stir in remaining ingredients; heat, covered, 3 minutes
at HIGH.
Set Power Select at MEDIUM. Heat, covered, 5 to 6
minutes or until shrimp is tender, stirring once. Let
STAND, covered, 3 minutes before serving.

SHRIMP SCAMPI

Power Select: HIGH
                 MEDIUM→STAND
Approx. Cooking Time: 7 minutes
Yield: about 4 servings

½ cup butter or margarine
½ tablespoon finely chopped garlic or to taste
2 tablespoons lemon juice
1 tablespoon parsley flakes
½ teaspoon salt
1 pound medium shrimp, shelled and cleaned
Paprika (optional)

Set Power Select at HIGH. In round baking dish, heat butter and garlic 1½ to 2 minutes or until butter is melted. Add lemon juice, parsley and salt; stir in shrimp.
Set Power Select at MEDIUM. Heat, covered, 4 to 5 minutes or until shrimp is done, stirring once. Let STAND, covered, 5 minutes; sprinkle with paprika before serving.

Note: **For TWO servings,** *follow above procedure; halve all ingredients. Heat butter ¾ to 1 minute and shrimp 2½ to 3 minutes.*

SHRIMP AND VEGETABLES MANDARIN

Power Select: HIGH
                 HIGH→MEDIUM
Approx. Cooking Time: 13 minutes
Yield: about 4 servings

Water
1 can (11 oz.) mandarin oranges, drained
   (reserve liquid)
2 envelopes (¼ oz. ea.) instant chicken broth
1½ tablespoons cornstarch
⅛ teaspoon garlic powder
1 pound medium shrimp, shelled and cleaned
1 bunch green onions (scallions), thinly sliced
   (about ½ cup)
1 package (6 oz.) frozen pea pods, thawed*
1 jar (4½ oz.) sliced mushrooms, drained
Slivered almonds

Set Power Select at HIGH. Add enough water to reserved syrup to equal 1½ cups.
In 2-quart casserole dish, combine syrup mixture, broth, cornstarch and garlic. Heat 3½ to 4½ minutes or until mixture is thickened, stirring twice. Stir in shrimp, onions, pea pods and mushrooms. Heat, covered, 2 minutes at HIGH.
Set Power Select at MEDIUM. Heat, covered, 5 to 6 minutes or until shrimp is tender, stirring once. Stir in oranges and almonds and let stand, covered, 5 minutes before serving.

*Hint: *To quickly thaw frozen vegetables in your microwave oven, see page 139.*

SIMPLE SEAFOOD NEWBURG

Power Select: MEDIUM
                 MEDIUM→STAND
Approx. Cooking Time: 10 minutes
Yield: about 4 servings

1 can (10¾ oz.) condensed cream of mushroom soup
1 package (10 oz.) frozen peas, thawed (see page 139)
¼ cup milk or half 'n half
1 pound seafood, cooked (see page 68) and cut into
   bite-size pieces
1 jar (2½ oz.) sliced mushrooms, drained
2 to 3 tablespoons sherry

Set Power Select at MEDIUM. In 1½-quart casserole dish, combine soup, peas and milk. Heat, covered, 4 to 5 minutes, stirring once. Add remaining ingredients. Heat, covered, 4 to 5 minutes at MEDIUM or until heated through, stirring once. Let STAND, covered, 3 minutes before serving.

STEAMED WHOLE LOBSTER

Power Select: HIGH
                 MEDIUM→STAND
Approx. Cooking Time: 22 minutes
Yield: about 2 servings

1 quart hot water
½ teaspoon salt
1 fresh lobster (about 1½ to 2 lb.), pegged

Set Power Select at HIGH. In 5-quart casserole dish, heat, covered, water and salt 5 to 6 minutes or until boiling. Tilt dish; place lobster in dish, head first.
Set Power Select at MEDIUM. Heat, covered, 14 to 16 minutes or until shell turns red. Let STAND, covered, 2 minutes. To test for doneness, slit tail section; lobster meat should be opaque. If necessary, heat, covered, an additional 1 to 2 minutes.

TROUT AMANDINE

Power Select: HIGH
                 HIGH→STAND
Approx. Cooking Time: 11 minutes
Yield: 2 or 4 servings

⅓ cup butter or margarine
½ cup slivered almonds
2 whole trout, cleaned
   (about 12 oz. ea.)
Salt and pepper to taste
Lemon juice

Set Power Select at HIGH. In 2-cup glass measure, heat butter and almonds 3 to 4 minutes or until almonds are lightly browned, stirring twice.
In oblong baking dish, arrange fish; season inside of fish with salt, pepper and lemon juice. Pour butter and almonds inside and over fish. Heat, covered with wax paper, 6 to 7 minutes at HIGH or until fish is tender. Let STAND covered, 5 minutes before serving.

Only time for a quick put-something-together supper? You do not have to forfeit a piping hot, hearty meal just because you have only 30 minutes to prepare dinner. With help from your microwave oven you can have a favorite recipe ready and on the table in no time!

We have gathered some popular recipes to get you started. Also, use these as a guide when converting your own recipe into a microwave specialty.
As you make your casserole, remember to cut pieces into uniform sizes whenever possible.

BAKED ZITI

Power Select: MEDIUM-HIGH→STAND
Approx. Cooking Time: 9 minutes
Yield: about 4 servings

1 package (8 oz.) ziti macaroni, cooked (see p. 106)
1 jar (15½ oz.) spaghetti sauce
½ cup shredded Mozzarella cheese (about 2 oz.)

Set Power Select at MEDIUM-HIGH. In 2-quart casserole dish combine ziti and spaghetti sauce. Heat, covered, 8 to 9 minutes; stir once. Sprinkle with cheese. Let STAND, covered, 10 minutes before serving.

CHICKEN A LA KING

Power Select: HIGH
HIGH→MEDIUM
Approx. Cooking Time: 20 minutes
Yield: about 6 servings

⅓ cup butter or margarine
2 tablespoons finely chopped green pepper
⅓ cup flour
1 teaspoon salt
⅛ teaspoon pepper
1¼ cups chicken broth
1¼ cups milk or half 'n half
3 cups cut-up cooked chicken or turkey
1 jar (4 oz.) sliced pimento, drained (about ⅓ cup)
1 can (4 oz.) sliced mushrooms, drained
2 tablespoons dry sherry (optional)

Set Power Select at HIGH. In 3-quart casserole dish, heat butter and green pepper 3 to 4 minutes or until green pepper is tender; stir in flour, salt and pepper. Gradually add broth and milk, stirring until smooth. Heat 2 to 3 minutes at HIGH.
Set Power Select at MEDIUM. Heat 4 to 5 minutes or until sauce is thickened, stirring twice. Add remaining ingredients. Heat 7 to 8 minutes or until heated through, stirring twice. Serve over toast, noodles or rice.

CHICKEN AND DUMPLINGS

Power Select: HIGH→MEDIUM
MEDIUM
MEDIUM→STAND
Approx. Cooking Time: 48 minutes
Yield: about 6 servings

3 pounds chicken parts
3¾ cups water
2 bay leaves
1 teaspoon salt
8 peppercorns
1 tablespoon parsley flakes
¼ teaspoon dried sage
5 tablespoons cornstarch
1 package (10 oz.) frozen peas and carrots, thawed
1 package (8 oz.) refrigerated buttermilk biscuits

Set Power Select at HIGH. In 5-quart casserole dish, combine chicken, 3 cups water, bay leaves, salt and peppercorns. Heat, covered, 10 minutes.
Set Power Select at MEDIUM. Heat, covered, 20 minutes or until chicken is tender. Remove chicken; strain broth into 4-quart casserole dish. Add parsley, sage, and cornstarch blended with remaining water. Heat 5 to 6 minutes at MEDIUM or until broth is thickened, stirring once. Meanwhile, remove chicken meat from bone. Stir into gravy with peas and carrots; place biscuits, halved on top. Heat, covered, 10 to 12 minutes at MEDIUM. Let STAND 7 minutes before serving.

CHILI 'N RICE CASSEROLE

Power Select: HIGH
HIGH→MEDIUM-LOW→STAND
Approx. Cooking Time: 55 minutes
Yield: about 4 servings

1 pound ground beef
1 cup chopped green pepper
1 cup chopped onion
1 clove garlic, finely chopped
Water
1 can (16 oz.) whole tomatoes, chopped and drained (reserve liquid)
1 can (15 oz.) tomato sauce
1 cup rice
2 to 3 tablespoons chili powder
1 teaspoon salt

Set Power Select at HIGH. In 4-quart casserole dish, crumble ground beef; stir in green pepper, onion and garlic. Heat 4½ to 5½ minutes or until beef is browned and onion is tender, stirring twice; drain. Add enough water to reserved liquid to equal 2 cups; add to beef and stir in remaining ingredients. Heat, covered, 8 to 9 minutes at HIGH.
Set Power Select at MEDIUM-LOW. Heat, covered, 40 minutes or until rice is almost tender.
Let STAND, covered, 15 minutes before serving.

CORN DOGGIES

Power Select: MEDIUM-LOW→STAND
Approx. Cooking Time: 15 minutes
Yield: 4 servings

¾ cup yellow cornmeal
¾ cup all-purpose flour
½ cup chopped onion
1 tablespoon baking powder
½ teaspoon salt
¼ teaspoon dry mustard powder
1 egg
1 can (8 oz.) cream-style corn
½ cup milk
⅛ teaspoon hot pepper sauce
4 frankfurters, halved crosswise

Set Power Select at MEDIUM-LOW. Combine cornmeal, flour, onion, baking powder, salt and mustard; stir in egg, corn, milk and hot pepper sauce. Spoon batter into greased round baking dish with inverted glass in center. Place frankfurter halves around dish in spoke-like fashion. Heat 13½ to 14½ minutes or until cornbread is done. Remove glass; let STAND, covered, 7 minutes before serving.

COUNTRY HAM CASSEROLE

Power Select: MEDIUM-HIGH
                MEDIUM-HIGH→STAND
Temperature Select: 145°F
Approx. Cooking Time: 14 minutes
Yield: about 4 servings

1 package (8 oz.) noodles, cooked (see page 106)
2 cups cut-up cooked ham (about ½ lb.)
1½ cups shredded Swiss cheese (about 6 oz.)
1 can (10¾ oz.) condensed cream of celery soup
1 can (8 oz.) green peas, drained*
¾ cup milk
½ teaspoon dry mustard powder (optional)
French fried onion pieces or crushed corn chips

Set Power Select at MEDIUM-HIGH. In 3-quart casserole dish, combine noodles, ham, 1¼ cups cheese, soup, peas, milk and mustard. Heat, covered, 5 to 6 minutes stirring once. Top with remaining cheese and onion pieces.

TO HEAT BY TEMPERATURE: Insert probe into center of casserole. Set Temperature Select at 145°F.

TO HEAT BY TIME: Set time 7 to 8 minutes at MEDIUM-HIGH.

Heat; let STAND, covered, 5 minutes before serving.

*Variation: *Use one cup cut-up cooked asparagus for peas.*

EASY LASAGNA

Power Select: HIGH
                HIGH→MEDIUM-LOW→STAND
Approx. Cooking Time: 43 minutes
Yield: about 6 servings

½ pound ground beef
1 jar (32 oz.) spaghetti sauce
½ cup water
1½ cups ricotta or cottage cheese
1 egg
½ teaspoon pepper
8 lasagne noodles (uncooked)
½ pound Mozzarella cheese, thinly sliced
½ cup grated Parmesan cheese

Set Power Select at HIGH. In large glass bowl, crumble ground beef. Heat 2 to 3 minutes or until beef is browned, stirring once; drain. Stir in spaghetti sauce and water.
Meanwhile, combine ricotta cheese, egg and pepper. In oblong baking dish, spoon ½ cup sauce; alternately layer noodles, egg mixture, mozzarella cheese and sauce, forming 2 layers. Heat, covered, 8 minutes at HIGH.
Set Power Select at MEDIUM-LOW. Heat, covered, 30 to 32 minutes or until noodles are tender. Top with parmesan cheese; let STAND, covered, 15 minutes before serving.

EGGPLANT PARMESAN

Power Select: HIGH
                HIGH→STAND
Temperature Select: 160°F
Approx. Cooking Time: 17 minutes
Yield: about 4 servings

1 medium eggplant (about 1¾ lb.)
1 slice white bread, crumbed
¼ cup grated Parmesan cheese
2 tablespoons butter or margarine, melted
2 cups spaghetti sauce
1½ to 2 cups shredded Mozzarella cheese (about 6 to 8 oz.)

Set Power Select at HIGH. Pierce skin of eggplant several times; arrange eggplant on paper towel on glass oven tray. Heat 4½ to 5½ minutes or until eggplant is almost tender; let cool, then peel, if desired, and slice into ½-inch pieces.
Meanwhile, combine bread, parmesan cheese and butter. In 1½-quart casserole dish, alternately layer spaghetti sauce, eggplant, crumb mixture and mozzarella cheese.

TO HEAT BY TEMPERATURE: Insert probe into center of casserole. Set Temperature Select at 160°F.

TO HEAT BY TIME: Set time for 10½ to 11½ minutes at HIGH or until heated through.

Heat; let STAND, covered 5 minutes before serving.

HAMBURGER MEDLEY

Power Select: HIGH
                HIGH→MEDIUM-LOW→STAND
Approx. Cooking Time: 25 minutes
Yield: about 4 servings

1 pound ground beef
½ cup chopped green pepper or onion
2 cups water
1 can (15 oz.) tomato sauce
1 can (8 oz.) whole kernel corn, undrained
½-8 ounce package elbow macaroni
⅛ teaspoon hot pepper sauce
1 cup corn chips, crushed

Set Power Select at HIGH. In 3-quart casserole dish, crumble ground beef; stir in green pepper. Heat 4½ to 5½ minutes or until beef is browned, stirring once; drain. Stir in water, tomato sauce, corn, macaroni and hot pepper sauce. Heat, covered, 10 minutes at HIGH. Set Power Select at MEDIUM-LOW. Heat, covered, 8 to 9 minutes or until macaroni is almost tender, stirring once. Let STAND, covered, 10 minutes; top with corn chips and serve.

HONEYED HAM AND APPLE RING

Power Select: MEDIUM-HIGH→STAND
                HIGH
Approx. Cooking Time: 20 minutes
Yield: about 6 servings

1¼ pounds cooked ham, ground (about 3½ cups)
5 small apples
3 eggs
1 cup soft bread crumbs
½ cup milk
⅓ cup finely chopped onion
5 tablespoons honey
¼ teaspoon ground cloves
⅛ teaspoon ground ginger
Pepper to taste
2 tablespoons butter or margarine

Set Power Select at MEDIUM-HIGH. Combine ham, 1 apple peeled and chopped, eggs, bread crumbs, milk, onion, 4 tablespoons honey, cloves, ginger and pepper. Spoon mixture into 9-inch glass pie plate with inverted glass in center. Heat 12 to 13 minutes or until mixture is set. Let STAND, covered, 7 minutes. Meanwhile, peel and slice remaining apples. In small glass bowl, combine apples, butter and remaining honey.
Set Power Select at HIGH. Heat, covered, 6 to 7 minutes or until apples are tender. Invert ham onto serving platter; arrange apples on top of ring.

HOT ENCHILADA DOGS

Power Select: MEDIUM-HIGH
Approx. Cooking Time: 8 minutes
Yield: 4 servings

1 can (16 oz.) chili without beans
3 tablespoons finely chopped green chili peppers
⅛ teaspoon hot pepper sauce
8 tortillas, softened*
8 frankfurters, ends slit
1 can (8 oz.) tomato sauce
1 cup shredded Cheddar cheese (about 4 oz.)

Set Power Select at MEDIUM-HIGH. Combine chili, chili peppers and hot pepper sauce. Place 2 tablespoons chili mixture on each tortilla; place frankfurters in center and roll up. In oblong baking dish, arrange tortillas seam-side down. Combine tomato sauce with remaining chili mixture; pour over tortillas. Heat, covered, 6½ to 7½ minutes or until heated through. Top with cheese; let stand, covered, 5 minutes before serving.

*__Hint__   *To soften tortillas in your microwave oven, in oblong baking dish, arrange tortillas between layers of damp paper towels. Heat, covered, at Power Select HIGH. Eight tortillas will soften in 4½ to 6 minutes.*

LAST MINUTE DINNER

Power Select: MEDIUM-HIGH→STAND
Approx. Cooking Time: 11 minutes
Yield: about 4 servings

1 can (10¾ oz.) condensed cream of chicken or
  cream of mushroom soup
¾ cup water
¼ cup white wine*
2 teaspoons soy sauce
1½ to 2 cups cut-up cooked chicken or turkey
1½ cups packaged precooked rice
1 can (8 oz.) green peas, drained
2 tablespoons chopped pimento

Set Power Select at MEDIUM-HIGH. In 2-quart
casserole dish, blend soup, water, wine and soy
sauce; stir in remaining ingredients. Heat, covered,
9½ to 10½ minutes or until heated through, stirring
twice. Let STAND, covered, 5 minutes. Top, if desired,
with crushed crackers or buttered bread crumbs.

*If desired, omit wine and increase water to 1 cup.

MERMAID'S IMPERIAL DELIGHT

Power Select: HIGH
                MEDIUM
Approx. Cooking Time: 15 minutes
Yield: about 6 servings

¼ cup chopped green pepper
2 tablespoons butter or margarine
1 pound medium shrimp, shelled and cleaned
2 cups cooked rice (see page 108)
1½ cups mayonnaise
1 can (8 oz.) peas, drained
1 package (6 oz.) crabmeat, drained and flaked
  (canned or frozen, thawed)
Salt and pepper to taste

Set Power Select at HIGH. In 2-quart casserole dish,
heat green pepper and butter 1½ to 2½ minutes,
stirring once. Add shrimp and heat 3 to 4 minutes,
stirring once. Stir in remaining ingredients.
Set Power Select at MEDIUM. Heat, covered, 6½ to 7½
minutes or until heated through, stirring once. Top,
if desired, with buttered bread crumbs.

NONA'S ITALIAN SAUSAGE

Power Select: HIGH
                HIGH→STAND
Approx. Cooking Time: 22 minutes
Yield: about 6 servings

1½ pounds Italian sausage links, cut into 1¼-inch
    pieces
3 medium potatoes, peeled and cut into small chunks
1 clove garlic, finely chopped
3 medium green peppers, cut into chunks
3 medium onions, cut into chunks
2 cans (8 oz. ea.) tomato sauce
½ teaspoon salt
½ teaspoon ground oregano
¼ teaspoon pepper

Set Power Select at HIGH. In 3-quart casserole dish,
combine sausage, potatoes and garlic; heat, covered,
9 to 11 minutes or until sausage is almost cooked,
stirring once. Drain; stir in remaining ingredients and
heat, covered, 9 to 11* minutes at HIGH or until
vegetables are tender, stirring twice. Let STAND,
covered, 5 minutes before serving.

*If desired, add an additional can (8 oz.) tomato sauce.

Easy Lasagne, page 77

PAELLA 🔳

Power Select: HIGH
MEDIUM
MEDIUM→STAND
Approx. Cooking Time: 58 minutes
Yield: about 6 servings

5½ cups hot tap water
½ teaspoon ground cinnamon
Pinch saffron
2 packages (6 oz. ea.) chicken flavored rice mix with
  flavor packet
12 small clams, scrubbed
12 medium shrimp, shelled and cleaned
¾ pound cooked ham, cubed
6 pieces frozen fried chicken, thawed
1 package (9 oz.) frozen artichoke hearts, thawed
½ cup sliced pitted ripe olives (optional)
3 tablespoons chopped pimento (optional)

Set Power Select at HIGH. In 5-quart casserole dish,
combine water, cinnamon, saffron and flavor packets
(from rice mix). Heat, covered, 10 to 12 minutes or
until liquid is boiling. Add rice and heat, covered,
10 to 11 minutes. Add clams and let stand, covered,
10 to 12 minutes.
Set Power Select at MEDIUM. Add shrimp and ham
and heat, covered, 11 to 12 minutes, stirring once.
Add chicken, artichokes, olives and pimento. Heat,
covered, 10 to 11 minutes at MEDIUM, stirring once. Let
STAND 10 minutes before serving.

PARTY TUNA CASSEROLE 🔳

Power Select: MEDIUM-HIGH
MEDIUM-HIGH→STAND
Approx. Cooking Time: 10 minutes
Yield: about 4 servings

2 tablespoons butter or margarine, melted
1 tablespoon soy sauce
1 teaspoon garlic powder
1 can (3 oz.) chow mein noodles
1 can (10¾ oz.) condensed cream of mushroom soup
1 can (7 oz.) tuna, drained and flaked
1 cup finely chopped celery*
¼ pound salted cashew nuts
2 teaspoons dried onion flakes
¼ cup water

Set Power Select at MEDIUM-HIGH. Combine butter,
soy sauce, garlic and noodles; toss well and reserve.
In 8-inch round baking dish, combine soup, tuna,
celery, nuts, onion and water. Heat 8 to 9 minutes or
until heated through, stirring twice. Top with noodles
and heat 1 minute at MEDIUM-HIGH. Let STAND, covered,
5 minutes.

*Variation: *Use 1 cup sliced water chestnuts for celery.*

QUICK CORNED BEEF AND CABBAGE 🔳

Power Select: HIGH
HIGH→STAND
Approx. Cooking Time: 19 minutes
Yield: about 4 servings

2 medium potatoes, thinly sliced (about 2 cups)
1 medium onion, sliced
¼ cup water
¾ teaspoon salt
⅛ teaspoon pepper
1 can (12 oz.) corned beef, crumbled
½ head cabbage, cut into 4 wedges (about 1¼ lb.)
¼ cup butter or margarine, melted*

Set Power Select at HIGH. In greased 3-quart
casserole dish, layer potatoes and onion; add water,
salt and pepper. Heat, covered, 7 to 8 minutes. Add
corned beef and cabbage; pour butter over cabbage.
Heat, covered, 10 to 11 minutes at HIGH or until
cabbage is tender. Let STAND, covered, 5 minutes
before serving.

*Hint: *To quickly melt butter in your microwave oven,
see Quick Tips page 140.*

SATURDAY NIGHT SUPPER 🔳

Power Select: HIGH
MEDIUM-HIGH
MEDIUM-HIGH→STAND
Temperature Select: 145°F
Approx. Cooking Time: 20 minutes
Yield: about 4 servings

4 slices bacon, diced
½ cup finely chopped onion
1 can (10¾ oz.) condensed cream of celery soup
1 can (16 oz.) sliced potatoes, drained
  (reserve ⅓ cup liquid)
1 package (9 oz.) frozen french-style green beans,
  thawed (see page 139)
2 cups cut-up cooked chicken*

Set Power Select at HIGH. In 2½-quart casserole dish,
heat bacon 2½ to 3 minutes, stirring once. Remove
bacon and add onion to bacon drippings; heat 2½ to
3½ minutes or until onion is tender. Blend in soup and
reserved liquid; stir in potatoes, green beans and
chicken.
Set Power Select at MEDIUM-HIGH. Heat, covered, 8 to
9 minutes, stirring twice; top with bacon.

TO HEAT BY TEMPERATURE: Insert probe into center
of casserole. Set Temperature Select at 145°F.

TO HEAT BY TIME: Set time for 3 to 4 minutes at MEDIUM-
HIGH.

Heat; let STAND, covered, 5 minutes before serving.

*Substitution: *Use 3 cans (5 oz. ea.) boned chicken or
1 pound frankfurters, cut up.*

PREPARING DRY CASSEROLE MIXES 🔳

"add ground beef"—(5½ to 8 oz. ea.)
Set Power Select at HIGH. In 3-quart casserole dish,
crumble 1 pound ground beef. Heat 3½ to 4½
minutes or until beef is browned, stirring once; drain.
Stir in sauce mix, noodles and hot water (amount
as package directs*). Heat, covered, 5 to 7 minutes
or until mixture boils at HIGH.
Set Power Select at MEDIUM-LOW. Heat, covered,
8 to 10 minutes or until noodles are almost tender.
Let stand, covered, 10 minutes before serving.

For thicker sauce, reduce water by ¼ cup.

SAUSAGE AND BEAN CASSOULET

Power Select: HIGH
                HIGH→MEDIUM
Approx. Cooking Time: 30 minutes
Yield: about 6 servings

1½ pounds Italian sausage links, cut into 1½-inch
   pieces
2 small onions, sliced
2 cans (16 oz. ea.) navy or small white beans, rinsed*
½ pound cooked ham, cut into 1-inch pieces
1 can (8 oz.) tomato sauce
½ cup catsup
¼ cup white wine (or water)
¼ cup brown sugar
1 teaspoon salt
½ teaspoon dry mustard powder
½ teaspoon pepper

Set Power Select at HIGH. In 3-quart casserole dish, combine sausage and onions. Heat, covered, 8 to 10 minutes or until sausage is almost cooked, stirring once; drain. Stir in remaining ingredients and heat, covered, 5 minutes at HIGH.
Set Power Select at MEDIUM. Heat, covered, 10 to 15 minutes or until flavors are blended, stirring twice.

*Note: *To use dried beans, see page 104.*

SIMPLE CHICKEN POT PIE

Power Select: MEDIUM-HIGH
                MEDIUM-HIGH→STAND
Temperature Select: 145°F
Approx. Cooking Time: 12 minutes
Yield: about 4 servings

2 cups cut-up cooked chicken or turkey
1 can (10¾ oz.) condensed cream of chicken soup
1 package (10 oz.) frozen mixed vegetables, thawed
   (see page 139)
½ cup milk
⅛ teaspoon pepper
Dash Worcestershire sauce
2 cups leftover stuffing*

Set Power Select at MEDIUM-HIGH. In 2-quart casserole dish, combine chicken, soup, vegetables, milk, pepper and Worcestershire. Heat 6 to 7 minutes, stirring once. Crumble stuffing over chicken mixture to form crust.

TO HEAT BY TEMPERATURE: Insert probe into center of casserole. Set Temperature Select at 145°F.

TO HEAT BY TIME: Set time for 4 to 5 minutes at MEDIUM-HIGH.

Heat; let STAND, covered, 7 minutes before serving.

*Substitution: *Use 2 cups seasoned croutons for leftover stuffing.*

SHEPHERD'S PIE

Power Select: HIGH
                MEDIUM-HIGH
Approx. Cooking Time: 18 minutes
Yield: about 4 servings

½ cup chopped onion
3 tablespoons butter or margarine
3 tablespoons flour*
½ tablespoon parsley
1½ cups beef broth*
2 cups cut-up cooked lamb or beef
   (about ¾-inch pieces)
1 package (10 oz.) frozen peas and carrots, thawed
   (see page 139)
1½ to 2 cups hot mashed potatoes
Paprika

Set Power Select at HIGH. In 2-quart casserole dish, heat onion and butter 2 to 2½ minutes or until onion is tender. Stir in flour and parsley; gradually add broth. Heat 2 to 3 minutes or until gravy is thickened, stirring once. Stir in lamb and peas and carrots.
Set Power Select at MEDIUM-HIGH. Heat 7½ to 8½ minutes or until heated through, stirring once. Spoon potatoes on top of casserole; sprinkle with paprika. Heat, if necessary, 2 to 3 minutes.

*Substitution: *Use 1½ cups leftover or canned gravy for flour and broth.*

SPICY SHRIMP AND SPAGHETTI BAKE

Power Select: HIGH
                HIGH→MEDIUM
                MEDIUM-HIGH
Approx. Cooking Time: 18 minutes
Yield: 4 to 6 servings

½ cup chopped green pepper
½ cup chopped onion
3 tablespoons butter
3 cans (8 oz. ea.) tomato sauce
1 can (16 oz.) whole tomatoes, chopped and drained
1 pound medium shrimp, shelled and cleaned
1 tablespoon Worcestershire sauce
1 teaspoon salt
⅛ teaspoon crushed red pepper (optional)
1 package (8 oz.) spaghetti, cooked and drained
   (see page 106)
¾ cup grated Parmesan cheese

Set Power Select at HIGH. In 3-quart casserole dish, combine green pepper, onion and butter; heat, covered, 3 to 4 minutes. Stir in tomato sauce, tomatoes, shrimp, Worcestershire sauce, salt and red pepper. Heat, covered, 3 minutes at HIGH.
Set Power Select at MEDIUM. Heat, covered, 3 to 4 minutes or until shrimp is almost done. Stir in spaghetti and ½ cup cheese; combine thoroughly. Top with remaining cheese.
Set Power Select at MEDIUM-HIGH. Heat, uncovered, 5 to 7 minutes or until heated through.

TURKEY TETRAZZINI 🍴

Power Select: HIGH
                MEDIUM
                MEDIUM→STAND
Temperature Select: 145°F
Approx. Cooking Time: 14 minutes
Yield: about 6 servings

¼ **cup butter or margarine**
¼ **cup flour**
1 teaspoon salt
¼ **teaspoon pepper**
1 cup chicken broth
1 cup half 'n half
3 cups cut-up cooked turkey or chicken
1 package (8 oz.) spaghetti, cooked and drained
  (see page 106)
1 can (4 oz.) sliced mushrooms, drained
2 tablespoons sherry (optional)
¼ **cup grated Parmesan cheese**
Paprika

Set Power Select at HIGH. In 3-quart casserole dish, heat butter 1 to 2 minutes or until melted; stir in flour, salt and pepper. Gradually add broth and cream, stirring until smooth.

Set Power Select at MEDIUM. Heat 4½ to 5 minutes or until sauce is thickened, stirring twice. Stir in turkey, spaghetti, mushrooms and sherry; top with parmesan cheese and paprika.

TO HEAT BY TEMPERATURE: Insert probe into center of casserole. Set Temperature Select at 145°F

TO HEAT BY TIME: Set time for 6 to 7 minutes at MEDIUM.

Heat; let STAND, covered, 7 minutes before serving.

NOTES

Has a good weekday breakfast become a memory? Do you look forward to the weekend brunch of your favorite eggs and all the trimmings? Turn your fond memories into reality: with the assistance of your microwave oven you can have poached eggs in minutes. Cook directly in the serving bowl. And, you won't be left with the dirty dishes that could turn breakfast dreams into nightmares.

Creamy scrambled eggs, smooth Welsh Rarebit, easy Omelets—all this and more awaits you in this chapter...What an eye-opener!

SPECIAL HINTS FOR EGGS

Baked Eggs

- Use 6-ounce custard cup or coffee cup, generously greased, for each egg.
- Break egg into cup and with toothpick, pierce egg yolk twice and egg white several times.
- Top with one teaspoon milk.
- Heat, covered with plastic wrap, at Power Select MEDIUM.
- Let STAND, covered, before serving.

NUMBER OF EGGS	APPROXIMATE HEATING TIME (in minutes) at Power Select MEDIUM*	→	STANDING TIME
1	¾ to 1	→	1
2	1¼ to 1½	→	1
4	1¾ to 2¼	→	1½
6	2½ to 3	→	2

Poached Eggs

- Use 10-ounce custard cup or small glass bowl for each egg.
- Heat ¼ cup hot water, dash <u>each</u> vinegar and salt in each cup at Power Select HIGH.
- Break egg into boiling water and with toothpick, pierce egg yolk twice and egg white several times.
- Heat, covered with plastic wrap, at Power Select MEDIUM.
- Let STAND, covered, before serving.

NUMBER OF EGGS	APPROXIMATE HEATING TIME (in minutes)		→	STANDING TIME
	TO BOIL WATER at Power Select HIGH	TO POACH EGGS at Power Select MEDIUM*		
1	1	½ to ¾	→	1
2	3	1½ to 1¾	→	2
4	4	2¼ to 2½	→	2
6	6 to 6½	3½ to 3¾	→	2

Scrambled Eggs

- Beat eggs and stir in one tablespoon milk and dash salt for each egg.
- Pour into greased dish.
- Heat, covered with plastic wrap; stir vigorously once between heating times.
- Stir and let stand, covered. Stir again before serving.

NUMBER OF EGGS	CONTAINER	APPROXIMATE HEATING TIME (in minutes) at Power Select MEDIUM*		STANDING TIME
		FIRST HEATING	SECOND HEATING	
1	10 oz. custard cup or small glass bowl	½ to ¾	¼ to ½	1
2	10 oz. custard cups or small glass bowls	1 to 1¼	½ to ¾	1½
4	8-in. round cake dish	2 to 2¼	1 to 1¼	1½
6	8-in. round cake dish	3 to 3¼	1½ to 2	2
8	8-in. round cake dish	3½ to 4	2 to 2½	2

Important Note: *Eggs will be slightly underdone after heating time. The cooking will be completed during standing time.*

Pictured on the preceding page: Swiss Cheese Fondue, Eggs Benedict, Baked Eggs In Bologna.

PREPARING HARD-COOKED EGGS

Cooking eggs in their shell is a microwave oven NO. Because you are unable to pierce the shell or the egg membrane, there is no place for the steam to escape. The result would be a messy egg, bursting inside the oven.

HOWEVER, if the hard cooked egg will be chopped, you can do this in the microwave oven.

In greased small glass bowl, break egg; with toothpick, pierce egg yolk twice and egg white several times. Heat, covered, at Power Select MEDIUM. Let stand to cool before slicing, chopping, etc.

Pierce egg yolk and egg white before heating

NUMBER OF EGGS	APPROXIMATE HEATING TIME (in minutes) at Power Select MEDIUM
1	1 to 1½
2	2 to 2½
4	3½ to 4

Scrambled Eggs, page 84

EGGS ❦❦❦❦❦❦❦❦❦❦❦❦❦❦❦❦❦

BAKED EGGS IN BOLOGNA CUPS

Power Select: HIGH
                MEDIUM
Approx. Cooking Time: 3 minutes
Yield: 4 servings

4 slices bologna
4 eggs
4 teaspoons milk
Salt and pepper to taste

Set Power Select at HIGH. Heat bologna in single layer between layers of paper towel ½ to ¾ minute. For each serving, line custard cups (6 oz. ea.) with bologna. Break egg into center; with toothpick, pierce egg yolk twice and egg white several times. Top with 1 teaspoon milk; season with salt and pepper.
Set Power Select at MEDIUM. Heat, covered with plastic wrap, 2 to 2¼ minutes. Let stand, covered, 2 minutes before serving.

Note: **For TWO baked eggs,** *follow above procedure; halve all ingredients. Heat bologna ½ to ¾ minute and eggs 1½ to 1¾ minutes; let stand 1 minute.*
For ONE baked egg, *heat bologna ¼ to ½ minute and egg 1 to 1½ minutes; let stand 1 minute.*

BASIC OMELET

Power Select: HIGH
                MEDIUM→STAND
Approx. Cooking Time: 4 minutes
Yield: 1 serving

1 tablespoon butter or margarine
2 eggs
2 tablespoons milk
⅛ teaspoon salt
Dash pepper

Set Power Select at HIGH. In 9-inch glass pie plate, heat butter ½ to ¾ minute or until melted, turn plate to coat bottom with butter.
Meanwhile, combine remaining ingredients; pour into pie plate.
Set Power Select at MEDIUM. Heat, covered, 2 to 3 minutes or until omelet is almost set, stirring after 1 minute; let STAND, covered, 2 minutes. With spatula, loosen edges of omelet from plate; fold into thirds to serve.

Note: *Try one of these easy variations-*
For CHEESE Omelet, *before folding, sprinkle ¼ cup shredded cheese down center of omelet.*
For HAM Omelet, *before folding, sprinkle ¼ cup finely chopped cooked ham down center of omelet.*
For HERB Omelet, *blend in ⅛ teaspoon basil, thyme or crushed rosemary with eggs and milk.*
For JELLY Omelet, *before folding, spoon ¼ cup jelly down center of omelet.*

BREAKFAST STACKS

Power Select: MEDIUM
                HIGH
                MEDIUM
Approx. Cooking Time: 9 minutes
Yield: 4 servings

4 eggs
¼ cup milk
Salt and pepper to taste
4 slices Canadian bacon (about ½-in. thick)
4 English muffins, split and toasted
4 slices American cheese

Set Power Select at MEDIUM. Combine eggs, milk, salt and pepper; prepare Scrambled Eggs according to chart, page 84.
Set Power Select at HIGH. While eggs are standing, heat bacon, in single layer on paper towel lined paper plate, 2 to 3 minutes. Place bacon on 4 muffins; top with eggs, cheese, then remaining muffins. Wrap each stack in paper napkin; arrange on glass oven tray.
Set Power Select at MEDIUM. Heat 1½ to 2 minutes.

Note: **For TWO servings,** *follow above procedure; halve all ingredients. Heat bacon 1¼ to 1¾ minutes and Stacks 1 to 1½ minutes.*
For ONE serving, *heat ham ¾ to 1 minute and Stack ½ to ¾ minute.*

CORNED BEEF HASH AND EGGS

Power Select: MEDIUM-HIGH
                MEDIUM→STAND
Approx. Cooking Time: 9 minutes
Yield: 4 servings

1 can (24 oz.) corned beef hash
2 tablespoons catsup
1 tablespoon Worcestershire sauce
½ teaspoon onion powder
⅛ teaspoon pepper
4 eggs

Set Power Select at MEDIUM-HIGH. In 8-inch round baking dish, combine hash, catsup, Worcestershire, onion powder and pepper. Heat, covered, 3 to 4 minutes; stir. Lightly pat mixture into dish and form 4 wells. Into each well, break 1 egg; with toothpick, pierce egg yolk twice and egg white several times.
Set Power Select at MEDIUM. Heat, covered, 3½ to 4½ minutes or until eggs are almost set.
Let STAND, covered, 5 minutes before serving.

COUNTRY BREAKFAST

Power Select: HIGH
                MEDIUM→STAND
Approx. Cooking Time: 18 minutes
Yield: about 4 servings

2 medium baking potatoes (about 6 oz. ea.)*
¼ cup butter or margarine
¼ cup chopped green pepper
¼ cup chopped onion
4 eggs
½ cup milk
½ teaspoon salt
⅛ teaspoon pepper
2 slices American cheese, halved (optional)

Set Power Select at HIGH. Heat potatoes according to directions for baking potatoes (page 104). Let stand 5 minutes; peel and slice.
Meanwhile, in 9-inch baking dish, heat butter, green pepper and onion 3 to 4 minutes or until vegetables are tender; add sliced potatoes. Combine eggs, milk, salt and pepper; stir into potatoes.
Set Power Select at MEDIUM. Heat, covered, 5 to 6 minutes or until eggs are set, stirring twice. Top with cheese; let STAND, covered, 5 minutes before serving.

Substitution: *Use 1 or 2 cans (16 oz. ea.) sliced potatoes, drained for baked potatoes.*

EGGS BENEDICT

Power Select: HIGH
                      MEDIUM
Approx. Cooking Time: 12 minutes
Yield: 4 servings

1 package (1¼ oz.) hollandaise sauce mix
Ingredients as sauce mix package directs
4 eggs
4 thin slices cooked ham
2 English muffins, split and toasted

Set Power Select at HIGH. In 2-cup glass measure, combine sauce mix and ingredients as package directs. Heat 2 to 2½ minutes or until sauce is thickened, stirring once.
Set Power Select at MEDIUM. Prepare Poached Eggs according to chart, page 84. While eggs are standing, heat ham, arranged in single layer on paper towel lined paper plate, 1 to 1½ minutes.
To serve, place ham on muffin; top with egg, then sauce. If necessary, reheat ½ to 1 minute.

NORMANDY OMELET

Power Select: HIGH
                      MEDIUM→STAND
Approx. Cooking Time: 10 minutes
Yield: 2 servings

1 small apple, sliced
2 tablespoons butter or margarine
1 tablespoon honey
Dash ground cinnamon
4 eggs, separated
Salt and pepper to taste

Set Power Select at HIGH. In small glass bowl, combine apple, 1 tablespoon butter, honey and cinnamon. Heat, covered, 3 to 4 minutes or until apples are tender; reserve.
In 9-inch glass pie plate, heat remaining butter ½ to ¾ minute or until melted; turn plate to coat bottom with butter.
Meanwhile, beat egg whites until stiff, but not dry; beat egg yolks, salt and pepper until thickened. Fold egg yolks into egg whites; carefully pour mixture into pie plate.
Set Power Select at MEDIUM. Heat 4 to 5 minutes; let STAND 2 minutes. With spatula, loosen edges of omelet from plate; spoon apples onto half. Fold other half omelet over apples; sprinkle, if desired, with confectioners' sugar.

RANCHERO EGGS

Power Select: HIGH
                      MEDIUM
Approx. Cooking Time: 11 minutes
Yield: 6 servings

1 can (28 oz.) stewed tomatoes, chopped
3 tablespoons chopped green chilies
1 tablespoon dried onion flakes
⅛ teaspoon garlic powder
Salt and pepper to taste
6 eggs
¾ cup shredded Monterey Jack or Cheddar cheese (about 3 oz.)

Set Power Select at HIGH. In oblong baking dish, combine tomatoes, chilies, onion, garlic, salt and pepper. Heat, covered, 4½ to 5½ minutes, stirring once. Break eggs into tomato mixture (around outside edge); with toothpick, pierce egg yolks twice and egg whites several times.
Set Power Select at MEDIUM. Heat, covered, 4½ to 5½ minutes or until eggs are almost set.
Sprinkle with cheese; let stand, covered, 5 minutes. If desired, serve over corn bread.

SATURDAY'S HAM AND EGG SCRAMBLE

Power Select: HIGH
                      MEDIUM→STAND
Approx. Cooking Time: 9 minutes
Yield: about 4 servings

1 cup cut-up cooked ham
2 tablespoons butter or margarine
1 package (3 oz.) cream cheese, softened (see page 140)
⅓ cup milk
5 eggs
Salt and pepper to taste

Set Power Select at HIGH. In 9-inch baking dish, heat ham and butter, covered with wax paper, 2 to 3 minutes, stirring once.
Set Power Select at MEDIUM. Combine cream cheese and milk; blend in eggs, salt and pepper. Add to ham and heat, covered, 5 to 6 minutes or until eggs are almost set, stirring twice. Let STAND, covered, 3 minutes before serving.

CHEESE

ALPINE SHRIMP FONDUE

Power Select: MEDIUM
Approx. Cooking Time: 8 minutes
Yield: about 4 servings

1 can (10¾ oz.) condensed cream of shrimp soup
1 cup shredded Swiss cheese (about 4 oz.)
¼ cup white wine
½ teaspoon Worcestershire sauce
French bread, cut into 1-inch cubes or bread sticks

Set Power Select at MEDIUM. In 1-quart casserole dish*, combine soup, cheese, wine and Worcestershire. Heat 7 to 8 minutes or until cheese is melted, stirring every 2 minutes. Serve hot with French bread.

If desired, a microwave oven safe pottery or ceramic fondue dish can be used.

MACARONI AND CHEESE

Power Select: MEDIUM
Approx. Cooking Time: 13 minutes
Yield: about 4 servings

**1 package (8 oz.) elbow macaroni, cooked and
 drained (see page 106)**
**¾ pound pasteurized process cheese spread, cut
 into cubes**
¾ to 1 cup milk
½ to ¾ teaspoon salt
¼ teaspoon onion powder
⅛ teaspoon dry mustard powder (optional)
¼ teaspoon pepper
Buttered bread crumbs

Set Power Select at MEDIUM. In 3-quart casserole
dish, combine macaroni, cheese, milk, salt, onion,
mustard and pepper. Heat, covered, 9 to 10 minutes;
stirring twice. Top with bread crumbs and heat,
uncovered, 3 minutes.

*Variation: Use ½ cup tomato sauce for ¼ cup milk and
⅛ teaspoon oregano for dry mustard.*

ONION CHEESE PIE

Power Select: MEDIUM→STAND
Approx. Cooking Time: 8 minutes
Yield: about 6 servings

3 eggs
1 cup shredded Swiss cheese (about 4 oz.)
½ cup half and half or whipping cream
3 drops hot pepper sauce
8-inch pastry crust, baked (see page 131)
1 can (3 oz.) french fried onions, chopped
Parsley flakes

Set Power Select at MEDIUM. Combine eggs, cheese,
cream and pepper sauce; pour into prepared crust.
Top with onions and parsley. Heat 6 to 7½ minutes, or
until center is almost set, gently stirring after 2
minutes. Let STAND, covered, 7 minutes before serving.

SPINACH CHEESE RING

Power Select: MEDIUM
                MEDIUM→STAND
Approx. Cooking Time: 7 minutes
Yield: about 4 servings

**2 packages (10 oz. ea.) frozen chopped spinach,
 cooked and drained (see page 98)**
1 cup (½ pt.) cottage cheese
2 eggs
3 tablespoons Parmesan cheese
½ teaspoon caraway seeds
½ teapoon salt
Dash pepper
¼ cup buttered bread crumbs
¼ teaspoon paprika

Set Power Select at MEDIUM. Thoroughly combine
spinach, cottage cheese, eggs, 2 tablespoons parmesan cheese, caraway, salt and pepper. Spoon into
9-inch glass pie plate with small glass inverted in
center; heat, covered, 4 to 5 minutes or until almost
set. Sprinkle bread crumbs blended with remaining
cheese and paprika around outside edge. Heat 1 to 1½
minutes at MEDIUM. Let STAND, covered, 5 minutes
before serving.

Hint: *To cover pie plate with glass in center, use plastic
wrap; make a cut for glass to fit through. This also
serves as a vent hole!*

SWISS CHEESE FONDUE

Power Select: HIGH
                MEDIUM
Approx. Cooking Time: 9 minutes
Yield: about 6 servings

1 pound Swiss cheese, shredded (about 4 cups)
¼ cup flour
⅛ teaspoon garlic powder
⅛ teaspoon pepper
Dash ground nutmeg
1 cup white wine or apple juice
2 tablespoons Kirsch (optional)
French bread, cut into cubes or bread sticks

Set Power Select at HIGH. Toss cheese with flour,
garlic, pepper and nutmeg.
In 2-quart casserole dish,* heat wine 2 to 2½ minutes;
gradually add ½ cheese, stirring until smooth.
Set Power Select at MEDIUM. Heat 2 to 3 minutes,
stirring once. Add remaining cheese and Kirsch,
stirring until smooth. Heat 2 to 3 minutes or until
cheese is melted, stirring once. Serve hot with French
bread.

**If desired, a microwave oven safe pottery or ceramic
fondue dish can be used.*

WELSH RAREBIT

Power Select: HIGH
                MEDIUM
Approx. Cooking Time: 8 minutes
Yield: about 4 servings

1 pound Cheddar cheese, shredded (about 4 cups)
3 tablespoons flour
⅔ cup beer
½ teaspoon Worcestershire sauce
½ teaspoon dry mustard powder

Set Power Select at HIGH. Toss cheese with flour.
In 4-cup glass measure, heat beer 1½ to 2 minutes or
until boiling.
Set Power Select at MEDIUM. Gradually add ½ cheese,
Worcestershire, and mustard, stirring until smooth.
Heat 1½ to 2½ minutes, stirring once. Add remaining
cheese and heat 2 to 3 minutes or until cheese is
completely melted, stirring once. Serve, traditionally,
over toast points.

Sandwiches have grown to be a lunch and snack time institution. Now, with the help of your microwave oven, those cold luncheon meat sandwiches can turn into something warm and flavorful. Imagine the delicious sandwiches you can create with a variety of cheeses or gravies. So, now when you are in a hurry, you can create a hearty hot meal in minutes...that is better than a cold sandwich from the refrigerator. No extra clean-up either...sandwiches with cheeses can be heated on a paper plate covered with a paper napkin. It's that simple.

We have not forgotten about the king and queen of sandwiches: the hamburger and frankfurter...directions for these favorites and others follow.

ARMENIAN LUNCH

Power Select: HIGH
 HIGH→MEDIUM
Approx. Cooking Time: 11 minutes
Yield: 4 servings

1 envelope (1 oz.) onion-mushroom soup mix
1 cup (8 oz.) plain yogurt
½ cup chopped green pepper
Pinch dried mint leaves
1½ pounds ground beef
2 cloves garlic, finely chopped
1 can (8 oz.) stewed tomatoes, chopped and drained
1 tablespoon parsley flakes
4 individual loaves Middle Eastern pocket (pita) bread

Set Power Select at HIGH. Combine 1 tablespoon soup mix, yogurt, green pepper and mint; reserve.
In 2-quart casserole dish, crumble ground beef; stir in remaining soup mix and garlic. Heat, covered, 4½ to 5½ minutes or until beef is browned, stirring once; drain. Stir in tomatoes and parsley. Heat, covered, 1 minute at HIGH.
Set Power Select at MEDIUM. Heat, covered, 3 to 4 minutes stirring once.
Meanwhile, cut bread in half; gently open. Fill ''pocket'' with beef mixture; top with yogurt dressing.

BARBECUED BEEF SANDWICHES

Power Select: MEDIUM
Approx. Cooking Time: 4 minutes
Yield: 4 servings

½ to ¾ pound sliced cooked roast beef
8 slices rye bread or 4 hamburger rolls
¼ to ½ cup barbecue or chili sauce

Set Power Select at MEDIUM. Arrange ½ beef on 4 slices bread; spread generously with barbecue sauce. Top with remaining beef, then bread. Wrap each sandwich in paper napkin; arrange on glass oven tray. Heat 3 to 4 minutes or until heated through.

Note: For TWO sandwiches, *follow above procedure. Halve all ingredients; heat 1½ to 2 minutes. For ONE sandwich, heat 1 to 1¼ minutes.*

CHILI TACOS

Power Select: HIGH
 HIGH→MEDIUM
Approx. Cooking Time: 11 minutes
Yield: 6 servings

1 pound ground beef
1 package (1¼ oz.) taco seasoning mix
½ cup water
12 taco shells
1 cup shredded lettuce
⅔ cup chopped tomatoes
¼ cup chopped green pepper or onion
1 cup shredded Cheddar or Monterey Jack cheese (about 4 oz.)

Set Power Select at HIGH. In 2-quart casserole dish, heat ground beef 3 to 4 minutes or until browned, stirring once; drain. Add seasoning mix and water; heat, covered, 2 minutes at HIGH.
Set Power Select at MEDIUM. Heat, covered, 5 minutes, stirring once. Fill each taco shell with 2 tablespoons beef mixture, then top with lettuce, tomato, green pepper and cheese*.

*Hint: *If desired, arrange taco shells in oblong baking dish; fill as directed above. Heat 3 to 4 minutes (at Power Select MEDIUM) to melt cheese.*

HAMBURGERS......YOUR WAY

Power Select: MEDIUM-HIGH
Approx. Cooking Time: 5 minutes
Yield: 4 servings

1 pound ground beef
4 slices each cheese, onion and tomato
4 hamburger rolls
Catsup or creamy Russian dressing

Set Power Select at MEDIUM-HIGH. Shape ground beef into 4 patties (about 4-in. in diameter). In baking dish, arrange patties and heat 3½ to 4½ minutes, turning patties over and draining liquid once. Top with cheese; let stand, covered, 2 minutes. Place each hamburger in roll and top with remaining ingredients, as desired.

Note: For TWO servings, *follow above procedure. Halve all ingredients; heat patties 1½ to 2 minutes. For ONE serving, heat patty ¾ to 1¼ minutes.*

Pictured on the preceding page: Reuben Deli Delight, Chili Tacos, Armenian Lunch, Round-About Dogs.

HEAVENLY FRENCH DIP

Power Select: HIGH
MEDIUM
Approx. Cooking Time: 7 minutes
Yield: 2 servings

1 medium onion, cut into rings
2 tablespoons butter or margarine
½ loaf French bread (about 12 in. long)*
¼ to ⅓ pound sliced cooked roast beef
Salt and pepper to taste
1 can (10¼ oz.) beef gravy
2 tablespoons red wine (optional)

Set Power Select at HIGH. In small glass bowl, combine onion and butter. Heat, covered, 2 to 3 minutes or until onion is tender, stirring once.
Meanwhile, slice bread in half lengthwise and then crosswise, forming 2 sandwiches. Arrange beef on 2 pieces bread; top with onions, then season with salt and pepper. Close sandwich; wrap individually in paper napkin.
In same glass bowl, heat gravy and wine 1½ to 2 minutes or until heated through, stirring once.
Set Power Select at MEDIUM. Heat sandwiches 1 to 2 minutes or until warm. Serve with gravy for dipping.

*****Substitution:** *Use 2 Italian rolls (6 in. ea.) for French bread.*

Hamburgers ··· Your Way, page 90

MEAT LOAF MELTWICH

Power Select: MEDIUM
Approx. Cooking Time: 4 minutes
Yield: 4 servings

Chili sauce
8 slices rye bread
8 thin slices cooked meat loaf
4 slices (rectangular) Muenster cheese, halved

Set Power Select at MEDIUM. Spread chili sauce on bread. On four slices, place meat loaf and cheese; top with remaining bread. Wrap each sandwich in paper napkin; arrange on glass oven tray. Heat 2½ to 3½ minutes or until heated through.

Note: **For TWO sandwiches,** *follow above procedure; halve all ingredients. Heat 1½ to 2 minutes.*
For ONE sandwich, *heat 1 to 1½ minutes.*

MEXICAN MEAT PIES

Power Select: MEDIUM-HIGH
MEDIUM
Approx. Cooking Time: 6 minutes
Yield: 3 to 4 servings

6 corn toaster cakes*
1 can (16 oz.) chili without beans
½ cup shredded Monterey Jack or Cheddar cheese (about 2 oz.)
Sliced black olives, chopped green pepper and chopped onion

Set Power Select at MEDIUM-HIGH. On 12-inch glass pizza dish, arrange corn toaster cakes; spoon on chili. Heat 3½ to 4 minutes; top with cheese.
Set Power Select at MEDIUM. Heat 1½ to 2 minutes or until cheese is melted. Top, as desired, with olives, green pepper and onions.

*****Substitution:** *Use 3 cheese-flavored English muffins, split and toasted for corn cakes.*

MINI-PIZZA SNACKS

Power Select: MEDIUM
Approx. Cooking Time: 2 minutes
Yield: 2 servings

2 English muffins, split and toasted
¼ to ½ cup spaghetti sauce
¼ cup shredded Mozzarella cheese (about 1 oz.)
Oregano

Set Power Select at MEDIUM. On paper plate, arrange muffins; spread with spaghetti sauce. Top with cheese and season with oregano. Heat 1 to 2 minutes or until cheese is melted.

Note: **For ONE serving,** *follow above procedure; halve all ingredients. Heat ½ to 1 minute.*

OPEN FACED SANDWICHES WITH GRAVY

Power Select: HIGH
                           MEDIUM-HIGH
Approx. Cooking Time: 5 minutes
Yield: 4 servings

1 envelope (⅞ oz.) turkey gravy mix*
1 cup water*
½ pound sliced cooked turkey
4 slices white bread

Set Power Select at HIGH. In 2-cup glass measure, combine gravy mix and water; heat 2½ to 3 minutes or until thickened, stirring twice.
Set Power Select at MEDIUM-HIGH. In baking dish, arrange turkey in four piles (to fit bread). Heat, covered, 1½ to 2 minutes or until heated through. To serve, arrange turkey on bread; top with gravy.

Substitution: *Use 1 can (10½ oz.) mushroom gravy or 1 cup leftover gravy for mix and water. Heat 1½ to 2 minutes, stirring once.*
Note: *Chicken, pork or beef gravy and meat may be used.*

OPEN FACED TUNA TEMPTER

Power Select: MEDIUM
Approx. Cooking Time: 5 minutes
Yield: 4 servings

1 can (7 oz.) tuna, drained and flaked
⅓ cup mayonnaise
Celery seed
Onion powder
Salt and pepper
4 slices whole wheat bread, toasted
4 thin slices tomato
4 slices American cheese

Set Power Select at MEDIUM. Combine tuna and mayonnaise; season with celery, onion, salt and pepper. Spread tuna on toast; top with tomato. On paper plate, heat sandwiches 2 to 2½ minutes; top with cheese. Heat 1¾ to 2¼ minutes or until cheese is melted.

PIZZA HEROES

Power Select: HIGH
                           MEDIUM
Approx. Cooking Time: 8 minutes
Yield: 4 servings

1 pound ground beef
¼ cup finely chopped onion
½ cup spaghetti sauce
½ teaspoon salt
¼ teaspoon oregano
2 Italian rolls, split lengthwise (about 6 to 8-in. ea.)
Pizza Toppings*
½ to ¾ cup shredded Mozzarella cheese
  (about 2 to 3 oz.)

Set Power Select at HIGH. In baking dish, crumble ground beef and stir in onion. Heat 3 to 4 minutes or until beef is browned, stirring once; drain. Stir in sauce, salt and oregano.
In oblong baking dish, arrange rolls; spoon on beef mixture. Top with Pizza Toppings, then cheese.

Set Power Select at MEDIUM. Heat 3 to 4 minutes or until cheese is melted and hero is heated through.

***Pizza Toppings**
Use your favorite combination: anchovies, canned sliced mushrooms, green pepper rings, sliced tomatoes or thinly sliced pepperoni.

Note: **For TWO servings,** *follow above procedure; halve all ingredients. Heat ground beef 2 to 2½ minutes and cheese 2 to 2½ minutes.*

POTATO DOGS

Power Select: HIGH
Approx. Cooking Time: 5 minutes
Yield: 2 servings

⅓ cup water
1 tablespoon milk
2 teaspoons butter or margarine
Dash dry mustard powder (optional)
⅔ cup instant mashed potato flakes
2 frankfurters
Pork flavored seasoned coating mix

Set Power Select at HIGH. In small glass bowl, heat water, milk, butter and dry mustard 1 to 1½ minutes or until boiling. Stir in instant mashed potatoes; cool. Meanwhile, cut "X" slit in ends of frankfurters. Pat potato mixture around frankfurters, leaving ends exposed; roll in coating mix. On paper plate, arrange coated frankfurters; heat 2¼ to 2¾ minutes. If potato coating cracks, press together with fingers.

RED DELICIOUS SANDWICH

Power Select: MEDIUM-HIGH
                           MEDIUM
Approx. Cooking Time: 5 minutes
Yield: 4 servings

4 slices raisin bread, toasted
Mustard
½ pound sliced cooked ham
½ apple, sliced
4 slices American cheese

Set Power Select at MEDIUM-HIGH. Spread bread with mustard; arrange on paper plate. Place ½ ham on bread; top with apple, then remaining ham. Heat 2 to 2¼ minutes; top with cheese.
Set Power Select at MEDIUM. Heat 2 to 2½ minutes or until cheese begins to melt.

Note: **For TWO servings,** *follow above procedure; halve all ingredients. Heat ham 1 to 1½ minutes and cheese 1½ to 2 minutes.*
          For ONE serving, *heat ham ½ to 1 minute and cheese ¾ to 1¼ minutes.*

Sloppy Joes, page 94

REUBEN DELI DELIGHT

Power Select: MEDIUM-HIGH
              MEDIUM
Approx. Cooking Time: 4 minutes
Yield: 4 sandwiches

½ pound thinly sliced cooked corned beef
4 slices rye or pumpernickel bread
¼ cup creamy Russian dressing
1 can (8 oz.) sauerkraut, rinsed and drained
4 slices (rectangular) Swiss cheese, halved

Set Power Select at MEDIUM-HIGH. Arrange corned
beef on bread; top with dressing. Add sauerkraut and
arrange sandwiches on paper towel lined glass oven
tray. Heat 1½ to 2 minutes; top with cheese.
Set Power Select at MEDIUM. Heat 1½ to 2 minutes
or until cheese is melted.

Hint: *If a closed sandwich is desired, top with additional*
bread; wrap each sandwich in paper napkin and heat
½ to 1 minute.

Note: **For TWO sandwiches,** *follow above procedure;*
halve all ingredients. Heat sandwiches 1 to 1½
minutes and cheese 1 to 1½ minutes.
For ONE serving, *heat sandwich ½ to ¾ minute*
and cheese ½ to 1 minute.

ROUND-ABOUT DOGS

Power Select: MEDIUM-HIGH
Approx. Cooking Time: 7 minutes
Yield: 2 servings

1 can (8 oz.) pork and beans
1 tablespoon sweet pickle relish or catsup
4 frankfurters
2 slices rye bread
Mustard
2 slices bacon, crisp cooked and crumbled (see page 54)
¼ cup shredded Cheddar cheese (about 1 oz.)

Set Power Select at MEDIUM-HIGH. In small glass
bowl, heat beans and relish, covered, 1½ to 2 minutes
or until heated through, stirring once.
Along one side of each frankfurter, make deep
slits every ¾-inch. On paper towel lined paper plate,
arrange franks cut-side out. Heat 2½ to 3 minutes or
until heated through and curled.
Spread mustard on bread; place on serving plate.
Arrange two franks on each bread to form ring.
Fill ring with beans; top with bacon and cheese. Heat
1 to 1¼ minutes or until cheese beigns to melt.

Variation: *Arrange cooked frankfurter on toasted*
English muffin half; fill center with heated sauerkraut and
top with poppy seeds.

SEAFARER'S SANDWICH

Power Select: MEDIUM-HIGH
                MEDIUM
Approx. Cooking Time: 8 minutes
Yield: 4 sandwiches

1 package (8 oz.) frozen fried fish fillets (4 fillets)
4 slices American cheese
½ cup cole slaw (optional)
4 hamburger rolls
4 tablespoons tartar sauce or cocktail sauce

Set Power Select at MEDIUM-HIGH. In square baking dish, heat fillets* 3½ to 4½ minutes.
Set Power Select at MEDIUM. Top with cole slaw and cheese; heat 2½ to 3½ minutes or until cheese is melted. Place fillet in roll; top with tartar sauce.

*Hint: *Fish heats well on microwave oven safe roasting rack set in oblong baking dish.*

Note: **For TWO servings,** *follow above procedure; halve all ingredients. Heat fillets 1½ to 2 minutes and cheese 1¼ to 1¾ minutes.*
For ONE serving, *heat fillet ¾ to 1¼ minutes and cheese ½ to 1 minutes.*

SLOPPY JOES

Power Select: HIGH
                HIGH→MEDIUM
Approx. Cooking Time: 11 minutes
Yield: 4 servings

1 pound ground beef
½ cup finely chopped onion
½ to ¾ cup catsup
¼ cup sweet pickle relish
Salt and pepper to taste
4 hamburger rolls

Set Power Select at HIGH. In baking dish, crumble ground beef and stir in onion. Heat 3 to 4 minutes or until beef is browned, stirring once; drain. Stir in catsup, relish, salt and pepper. Heat, covered, 1½ to 2½ minutes at HIGH.
Set Power Select at MEDIUM. Heat, covered, 3 to 4 minutes, stirring once. Serve in split hamburger rolls.

Variation: *Add ½ pound frankfurters, sliced with ground beef.*

SURPRISE BURGERS

Power Select: MEDIUM-HIGH
                MEDIUM-HIGH→STAND
Approx. Cooking Time: 7 minutes
Yield: 4 servings

1 pound ground beef
½ teaspoon salt
½ teaspoon pepper
Surprise Fillings*
4 hamburger rolls

Set Power Select at MEDIUM-HIGH. Combine ground beef, salt and pepper; shape into 8 thin patties. Arrange Surprise Filling on 4 patties; top with remaining patties, sealing edges tightly.
In square baking dish lined with paper towel, arrange burgers; heat, covered with paper towel, 5 to 7 minutes at MEDIUM-HIGH. Let STAND, covered, 2 minutes before serving in split rolls.

*Surprise Fillings:
Use one of the following: *cheese, onion or tomato slice, sliced mushrooms, pickle slices or chopped olives.*

TEXAS TOMMIES

Power Select: HIGH
Approx. Cooking Time: 7 minutes
Yield: 2 servings

8 slices bacon
4 frankfurters
1 slice American cheese, cut into thin strips
4 frankfurter rolls

Set Power Select at HIGH. In oblong baking dish, heat bacon between layers of paper towel 2½ to 2¾ minutes or until partially cooked.
Meanwhile, make lengthwise slit in each frankfurter, leaving ½-inch uncut on each end; make an "X" cut in each end. Stuff slit with cheese; wrap 2 slices of bacon around each frankfurter and secure with wooden toothpicks.
Discard paper towels from baking dish and arrange frankfurters in dish. Heat 2½ to 3½ minutes or until heated through. Remove toothpicks and serve in split rolls.

Note: **For ONE serving,** *follow above procedure; halve all ingredients. Heat bacon 1 to 1¼ minutes and frankfurters 1½ to 1¾ minutes.*

Wish your family would get excited over vegetables! Consider it done with the assistance of your new found friend—your microwave oven. Once they have tested these vegetables cooked to perfection, vegetables will not take the back seat to other parts of the meal.

Fresh vegetables retain their vibrant color, delicious flavor and crisp texture. Using only a small amount of water and seasoning the vegetables after cooking will become the easiest way ever to serve garden-fresh tasting vegetables.

Simple ways to heat frozen vegetables in your microwave oven will amaze you...and no added water or salt to detract from the delicate flavor. Follow the instructions in the chart for the best way to prepare your favorite frozen vegetables.

PREPARING FRESH AND FROZEN VEGETABLES

For FRESH Vegetables

- Weights given for fresh vegetables are purchase weights, before peeling, trimming etc.
- Pierce skins of vegetables to be heated whole and unpeeled (i.e. eggplant, potatoes, squash). This allows steam to escape and prevents vegetables from popping or bursting. Arrange vegetables on paper towel lined glass oven tray.
- Add only 2 to 3 tablespoons water per pound. Often, rinsing vegetables before cooking is sufficient. Salt just before serving.
- Heat, covered, in casserole dish; stirring once. Heat corn on the cob in oblong baking dish; rearrange once during heating.
- Let stand, covered, as specified in the chart or recipe.

For FROZEN Vegetables

- Prepare frozen vegetables (10 oz.) in original package. Pierce top of package and set on glass saucer. If vegetables are frozen in pouches, pierce top of pouch also. If packages are foil-wrapped; remove foil.
- Place desired amount of frozen vegetables (packed in poly-bags) in covered casserole dish. Do not add water or salt. Stir once during heating.
- Heat vegetables marked with an asterisk (*) in covered casserole dish; stir once during heating. This insures even heating without overcooking some portions. Arrange corn on the cob in oblong baking dish; rearrange once during heating.

Note: Timings for canned vegetables are not included in the vegetable preparation chart. These are already cooked and need only to be reheated. Empty vegetables with liquid, into serving dish and heat, covered. For 8-onuce size cans heat 1½ to 2 minutes; 16-ounce cans 2½ to 3 minutes at Power Select MEDIUM-HIGH.

Ratatouille, page 101

Pictured on the preceding page: Orange Glazed Carrots, Green Bean Amandine, Mashed Potatoes, Corn on the Cob.

VEGETABLE	AMOUNT	APPROXIMATE HEATING TIME, covered, at Power Select HIGH (in minutes)	STANDING TIME (in minutes)
ARTICHOKES			
Fresh, about 6 to 8 oz. ea.	1	6 to 7½	5
(3-in. diameter)	2	8½ to 10	5
See recipe, page 99	4	12½ to 14	5
Frozen, hearts	1 package (9 oz.)	5 to 6	3
ASPARAGUS			
Fresh, cut into 1½-in. pieces	1 pound plus ¼ cup water	5 to 6½	3
Frozen, spears	1 package (10 oz.)	5½ to 7	3
BEANS, Green or Wax			
Fresh, cut into 1½-in. pieces	1 pound plus ¼ cup water	6½ to 8	3
Frozen*	1 package (9 oz.)	6 to 8	3
BEETS			
Fresh, sliced	1½ to 2 pounds plus ¼ cup water	10½ to 12	5
BROCCOLI			
Fresh, cut into spears	1 pound plus ¼ cup water	6 to 7½	3
Frozen, chopped or spears	1 package (10 oz.)	6½ to 8	3
BRUSSEL SPROUTS			
Fresh	1 tub (10 oz.) plus 2 tbsp. water	5½ to 7	5
	1 pound plus ¼ cup water	8 to 10	5
Frozen*	1 package (10 oz.)	7½ to 9	5
CABBAGE, Fresh			
Chopped or Shredded	4 cups (about 1 lb.) plus ¼ cup water	6½ to 8	5
Wedges	4 (about 1 lb.) plus ¼ cup water	6 to 7½	5
CARROTS, sliced ½-in thick			
Fresh	1 pound plus ¼ cup water	7 to 8½	5
Frozen	1 package (10 oz.)	5½ to 7	3
CAULIFLOWER			
Fresh, cut into flowerets	1 pound plus ¼ cup water	6½ to 8	5
whole	1 to 1¼ lb. plus ¼ cup water	11½ to 13	5
Frozen, flowerets	1 package (10 oz.)	5½ to 7	3
CORN, Whole Kernel			
Frozen*	1 package (10 oz.)	4 to 5½	3
CORN, On the cob			
Fresh (remove husk and silk)	1 ear plus 2 to 4 tablespoons water	2 to 3	3
	2 ears plus 2 to 4 tablespoons water	3 to 4	3
	4 ears plus 2 to 4 tablespoons water	8½ to 10	5
	6 ears plus 2 to 4 tablespoons water	13 to 14½	5
Frozen (rinse off any frost)*	1 ear	3½ to 4½	3
	2 ears	5 to 6½	3
	4 ears	9½ to 11	5
	6 ears	14 to 15½	5
EGGPLANT, Fresh			
Cubed	1 pound plus ¼ cup water	7 to 8½	3
Whole (pierce skin)	1 to 1¼ pounds	4½ to 6	3

*Heat in covered casserole.

VEGETABLE	AMOUNT	APPROXIMATE HEATING TIME, covered, at Power Select HIGH (in minutes)	STANDING TIME (in minutes)
LIMA BEANS Frozen*	1 package (10 oz.)	5½ to 7	3

OKRA, Frozen
  Sliced
  Whole
	1 package (10 oz.)
	1 package (10 oz.)
		5 to 6½
		5½ to 7
			3
			3

ONIONS Fresh, (small, whole)	8 to 10 plus ¼ cup water (about 1 lb.)	6½ to 8	3

PEAS, GREEN
  Fresh
  Frozen*
	1½ pounds plus ¼ cup water
	1 package (10 oz.)
		5 to 6½
		5½ to 7
			3
			3

PEAS, Snow (Peapods) Frozen*	1 package (6 oz.)	4½ to 5½	3
PEAS and CARROTS Frozen*	1 package (10 oz.)	5½ to 7	3
PEAS, Blackeyed Frozen*	1 package (10 oz.) plus 1½ cups water	20 to 22	5

SPINACH
  Fresh, leaf
  Frozen, leaf or chopped *
	1 pound plus ¼ cup water
	1 package (10 oz.)
		5½ to 7
		6½ to 8
			3
			3

SQUASH (Summer), sliced
  ½-in. thick
 	
  Fresh
  Frozen
	
	1 pound plus ¼ cup water
	1 package (10 oz.)
		
		6½ to 8
		5 to 6½
			
			3
			3

SQUASH (Winter)
  Fresh, whole
    (pierce skin)
  Frozen, whipped
	1 (1 lb.)
	2 (¾ lb. ea.)
	1 package (12 oz.)
		6 to 7½
		7½ to 9
		6½ to 8
			5
			5
			3

SUCCOTASH Frozen*	1 package (10 oz.)	5½ to 7	3
VEGETABLES, mixed Frozen*	1 package (10 oz.)	6½ to 8	3

ZUCCHINI, sliced ½-in. thick
  Fresh
  Frozen
	1 pound plus ¼ cup water
	1 package (10 oz.)
		6½ to 8
		5 to 6½
			3
			3

*Heat in covered casserole.

VEGETABLES ✿✿✿✿✿✿✿✿✿✿✿✿✿✿

ARTICHOKES FOR TWO

Power Select: HIGH
Approx. Cooking Time: 13 minutes
Yield: 2 servings

7 tablespoons butter or margarine
Garlic salt
2 fresh artichokes (8 oz. ea.)
1 lemon, thinly sliced and halved
¼ cup dry seasoned bread crumbs
2 tablespoons grated Parmesan cheese
¼ teaspoon paprika
¼ teaspoon parsley flakes

Set Power Select at HIGH. In small bowl, heat butter 1½ to 2 minutes or until melted; reserve 1 tablespoon. Into remaining butter, add garlic.
Cut stem off artichoke; trim tips of leaves, then rinse. Place lemon in between leaves; arrange artichokes in individual custard cup and pour butter mixture over each. Heat, covered with plastic wrap, 9 to 11 minutes.
Meanwhile, combine reserved melted butter with remaining ingredients. Sprinkle over cooked artichokes; let stand, covered, 5 minutes before serving.

Hint: To cook plain artichokes, after rinsing, wrap individually in wax paper. Heat according to vegetable chart, page 97.

Note: For FOUR servings, follow above procedure; double all ingredients. Heat butter 4 minutes, artichokes 13 to 15 minutes.
For ONE serving, halve all ingredients. Heat butter 1 minute; artichoke 7 to 9 minutes.

BETTER BAKED BEANS

Power Select: HIGH
                       HIGH→MEDIUM-LOW
Approx. Cooking Time: 20 minutes
Yield: about 6 servings

3 slices bacon, diced
½ cup chopped green pepper or onion
2 cans (16 oz. ea.) pork and beans
¼ cup molasses
¼ cup catsup
1 tablespoon prepared mustard
½ teaspoon Worcestershire sauce
Dash hot pepper sauce

Set Power Select at HIGH. In 1½-quart casserole dish, heat bacon and green pepper 3 to 4 minutes or until bacon is crisp. Stir in remaining ingredients; heat, covered with wax paper 3 to 4 minutes at HIGH or until mixture is bubbly.
Set Power Select at MEDIUM-LOW. Heat, covered with wax paper 10 to 12 minutes.

BROCCOLI EGG DIVINE

Power Select: HIGH
Approx. Cooking Time: 9 minutes
Yield: about 6 servings

1 package (1¼ oz.) hollandaise sauce mix
Ingredients as sauce mix package directs
1 pound fresh broccoli spears, cooked (see page 97) *
4 hard-cooked eggs, chopped (see page 85)
2 slices Swiss cheese, cubed
¼ cup dry bread crumbs
2 tablespoons butter or margarine, melted
Paprika

Set Power Select at HIGH. In 2-cup glass measure, combine hollandaise sauce mix and ingredients according to package directions; heat 2 to 3 minutes or until sauce is thickened, stirring once.
In glass pie plate, arrange broccoli in spoke fashion, flowerets towards center (trim stems if necessary); top with eggs and cheese. Pour sauce over cheese and top with bread crumbs blended with butter and paprika. Heat, covered, 4½ to 6 minutes or until heated through. Let stand, covered, 5 minutes before serving.

*Substitution: Use 2 packages (10 oz. ea.) frozen broccoli spears, cooked (see page 97) for fresh broccoli.

CHEESY VEGETABLE CASSEROLE

Power Select: HIGH
Temperature Select: 160°F
Approx. Cooking Time: 20 minutes
Yield: about 6 servings

4 medium onions, sliced (about 1 lb.)
1 teaspoon salt
½ teaspoon basil
¼ teaspoon pepper
3 tablespoons butter or margarine
½ cup seasoned dry bread crumbs
Paprika
4 medium tomatoes (about 1½ lb.), sliced
6 slices American cheese (1 oz. ea.)

Set Power Select at HIGH. In medium glass bowl, heat, covered, onions 4½ to 5½ minutes, stirring once; stir in salt, basil and pepper.
In small glass bowl, heat butter 1 to 1½ minutes or until melted; stir in bread crumbs and paprika.
In 2-quart casserole dish, alternately layer half the tomatoes, onions and cheese; top with remaining tomatoes and onions. Cover with plastic wrap.

TO HEAT BY TEMPERATURE: Insert probe through plastic wrap into center of casserole. Set Temperature Select at 160°F.

TO HEAT BY TIME: Set time for 10 to 12 minutes.

Heat; top with remaining cheese, then bread crumb mixture; let stand, covered, 5 minutes before serving.

CALICO CORN RELISH

Power Select: HIGH
Approx. Cooking Time: 7 minutes
Yield: about 6 servings

Water
2 cans (12 oz. ea.) whole kernel corn, drained (reserve liquid)
½ cup chopped celery
½ cup diced green pepper
¼ cup finely chopped onion
2 to 3 tablespoons sugar
1 tablespoon cornstarch
⅓ cup cider vinegar
2 tablespoons diced pimento

Set Power Select at HIGH. In 4-cup glass measure, add enough water to reserved liquid to equal 1¼ cups. Add celery, green pepper, onion and sugar; heat 3 to 4 minutes. Stir in cornstarch blended with vinegar and heat 2½ to 3 minutes or until mixture is slightly thickened, stirring occasionally. Add corn and pimento; chill before serving.

CARAWAY CABBAGE

Power Select: HIGH→STAND
Approx. Cooking Time: 11 minutes
Yield: 6 servings

¼ cup butter or margarine
1 small head cabbage, cut into 6 wedges (about 1½ lb.)
¼ teaspoon caraway seeds
¼ cup water

Set Power Select at HIGH. In oblong baking dish, heat butter 1 minute or until melted. Brush cabbage with butter and arrange, wide edge towards rim, in same dish; sprinkle with caraway and water. Heat, covered, 8 to 9½ minutes or until cabbage is almost tender; let STAND, covered, 5 minutes before serving.

CLASSIC COMPANY GREEN BEANS

Power Select: HIGH→STAND
Temperature Select: 160°F
Approx. Cooking Time: 17 minutes
Yield: about 6 servings

2 packages (9 oz. ea.) frozen french-style green beans
1 can (10¾ oz.) condensed cream of mushroom soup
1 can (3 oz.) french fried onions

Set Power Select at HIGH. In 2-quart casserole dish, heat beans, covered, 9 to 11 minutes, or until beans are tender, stirring twice. Stir in soup and ½ onion pieces; top with remaining onion pieces.

TO HEAT BY TEMPERATURE: Insert probe into center of casserole. Set Temperature Select at 160°F.

TO HEAT BY TIME: Set time for 5 to 6 minutes.

Heat; let STAND, 3 minutes before serving.

GARDEN SUCCOTASH

Power Select: HIGH
Approx. Cooking Time: 13 minutes
Yield: about 6 servings

1 package (10 oz.) frozen lima beans
1 package (10 oz.) frozen whole kernel corn
2 tablespoons chopped pimento (optional)
¼ cup milk or half 'n half
3 tablespoons butter or margarine
1 teaspoon salt
Dash pepper

Set Power Select at HIGH. In 2-quart casserole dish, combine lima beans, corn and pimento; heat, covered, 9 to 11 minutes or until vegetables are tender, stirring once. Stir in remaining ingredients; heat, covered, 1 to 1½ minutes or until heated through.

GREAT NORTHERN BEAN CASSEROLE

Power Select: HIGH→MEDIUM-LOW
MEDIUM-LOW
Approx. Cooking Time: 1¼ hours
Yield: 4 to 6 servings

1½ quarts hot water
1 package (16 oz.) dried great northern beans
4 slices bacon, diced
1 cup chopped onion
½ cup chopped green pepper
1 teaspoon salt
1 can (6 oz.) tomato paste
⅓ cup brown sugar
¼ cup dark corn syrup

Set Power Select at HIGH. In 4-quart casserole dish, combine water, beans, bacon, onion, green pepper and salt. Heat, covered, 10 to 12 minutes or until water is boiling.
Set Power Select at MEDIUM-LOW. Heat, covered, 45 minutes, stirring twice. Stir in tomato paste, sugar and syrup. Heat, covered, 15 minutes at MEDIUM-LOW or until beans are tender, stirring once.

GREEN BEANS AMANDINE

Power Select: HIGH
Approx. Cooking Time: 14 minutes
Yield: about 4 servings

¼ cup slivered almonds
3 tablespoons butter or margarine
1¼ to 1½ pounds fresh green beans, cut into 1½-inch pieces
¼ cup water
½ teaspoon salt
Dash ground nutmeg (optional)

Set Power Select at HIGH. In glass measure, heat almonds and butter 3 to 4 minutes or until almonds are lightly browned; reserve.
In 2-quart casserole dish, combine beans and water; heat, covered, 8½ to 10 minutes or until beans are tender, stirring once. Add remaining ingredients, almonds and butter; let stand, covered, 3 minutes before serving.

HERB BAKED TOMATOES

Power Select: HIGH→STAND
Approx. Cooking Time: 2 minutes
Yield: 4 servings

3 tablespoons seasoned dry bread crumbs
2 tablespoons butter or margarine, melted
2 tablespoons grated Parmesan cheese
½ teaspoon oregano or basil
2 medium tomatoes, cut in half

Set Power Select at HIGH. Combine bread crumbs, butter, cheese and oregano. In 8-inch square baking dish, arrange tomato halves; top with bread crumb mixture.
Heat, covered, 1½ to 2 minutes or until tomatoes are tender. Let STAND, 2 minutes before serving.

HONEY ACORN SQUASH

Power Select: HIGH→STAND
HIGH→STAND
Approx. Cooking Time: 10 minutes
Yield: 4 servings

2 acorn squash (about ¾ lb. ea.)
4 tablespoons honey
4 teaspoons butter or margarine
⅛ teaspoon grated lemon peel

Set Power Select at HIGH. Pierce skin of squash several times, arrange on paper towel lined glass oven tray. Heat 4 to 5 minutes, turning squash over once; let STAND 3 minutes. Cut squash in half; scoop out seeds. In oblong baking dish, arrange squash, cut-side up. Top with honey, butter and lemon. Heat, covered, 4 to 5 minutes at HIGH or until squash is tender; let STAND, covered, 2 minutes before serving.

Variations: *Use one of the following toppings for honey, butter and lemon–*
For FRUIT 'N HONEY SQUASH, *use 4 tablespoons finely chopped apple, 2 tablespoons flaked coconut, 4 tablespoons honey and 2 tablespoons butter.*
For HOLIDAY SPECIAL SQUASH, *use ½ cup chopped orange, ¼ cup whole berry cranberry sauce, 2 tablespoons brown sugar and ¼ teaspoon ground cinnamon.*

Fresh Asparagus, page 97

OKRA CREOLE

Power Select: HIGH
HIGH→STAND
Approx. Cooking Time: 21 minutes
Yield: about 6 servings

1 medium onion, sliced
¼ cup butter or margarine
2 packages (10 oz. ea.) frozen sliced okra
1 can (16 oz.) stewed tomatoes, chopped
½ teaspoon Worcestershire sauce
¼ teaspoon hot pepper sauce
Salt and pepper to taste

Set Power Select at HIGH. In 2-quart casserole dish, heat onion and butter 2½ to 3½ minutes or until onion is tender. Add okra, tomatoes, Worcestershire and pepper sauce; heat, covered, 15 to 17 minutes at HIGH or until vegetables are tender, stirring twice. Let STAND, covered, 3 minutes. Season with salt and pepper.

ORANGE GLAZED CARROTS

Power Select: HIGH
Approx. Cooking Time: 9 minutes
Yield: about 4 servings

1 pound carrots, sliced ½-inch thick
¼ cup orange juice
3 tablespoons honey
3 tablespoons butter or margarine
½ teaspoon grated lemon peel (optional)
¼ teaspoon salt
Dash ground nutmeg

Set Power Select at HIGH. In 2-quart casserole dish, combine carrots and orange juice; heat, covered, 7 to 8½ minutes or until carrots are tender, stirring once. Stir in remaining ingredients: let stand, covered, 3 minutes before serving.

RATATOUILLE

Power Select: HIGH
HIGH→STAND
Approx. Cooking Time: 25 minutes
Yield: about 8 servings

2 medium onions, sliced
1 medium green pepper, sliced
⅓ cup oil
2 cloves garlic, finely chopped
1 medium eggplant (about 1½ lb.), peeled and cut into ½-inch pieces
3 medium tomatoes (about 1 lb.), chopped
2 medium zucchini (about 1 lb.), thinly sliced
1 cup vegetable juice cocktail or tomato juice
2 teaspoons each basil and parsley flakes
1 teaspoon salt
¼ teaspoon pepper

Set Power Select at HIGH. In 5-quart casserole dish, combine onions, green pepper, oil and garlic; heat, covered, 4 to 5 minutes, stirring once. Add remaining ingredients and heat, covered, 18 to 20 minutes at HIGH or until vegetables are tender, stirring occasionally. Let STAND, covered, 5 minutes before serving.

Variation: *Add ¼ pound fresh mushrooms, sliced or 1 can (4 oz.) sliced mushrooms, drained with eggplant.*

STUFFED ONIONS FLORENTINE

Power Select: HIGH
                     HIGH→STAND
Approx. Cooking Time: 25 minutes
Yield: 6 servings

6 large Spanish onions (about 3½ lb.)
¼ cup water
½ pound pork sausage, crumbled
1 package (10 oz.) frozen chopped spinach, thawed and drained
¾ cup shredded Cheddar or Swiss cheese (about 3 oz.)
1 egg
6 tablespoons buttered bread crumbs

Set Power Select at HIGH. Peel onions; cut ½ inch slice off sprout end and just enough off the root end to sit flat. In shallow baking dish, arrange onions, add water and heat 11 to 13 minutes or until onions are partially cooked. (Remove centers as they pop up). Carefully remove centers of onion, leaving a ¼ to ½-inch shell; chop ¼ cup onion centers.
In glass bowl, combine ¼ cup chopped onion, crumbled sausage and spinach. Heat 4 to 5 minutes or until sausage is cooked, stirring twice; drain. Stir in cheese and egg. Fill onion shells with spinach mixture and arrange in baking dish; top with bread crumbs. Heat, covered, 6 to 7 minutes at HIGH or until heated through. Let STAND, covered, 5 minutes before serving. Serve, if desired, with Cheese Sauce (page 26).

SWISS SCALLOPED CORN

Power Select: HIGH
                     MEDIUM-HIGH→STAND
Approx. Cooking Time: 15 minutes
Yield: about 6 servings

3 slices bacon
2 cans (16 oz.) whole kernel corn, drained
1 cup shredded Swiss cheese (about 4 oz.)
½ teaspoon onion powder
⅛ teaspoon pepper
1½ tablespoons flour
1 egg
1 can (5⅓ oz.) evaporated milk
¼ cup dry bread crumbs
1 tablespoon butter or margarine, melted
Dash paprika

Set Power Select at HIGH. In oblong baking dish, arrange bacon between layers of paper towels; heat 2½ to 3 minutes or until bacon is crisp. Remove paper towels; crumble bacon. Stir in corn, cheese, onion powder, pepper and flour blended with egg and milk. Top with bread crumbs blended with butter and paprika. Set Power Select at MEDIUM-HIGH. Heat 10 to 12 minutes or until corn is set. Let STAND, covered, 5 minutes before serving.

ZUCCHINI PARMESAN

Power Select: HIGH
Approx. Cooking Time: 9 minutes
Yield: about 4 servings

4 medium zucchini, cut into 1-inch slices (about 1½ lb.)
¼ cup grated Parmesan cheese
1 can (8 oz.) tomato sauce
½ cup shredded Mozzarella cheese (about 2 oz.)

Set Power Select at HIGH. In 8-inch round baking dish, combine zucchini, parmesan cheese and tomato sauce; heat, covered, 8 to 9 minutes or until zucchini is tender, strring once. Sprinkle with mozzarella cheese and let stand, covered, 5 minutes before serving.

POTATOES ❦❦❦❦❦❦❦❦❦❦❦❦❦❦❦

BAKED STUFFED POTATOES

Power Select: HIGH
Approx. Cooking Time: 6 minutes
Yield: 4 servings

4 medium potatoes, baked (see page 104)
½ cup shredded Cheddar cheese (about 2 oz.)
⅓ to ½ cup milk
2 tablespoons butter or margarine
1 egg
Salt and pepper to taste
Paprika

Set Power Select at HIGH. Cut a thin slice (lengthwise) from each potato. Scoop out potato, leaving a thin shell. Combine potato, cheese, milk, butter, egg, salt and pepper; mash until smooth. Spoon potato mixture into shell; sprinkle with paprika*. Heat on paper towel lined glass oven tray 4 to 5½ minutes or until heated through.

**Recipe can be prepared up to this point in advance. Adjust heating time as necessary.*

Note: **For TWO servings,** *follow above procedure; halve all ingredients (use whole egg). Heat 2 to 3 minutes.*

BUTTERED CRUMB POTATOES

Power Select: HIGH
                     HIGH→STAND
Approx. Cooking Time: 8 minutes
Yield: 4 servings

4 small potatoes, peeled (about 4 oz. ea.)
2 tablespoons butter or margarine, melted
½ cup seasoned dry bread crumbs

Set Power Select at HIGH. Roll potatoes in butter, then in bread crumbs. Arrange in baking dish; drizzle with remaining butter. Heat, covered, 7 to 8 minutes at HIGH or until potatoes are tender; let STAND, covered, 3 minutes before serving.

HOT GERMAN POTATO SALAD

Power Select: HIGH
Approx. Cooking Time: 11 minutes
Yield: about 4 servings

4 slices bacon, diced
¼ cup finely chopped onion
2 teaspoons flour
⅓ cup cider vinegar
2 tablespoons brown sugar
¼ teaspoon celery seed
Salt and pepper to taste
4 medium potatoes, baked, (see page 104) peeled and
**   sliced***

Set Power Select at HIGH. In oblong baking dish, heat
bacon and onion 3½ to 5 minutes, stirring occasionally.
Stir in flour, vinegar, sugar, celery seed, salt and
pepper; heat 1 to 1½ minutes or until slightly thickened,
stirring once. Add potatoes and heat 3 to 4 minutes
or until heated through, stirring once; serve warm.

*Substitution: Use 2 cans (16 oz. ea.) sliced potatoes,
drained, for baked potatoes.*

MASHED POTATOES

Power Select: HIGH→STAND
                 MEDIUM
Approx. Cooking Time: 14 minutes
Yield: about 6 servings

6 medium potatoes (about 2 lb.), peeled and quartered
½ to ¾ cup milk
¼ cup butter or margarine
Salt and pepper to taste

Set Power Select at HIGH. Rinse potatoes; drain. In
medium glass bowl, heat potatoes, covered, 9 to 10½
minutes or until potatoes are tender, stirring once.
Let STAND, covered, 5 minutes; drain.
Set Power Select at MEDIUM. Meanwhile, in small glass
bowl, combine remaining ingredients; heat 2 to 3 minutes
or until hot. Add to potatoes and mash until smooth.

Note: *For INSTANT mashed potatoes, follow
package directions; heat water, milk and salt in
glass bowl at Power Select HIGH (see Heating Liquids
chart, page 22). Stir in butter and instant potato flakes.*

POTATO DUMPLINGS

Power Select: HIGH
Approx. Cooking Time: 14 minutes
Yield: 4 to 6 servings

2 quarts hot water or broth
2 cups hot mashed potatoes (see above)
½ cup flour
1 egg
½ teaspoon salt
¼ teaspoon parsley flakes
⅛ teaspoon pepper
Dash ground nutmeg

Set Power Select at HIGH. In 3-quart casserole, heat
water, covered, 10 minutes or until water is boiling.
Meanwhile, combine remaining ingredients; drop by
heaping tablespoons into water. Heat 3 to 4 minutes
or until dumplings float; drain.

QUICK SCALLOPED POTATOES

Power Select: HIGH
                 MEDIUM
                 MEDIUM→STAND
Temperature Select: 175°F
Approx. Cooking Time: 35 minutes
Yield: about 6 servings

6 medium potatoes (about 6 oz. ea.)
¼ cup butter or margarine
1 tablespoon dried onion flakes
1 teaspoon salt
½ teaspoon pepper
¼ cup flour
2 cups milk

Set Power Select at HIGH. Following procedure for
baking potatoes (page 104), heat potatoes 10 to 11
minutes or until potatoes are almost tender. Let stand
5 minutes; peel and slice.
Meanwhile, in 4 cup glass measure, heat butter,
onion, salt and pepper 1 to 1½ minutes or until
butter is melted. Stir in flour; gradually add milk,
stirring until smooth.
Set Power Select at MEDIUM. Heat 6 to 7 minutes or
until sauce is smooth, stirring twice. In 2-quart
casserole dish, alternately layer potatoes and sauce
forming three layers. Cover with plastic wrap.

TO HEAT BY TEMPERATURE: Insert probe through
plastic wrap into center of casserole. Set Power
Select at MEDIUM; set Temperature Select at 175°F.

TO HEAT BY TIME: Heat at Power Select MEDIUM,
14 to 15 minutes, or until heated through. Let STAND,
covered, 5 minutes before serving.

SWEET POTATO PONE

Power Select: HIGH
Temperature Select: 160°F
Approx. Cooking Time: 11 minutes
Yield: about 6 servings

¼ cup butter or margarine
2 cans (16 oz. ea.) sweet potatoes or yams, drained
1 egg
½ cup milk
2 tablespoons brown sugar
2 tablespoons molasses
½ teaspoon ground cinnamon
¼ teaspoon ground nutmeg
Dash ground cloves
½ cup miniature marshmallows

Set Power Select at HIGH. In 1½-quart casserole dish,
heat butter 1 to 1½ minutes or until melted. In medium
bowl, combine butter, sweet potatoes, egg, milk,
sugar, molasses, cinnamon, nutmeg and cloves; mash
until smooth. Spread into same casserole dish; cover
with plastic wrap.

TO HEAT BY TEMPERATURE: Insert probe through
plastic wrap into center of casserole. Set Power
Select at HIGH; set Temperature Select at 160°F.

TO HEAT BY TIME: Heat at Power Select HIGH 8 to 9
minutes or until heated through. Top with marshmallows; heat, uncovered, 30 seconds.

PREPARING BAKED POTATOES

- Select potatoes of equal size, if possible*.
- Rinse potatoes; pat dry.
- Prick skin several times with fork to allow steam to escape and prevent bursting.
- Arrange in circular pattern on paper towel lined glass oven tray, equal distance apart.
- Heat according to chart at Power Select HIGH.
- Let STAND, covered, 3 to 5 minutes before serving.

Heating time will vary slightly with larger or smaller potatoes.

AMOUNT		APPROXIMATE HEATING TIME* at Power Select HIGH (in minutes)
Medium Baking Potatoes (about 6 oz. ea.)	1	4½ to 5½
	2	6 to 7½
	4	8½ to 10
	6	12 to 13½

Note: *Potatoes can be wrapped in aluminum foil after heating.*

PREPARING DRIED BEANS AND PEAS

- Bring beans and hot water to a boil at Power Select HIGH
- Heat, covered, at Power Select MEDIUM-LOW until tender.

ITEM	CONTAINER	AMOUNT OF HOT WATER	APPROXIMATE HEATING TIME (in minutes)	
			To Boil Water at Power Select HIGH	To Cook Beans at Power Select → MEDIUM-LOW
Black-eyed peas (1 lb.)	5-quart casserole dish	2½ quarts	10 to 12 →	70
Kidney beans, Lima beans (small) or Northern beans (1 lb.)	5-quart casserole dish	2 quarts	9 to 11 →	60
Lima beans (large) (1 lb.)	5-quart casserole dish	2½ quarts	10 to 12 →	75
Split peas or Lentils (1 lb.)	3-quart casserole dish	1½ quarts	8 to 10 →	45

Note: *For best results, heat beans or peas covered.*

To tempt you into trying rice, pasta and cereals the microwave way, here are delicious recipes you will not be able to resist.

A microwave oven can help solve a common problem. Does everyone need breakfast at a different time? Control this breakfast dilemma and let your microwave take over. Have everyone prepare their own favorite cereals when they are ready.

Guaranteed easy clean-up, too. Heat the cereal right in the cereal bowl, following the simple chart and instructions.

There are definite savings also in heating pastas and rice in your microwave oven: To heat pasta, you use less water. Bringing the water to a boil is done quicker and does not heat the kitchen at the same time. Rice is heated directly in the serving dish and the MEDIUM-LOW Power Select assures a controlled heating to gently cook the rice tender everytime. You will never have a sticky pan to worry about.

PASTAS

PREPARING PASTA

- Cover and heat hot water to a boil at Power Select HIGH.
- Add pasta and 1 teaspoon salt (½ tablespoon oil optional).
- Heat, uncovered, at Power Select HIGH, stirring twice.
- Test pasta for desired doneness before adding more heating time.
- Slightly undercook pasta that will be heated again in casseroles.
- Stir and let STAND, covered, 3 minutes.
- Drain and rinse before serving.

ITEM	CONTAINER	AMOUNT OF HOT WATER	APPROXIMATE TIME TO BOIL WATER at Power Select HIGH (in minutes)	APPROXIMATE TIME TO COOK PASTA at Power Select HIGH (in minutes)	STANDING TIME (in minutes)
Egg Noodles medium width (8 oz.)	3-qt. casserole dish	1½ quarts	7 to 8	5 to 6	3
Elbow Macaroni (8 oz.)	3-qt. casserole dish	1½ quarts	7 to 8	7 to 8	3
Lasagna Noodles (8 oz.)	oblong baking dish*	1½ quarts	7 to 8	13 to 15	3
Spaghetti (8 oz.-broken)	3-qt. casserole dish	2 quarts	8 to 9	7 to 8	3
Specialty Noodles bows, shells, etc. (8 oz.)	3-qt. casserole dish	1½ quarts	7 to 8	10½ to 11	3

*Heat water for lasagne in 2–qt. glass bowl. Pour over noodles in oblong baking dish.

CONVENIENCE MIXES can easily be prepared, also. Here are directions for two popular ones.

FLAVORED RICE MIX WITH VERMICELLI

Set Power Select at HIGH. In 2-quart casserole dish, heat 2 tablespoons butter 1 minute or until melted; stir in rice and vermicelli. Heat 2 to 3 minutes, stirring once. Add flavor packet and 2¾ cups hot water. Heat, covered, 3 to 4 minutes or until boiling. at HIGH.
Set Power Select at MEDIUM-LOW. Heat, covered, 11 to 13 minutes or until rice is tender. Let stand, 5 minutes.

MACARONI AND CHEESE DINNER (7¼ oz.)

Set Power Select at HIGH. In 3-quart casserole dish, heat, covered, 6 cups hot water 5 to 6 minutes or until boiling. Add macaroni and heat 5 to 6 minutes, stirring once. Let STAND covered, 3 minutes, then drain.
Meanwhile, in serving dish, heat ¼ cup butter, ¼ cup milk and cheese 1½ to 2¼ minutes, stirring once.
Toss with drained macaroni.

Pictured on the preceding page: Granola Cereal, Spanish Rice, Fettuccine Alfredo.

FETTUCCINE ALFREDO

Power Select: HIGH
Approx. Cooking Time: 17 minutes
Yield: about 4 side-dish servings

1 package (8 oz.) medium egg noodles
1 cup grated Parmesan cheese
½ cup butter or margarine, cut into quarters
½ cup whipping cream
Pepper to taste

Set Power Select at HIGH. Cook noodles according to chart, page 106.
While noodles are standing, in glass serving bowl, heat cheese, butter and cream 2½ to 3 minutes or until butter is melted, stirring twice. Stir in drained noodles; toss well. Season with pepper.

FLORIDA-STYLE NOODLES

Power Select: HIGH
Approx. Cooking Time: 16 minutes
Yield: about 4 servings

1 package (8 oz.) medium egg noodles
½ cup almonds
¼ cup butter or margarine
1 tablespoon poppy seeds
½ tablespoon grated lemon peel
½ tablespoon grated orange peel
½ teaspoon salt
⅛ teaspoon pepper
1 cup sour cream

Set Power Select at HIGH. Cook noodles according to chart, page 106.
While noodles are standing, in glass serving bowl, heat almonds and butter 1 to 1½ minutes or until butter is melted. Stir in drained noodles, poppy seeds, lemon and orange peel, salt and pepper, toss well. Serve with sour cream.

HOMEMADE PASTA

Power Select: LOW
Approx. Cooking Time: 16 minutes (to dry)
Yield: about 3 cups (cooked)

1 egg
2 tablespoons milk
½ teaspoon salt
1 cup flour

Set Power Select at LOW. Combine egg, milk and salt; gradually add flour, stirring until smooth after each addition of flour to form a soft dough.
On floured surface, knead dough until smooth, about 30 times. Roll dough very thin; roll up loosely in jelly-roll fashion. Slice dough ¼-inch thick. Unroll each slice and arrange on wax paper lined glass oven tray. (Cut noodles to fit tray if necessary).
Heat 14 to 16 minutes or until noodles are dry.

To Prepare for Eating: *In 3-quart casserole dish, add noodles to 6 cups boiling salted water. Heat 9½ to 11½ minutes or until noodles are tender. Let stand 3 minutes; drain and serve.*

NOODLE PUDDING

Power Select: MEDIUM
MEDIUM→STAND
Approx. Cooking Time: 34 minutes
Yield: about 8 servings

1 package (8 oz.) medium egg noodles
½ cup butter or margarine
4 eggs, beaten
1 cup cottage cheese
1 cup sour cream
¾ cup raisins
½ cup sugar
1 teaspoon ground cinnamon
¼ teaspoon ground nutmeg

Set Power Select at MEDIUM. Cook noodles according to chart, page 106.
In round baking dish, heat butter 1 minute or until melted. In large bowl, combine butter, remaining ingredients and drained noodles; pour into same round baking dish. Sprinkle, if desired, with additional cinnamon. Heat 17 to 18½ minutes at MEDIUM until pudding is set. Let STAND, covered, with wax paper. Serve warm or chilled.

SWISS NOODLE BAKE

Power Select: HIGH
MEDIUM-HIGH
Approx. Cooking Time: 26 minutes
Yield: about 6 servings

1 package (8 oz.) medium egg noodles
4 slices bacon, diced
¼ cup chopped onion
1¼ cups shredded Swiss cheese (about 5 oz.)
1 egg, beaten
2 tablespoons milk
½ teaspoon salt
¼ teaspoon ground nutmeg
Pepper to taste
Buttered bread crumbs
⅛ teaspoon paprika

Set Power Select at HIGH. Cook noodles according to chart, page 106.
In 2-quart casserole dish, heat bacon and onion 4 to 5 minutes, or until crisp, stirring once; drain. Stir in drained noodles, cheese, egg, milk, salt, nutmeg and pepper.
Set Power Select at MEDIUM-HIGH. Heat, covered, 4 to 5 minutes. Top with bread crumbs blended with paprika; heat 2 minutes or until heated through.

RICE AND OTHER GRAINS ❦❦❦❦❦❦❦❦❦❦❦❦❦❦❦❦❦❦❦❦❦❦❦❦❦❦❦❦❦❦❦❦❦❦

PREPARING RICE AND OTHER GRAINS

- Cover and heat hot water to a boil at Power Select HIGH.*
- Add grain, salt and butter (amounts of salt and butter as package directs).
- Heat, covered, at Power Select MEDIUM-LOW.
- Let STAND, covered, before serving.

Notes: **For instant (no cook) products,** *using package directions, bring hot water to a boil. (See Heating Liquids chart page 22). Stir in product; let stand covered.*

   ***For program cooking,** add rice or grain to hot water. Program oven at HIGH, then MEDIUM–LOW.*

ITEM	CONTAINER	AMOUNT OF HOT WATER	APPROXIMATE TIME TO BOIL WATER AT POWER SELECT HIGH (in minutes)	APPROXIMATE TIME TO COOK GRAIN AT POWER SELECT MEDIUM-LOW (in minutes)	STANDING TIME (in minutes)
RICE					
Brown (1 cup)	2-qt. casserole dish	3 cups	5 to 6 →	30 to 33	→ 25
Flavored Rice Mix (6 oz.)	2-qt. casserole dish	as package directs	4 to 5 →	20	→ 10
Long Grain (1 cup)	2-qt. casserole dish	2 cups	4 to 5 →	13½ to 16½	→ 10
Long Grain & Wild Rice Mix (6 oz.)	2-qt. casserole dish	2½ cups	4½ to 5 →	23 to 25	→ 5
Quick Rice (1 cup)	1-qt. casserole dish	1 cup	2 to 3 →	5	→ 5
Short Grain (1 cup)	2-qt. casserole dish	2 cups	4 to 5 →	10 to 12	→ 10
BARLEY					
Quick Cook (1 cup)	2-qt. casserole dish	3 cups	5 to 6 →	5½ to 6½	→ 3 (then drain)
GRITS (⅔ cup)	3-qt. casserole dish	3⅓ cups	5 to 6 →	10	→ 10

BARLEY MUSHROOM CASSEROLE

Power Select: HIGH
HIGH→MEDIUM-LOW→STAND
Approx. Cooking Time: 16 minutes
Yield: about 6 servings

6 tablespoons butter or margarine
2 medium onions, finely chopped
3 cloves garlic, finely chopped
1 pound fresh mushrooms, sliced
1 cup quick cooking barley
½ cup chicken broth
¼ cup chopped parsley
2 teaspoons basil
1 teaspoon salt
¼ teaspoon pepper

Set Power Select at HIGH. In 2½-quart casserole dish, heat, covered, butter, onion and garlic 3 to 4 minutes or until onion is tender. Stir in remaining ingredients. Heat, covered, 5 minutes at HIGH.
Set Power Select at MEDIUM-LOW. Heat, covered, 5½ to 6½ minutes or until barley is tender. Let STAND, covered, 5 minutes before serving.

HOPPIN' JOHN

Power Select: HIGH
HIGH→MEDIUM-LOW→STAND
Approx. Cooking Time: 24 minutes
Yield: about 6 servings

4 slices bacon, diced
1 medium onion, chopped
2½ cups hot water
1½ cups cooked black-eyed peas
1 cup long grain rice
1 teaspoon salt
¼ teaspoon pepper
Dash hot pepper sauce (optional)

Set Power Select at HIGH. In 2½-quart casserole dish, heat bacon and onion 4 to 5 minutes or until bacon is crisp, stirring once; stir in remaining ingredients. Heat, covered, 5 to 6 minutes or until liquid boils at HIGH
Set Power Select at MEDIUM-LOW. Heat, covered, 11 to 13 minutes or until rice is tender, stirring once. Let STAND, covered, 5 minutes before serving.

RICE PILAF

Power Select: HIGH
HIGH→MEDIUM-LOW→STAND
Approx. Cooking Time: 23 minutes
Yield: about 6 servings

¼ cup butter or margarine
1 cup long grain rice
2¼ cups chicken broth
¼ cup raisins (optional)
1 to 1½ teaspoons curry powder

Set Power Select at HIGH. In 2-quart casserole dish, heat butter 1 minute or until melted; stir in rice. Heat 2 to 3 minutes or until rice is browned, stirring once. Add remaining ingredients and heat, covered, 4 to 5 minutes at HIGH.
Set Power Select at MEDIUM-LOW. Heat, covered 12 to 14 minutes or until rice is tender. Let STAND, covered, 5 minutes.

Variation: *Heat ¼ cup slivered almonds with butter.*

SPANISH RICE

Power Select: HIGH
HIGH→MEDIUM-LOW→STAND
Approx. Cooking Time: 26 minutes
Yield: about 6 servings

½ cup chopped onion
¼ cup finely chopped green pepper
2 tablespoons butter or margarine
Water
1 can (16 oz.) stewed tomatoes, chopped and drained (reserve liquid)
1 cup long grain rice
1½ teaspoons salt
⅛ teaspoon pepper

Set Power Select at HIGH. In 2-quart casserole dish, heat onion, green pepper and butter 2½ to 3½ minutes, stirring once. Add enough water to reserved liquid to equal 2 cups. Add to dish with tomatoes, rice, salt and pepper. Heat, covered, 4 to 5 minutes at HIGH.
Set Power Select at MEDIUM-LOW. Heat, covered, 16 to 17 minutes or until rice is tender, stirring once. Let STAND, covered, 5 minutes before serving.

NICER RICE

For a special touch, try one of the following suggestions next time you serve rice.
- Substitute beef or chicken broth for water when heating rice.
- Add 2 envelopes (¼ oz. ea.) instant onion soup to 2 cups water before adding rice.
- While rice is standing, heat, covered, ½ cup chopped onion, 1 jar (2½ oz.) sliced mushrooms, drained and 1 tablespoon butter 1½ to 2 minutes or until onion is tender (at Power Select HIGH). Stir into rice.
- Just before serving, stir in 4 slices bacon, crisp-cooked and crumbled and 1 to 2 tablespoons chives.

CEREALS ❦❦❦❦❦❦❦❦❦❦❦❦❦❦❦❦❦❦❦❦❦❦❦❦❦❦❦❦❦❦❦❦❦❦❦❦❦

GRANOLA CEREAL

Power Select: HIGH
Approx. Cooking Time: 10 minutes
Yield: about 3 cups

2 cups quick or old fashion oats
⅔ cup soy nuts or coarsely chopped nuts
⅓ cup wheat germ (optional)
¼ cup brown sugar
¼ cup honey
1 teaspoon vanilla extract
⅓ cup raisins or coconut

Set Power Select at HIGH. In oblong baking dish, heat oats 3 to 5 minutes, stirring occasionally. Add nuts, wheat germ, and brown sugar; stir in honey and vanilla. Heat 3 to 5 minutes, stirring twice; add raisins. Cool completely, stirring occasionally to crumble mixture. Store in airtight container.

Note: *To make GRANOLA SNACK, follow above procedure. Add ¼ cup oil with honey.*

NICE AND SPICY OATMEAL

Power Select: HIGH
Approx. Cooking Time: 5 minutes
Yield: about 4 servings

4 cups hot water
2 cups quick-cooking oats
½ cup chopped dried apricots or raisins
¼ cup brown sugar
¼ teaspoon salt
½ cup wheat germ (optional)
1 teaspoon ground cinnamon

Set Power Select at HIGH. In 2-quart casserole dish, combine water, oats, apricots, sugar and salt. Heat 4 to 5 minutes or until slightly thickened, stirring once; stir in wheat germ and cinnamon. Let stand 3 minutes before serving.

PREPARING HOT CEREALS 🔳

- Combine cereal, hot water* and salt (optional) in bowl or individual dish.
- Heat, stirring once.
- Let stand; stir before serving.
- Top as desired, with sugar, spices, etc.

For Cream of Wheat, heat water to a boil, then add cereal.

CEREAL	CONTAINER	AMOUNT OF HOT WATER	AMOUNT OF CEREAL	APPROXIMATE TIME TO COOK CEREAL (in minutes)		STAND TIME (in minutes)
				at Power Select HIGH	at Power Select MEDIUM-LOW	
Cream of Wheat						
1 serving	2-cup glass bowl	1¼ cups	2½ tablespoons	1	4 to 6	1
2 servings	1-qt. glass bowl	2 cups	⅓ cup	1½	6 to 7	1
4 servings	2-qt. glass bowl	3¾ cups	⅔ cup	2	7 to 8	2
Farina						
1 serving	individual serving dish	⅔ cup	2 tablespoons	1½ to 2	—	1
2 servings	2 individual serving dishes	1⅓ cups	¼ cup	3¼ to 3¾	—	1
4 servings	1-qt. glass bowl	2⅔ cups	½ cup	4½ to 5½	—	2
Oatmeal (Quick)						
1 serving	individual serving dish	¾ cup	⅓ cup	1 to 1½	—	1
2 servings	2 individual serving dishes	1½ cups	⅔ cup	2 to 2½	—	1
4 servings	1-qt. glass bowl	3 cups	1⅓ cups	3½ to 4	—	2
Wheat-Bran Cereal						
1 serving	individual serving dish	¾ cup	¼ cup	3	—	1
2 servings	2 individual serving dishes	1½ cups	½ cup	5 to 6	—	1
4 servings	2-qt. glass bowl	3 cups	1 cup	7 to 8	—	2

Piping hot muffins, split open with lots of butter...warm coffeecake to complement breakfast...sounds good, doesn't it.

Now, you do not have to get up hours before everyone else to surprise them with a freshly baked treat or plan in advance for something to serve with coffee.

Your microwave oven brings you flexibility for spur of the moment fun. Most breads and coffeecakes bake in 10 to 15 minutes, muffins or buns in about 6 minutes! And what a time saver your microwave oven will be in thawing and raising frozen bread dough and proofing yeast recipes.

HINTS FOR BAKING QUICK BREADS, MUFFINS AND COFFEE CAKES

Follow the steps below to guarantee your baked goods will be the best ever!

- Prepare batter according to package or recipe directions.
- Use glass baking dish, or cupcake paper-lined container as indicated in charts or recipes.
- Grease bottom of baking dish when coffee cake will be served from dish.
- Grease and line bottom of baking dishes with wax paper if inverting to remove from dish. DO NOT GREASE AND FLOUR DISHES.

- Use cupcake paper-lined custard cups or microwave safe muffin pan when heating muffins.
- Check quick breads and coffee cakes halfway through heating. If some areas are heating faster than others, turn dish ½ turn; continue heating.
- Test for doneness with a toothpick inserted near the center—it should come out clean.
- Let stand, covered, on flat surface, 10 to 15 minutes to finish baking.
- Turn out of dish and carefully peel off wax paper. Cool.
- Store, covered, until ready to serve.

PREPARING BREAD MIXES

ITEM	POWER SELECT	CONTAINER	APPROXIMATE HEATING TIME (in minutes)	STANDING TIME, COVERED (in minutes)
Coffee cake (14 oz.)	MEDIUM	8-in. round dish	9½ to 11½	10
Fruit Variety (16 to 19 oz.)	MEDIUM	8-in. round dish	11½ to 13½	10
Cornbread (12 oz.)	MEDIUM	8-in. round dish	7½ to 9½	10
Gingerbread	MEDIUM	8-in. round or square dish	7½ to 9½	5
Muffins (8 to 12 oz.) (heat 6 at a time)	MEDIUM-LOW	cupcake paper in individual custard cups or muffin maker	4½ to 5½	5
Quick Bread (14½ to 17 oz.)	MEDIUM	glass loaf dish, bottom lined with wax paper	10½ to 12½	15

Pictured on the proceding page: Graham Streusel Coffee Cake. Muffins from Convenience Mixes. Cherry Brunch Rolls. Boston Brown Bread.

BREADS ❦❦❦❦❦❦❦❦❦❦❦❦❦❦❦❦

BASIC NUT BREAD

Power Select: MEDIUM
Approx. Cooking Time: 9 minutes
Yield: 1 loaf

½ cup sugar
3 tablespoons butter or margarine
2 eggs
¾ cup buttermilk
½ teaspoon vanilla extract
1½ cups flour
¾ cup chopped nuts
1½ teaspoon baking powder
½ teaspoon salt
½ teaspoon ground cinnamon

Set Power Select at MEDIUM. Cream together sugar and butter; stir in eggs, buttermilk and vanilla. Add remaining ingredients, stirring only until flour is moistened.
Into 8'' x 4'' x 2½'' greased glass loaf dish, bottom lined with wax paper, spoon batter; sprinkle with additional cinnamon. Heat 8 to 9 minutes; let stand, covered, 10 minutes. Invert and remove wax paper; let stand 5 minutes. Store, covered, until ready to serve.

Variations: Fold in any ½ cup of the following, tossed with 1 tablespoon flour:

- *Blueberries*
- *Chopped apricots*
- *Cranberries*
- *Raisins*

BOSTON BROWN BREAD 🔲

Power Select: MEDIUM→STAND
Approx. Cooking Time: 10 minutes
Yield: 1 loaf

1 cup buttermilk
⅓ cup molasses
½ cup raisins
½ teaspoon baking powder
½ teaspoon baking soda
½ teaspoon salt
½ cup flour
½ cup whole wheat flour
½ cup yellow cornmeal

Set Power Select at MEDIUM. Combine buttermilk and molasses; stir in raisins, baking powder, baking soda and salt. Add flours and cornmeal, stirring only until moistened. Pour batter into generously greased 30-ounce cylinder-shaped plastic container. Cover loosely with plastic wrap; secure wrap with rubber band.
Heat 8½ to 9½ minutes; let STAND, covered, 10 minutes. Remove from container; let stand 5 minutes. Store, covered, until ready to serve.

CHERRY BRUNCH ROLLS

Power Select: MEDIUM
Approx. Cooking Time: 5 minutes
Yield: 10 rolls

1 cup brown sugar
¼ cup chopped maraschino cherries
¼ cup flaked coconut
¼ teaspoon ground cinnamon
1 can (8 oz.) refrigerated biscuits
⅓ cup butter or margarine, melted

Set Power Select at MEDIUM. Combine ½ cup brown sugar, cherries, coconut and cinnamon; sprinkle into a 2 quart baking ring.
Dip each biscuit into melted butter and then in remaining brown sugar. Arrange biscuits on top of cherry mixture; sprinkle remaining sugar over ring. Heat 3½ to 4½ minutes. Let stand, covered, 5 minutes before inverting on serving platter. Store, covered, until ready to serve.

CRISPY CROUTONS 🔲

Power Select: HIGH→STAND
Approx. Cooking Time: 7 minutes
Yield: about 3 cups

⅓ cup butter or margarine
6 slices pumpernickel or rye bread*

Set Power Select at HIGH. In small glass bowl, heat butter 1 minute or until melted. Brush butter onto bread (one side only); cut bread into small cubes. In oblong baking dish, arrange bread; drizzle with remaining butter. Heat 5 to 6 minutes or until bread is crispy, stirring twice. Let STAND, 10 minutes; store, covered, until ready to serve.

Variation: Use your favorite kind of bread.

IRISH SODA BREAD 🔲

Power Select: MEDIUM→STAND
Approx. Cooking Time: 10 minutes
Yield: about 6 servings

3 cups flour
3 tablespoons sugar
¾ teaspoon baking powder
3 tablespoons butter or margarine
1½ cups raisins
1 tablespoon caraway seeds
1 cup buttermilk
1 egg
¾ teaspoon baking soda

Set Power Select at MEDIUM. Sift together flour, sugar and baking powder; cut in butter. Stir in raisins and caraway. Combine buttermilk, egg and baking soda; add to dry ingredients, stirring only until flour is moistened. On floured board, lightly knead dough until smooth, about 3 minutes. Shape into ball and place in 1-quart glass bowl, bottom lined with wax paper; cut an ''X'' across top of dough. Heat 9 to 10 minutes. Let STAND, 10 minutes; turn out of bowl. Let stand an additional 10 minutes; store, covered, until ready to serve.

PECAN STICKY BUNS

Power Select: MEDIUM
Approx. Cooking Time: 6 minutes
Yield: 8 buns

½ **cup brown sugar**
⅓ **cup finely chopped pecans**
1 teaspoon ground cinnamon
¼ **cup butter or margarine, melted**
1 can (8 oz.) refrigerated crescent dinner rolls

Set Power Select at MEDIUM. In small bowl, combine sugar, pecans and cinnamon. Unroll the 2 sections of dough, but do not separate. On each long rectangle, spoon 1 teaspoon butter and 1 tablespoon pecan mixture; re-roll. Cut each into quarters, forming 8 buns. Dip each bun into butter and then into pecan mixture.
In 8-inch round baking dish, arrange biscuits in ring (do not place any in center); sprinkle remaining pecan mixture over ring.
Heat 4½ to 5½ minutes; let stand, covered, 5 minutes before inverting onto platter. Cover until ready to serve.

SIESTA CORNBREAD

Power Select: MEDIUM
Approx. Cooking Time: 14 minutes
Yield: about 6 servings

1 package (12 oz.) corn muffin mix
½ **cup chopped onion**
2 tablespoons chopped pimento
2 tablespoons chopped jalapeno peppers
1 can (8¼ oz.) cream-style corn
1 egg
¼ **cup milk**

Set Power Select at MEDIUM. Combine corn muffin mix, onion, pimento and peppers; stir in corn, egg and milk. Spoon batter into greased 2 quart baking ring. Heat 12 to 14 minutes or until bread pulls away from center and sides of dish. Let stand, covered, 10 minutes. Store, covered, until ready to serve.

SOUTHERN CHEESE SPOON BREAD

Power Select: HIGH→MEDIUM
                 MEDIUM→STAND
Approx. Cooking Time: 14 minutes
Yield: about 6 servings

½ **cup yellow cornmeal**
2 cups milk
¾ **teaspoon salt**
2 eggs
1 cup shredded American cheese (about 4 oz.)
2 tablespoons butter or margarine

Set Power Select at HIGH. In medium glass bowl, combine cornmeal, milk and salt. Heat 3 minutes, stirring once.
Set Power Select at MEDIUM. Heat 3 to 4 minutes or until cornmeal is thickened, stirring once until smooth. Add eggs, cheese and butter, stirring until cheese and butter are almost melted.
Pour into greased 1-quart casserole dish and heat, covered, 6 to 7 minutes, or until set, at Power Select MEDIUM. Let STAND, covered, 10 minutes before serving.

Assorted Quick Breads, page 112 and Pecan Sticky Buns, page 114

MUFFINS

EASY MORNING MUFFINS

Power Select: MEDIUM-LOW
Approx. Cooking Time: 10 minutes
Yield: 12 muffins

½ cup milk
½ cup oil
2 eggs
½ cup sugar
2 cups flour
1 tablespoon baking powder
½ teaspoon salt

Set Power Select at MEDIUM-LOW. Combine milk, oil, eggs and sugar; add remaining ingredients, stirring only until flour is moistened.
Fill 6 custard cups (6 oz. ea.)*, lined with cupcake paper, ⅔ full; arrange in circular pattern on glass oven tray.
Heat 4 to 5 minutes; repeat procedure with remaining batter. Let stand 5 minutes. If desired, dip tops of muffins in melted butter, then in cinnamon sugar. Store, covered, until ready to serve.

Or use a microwave oven safe muffin pan.

Variations: *Add any ½ cup of the following tossed with 1 tablespoon flour:*
- *Blueberries*
- *Chopped nuts*
- *Raisins*

Muffins from Convenience Mixes, page 112

PEACHY MUFFINS

Power Select: MEDIUM-LOW
Approx. Cooking Time: 9 minutes
Yield: 9 muffins

1 can (8 oz.) sliced peaches, drained (reserve ¼ cup)
⅓ cup brown sugar
3 tablespoons butter or margarine
1 egg
1 cup flour
½ cup chopped pecans
1 teaspoon baking powder
½ teaspoon salt

Set Power Select at MEDIUM-LOW. Finely chop ¼ cup peaches; set aside. Cream together remaining peaches, sugar and butter; stir in egg and reserved syrup. Add flour, pecans, baking powder and salt, stirring only until flour is moistened; stir in chopped peaches.
Fill 6 custard cups (6 oz. ea.)* lined with cupcake paper ⅔ full; arrange in circular pattern on glass oven tray.
Heat 4½ to 5½ minutes; repeat procedure with remaining batter, filling 3 cups. Heat 2½ to 3 minutes. Let stand 5 minutes; store, covered, until ready to serve.

Or use a microwave oven safe muffin pan.

PUMPKIN PECAN MUFFINS

Power Select: MEDIUM-LOW
Approx. Cooking Time: 11 minutes
Yield: 9 muffins

⅔ cup sugar
½ cup cooked pumpkin
1 egg
½ cup chopped pecans or walnuts
½ cup raisins
¼ cup milk
3 tablespoons oil
1 to 1¼ teaspoons pumpkin pie spice
⅛ teaspoon salt
1 cup flour
1 teaspoon baking powder

Set Power Select at MEDIUM-LOW. Combine sugar, pumpkin, egg, pecans, raisins, milk, oil, pumpkin pie spice and salt; add flour and baking powder, stirring only until flour is moistened. Fill 6 custard cups (6 oz. ea.)*, lined with cupcake paper, ⅔ full; arrange in circular pattern on glass oven tray.
Heat 6 to 7 minutes; repeat procedure with remaining batter, filling 3 cups. Heat 3½ to 4 minutes. Let stand 5 minutes; store, covered, until ready to serve.

Or use microwave oven safe muffin pan.

RAISIN BRAN MUFFINS

Power Select: MEDIUM-LOW
Approx. Cooking Time: 12 minutes
Yield: 12 muffins

2½ cups bran flakes cereal
1 cup milk
1¼ cups flour
½ to ¾ cup raisins
⅓ cup sugar
1 tablespoon baking powder
½ teaspoon salt
¼ teaspoon ground cinnamon
1 egg
¼ cup oil

Set Power Select at MEDIUM-LOW. In large bowl, combine bran flakes and milk, stirring until flakes are moistened; let stand 2 to 3 minutes.
Meanwhile, combine flour, raisins, sugar, baking powder, salt and cinnamon.
Stir egg and oil into cereal mixture; add flour mixture, stirring only until flour is moistened. Fill 6 custard cups (6 oz. ea)*, lined with cupcake paper, ⅔ full; arrange in circular pattern on glass oven tray. Heat 5 to 6 minutes; repeat procedure with remaining batter. Let stand 5 minutes; store, covered, until ready to serve.

Or use microwave oven safe muffin pan.

SUGARY JAM MUFFINS

Power Select: MEDIUM-LOW
Approx. Cooking Time: 8 minutes
Yield: 6 muffins

¼ cup shortening
¼ cup sugar
1 egg
¼ cup milk
1 cup flour
¾ teaspoon baking powder
¼ teaspoon salt
2 tablespoons jam
2 tablespoons butter or margarine
2 tablespoons cinnamon sugar

Set Power Select at MEDIUM-LOW. Cream together shortening and sugar; stir in egg and milk. Add flour, baking powder and salt, stirring only until flour is moistened. Divide ½ batter into 6 custard cups (6 oz. ea.)* lined with cupcake paper; spoon 1 teaspoon jam into center of each. Top with remaining batter, spreading to cover jam. Arrange dishes in circular pattern on glass oven tray.
Heat 5 to 6 minutes; let stand, covered, 3 minutes. Meanwhile, heat butter 1½ minutes or until melted. Dip tops of muffins in butter, then in cinnamon sugar. Store, covered, until ready to serve.

Or use microwave oven safe muffin pan.

COFFEE CAKES ♕♕♕♕♕♕♕♕♕♕♕♕

BANANA NUT COFFEE CAKE

Power Select: MEDIUM →STAND
Approx. Cooking Time: 10 minutes
Yield: about 8 servings

¼ cup shortening, melted
¼ cup milk
1 egg
½ cup mashed ripe banana (about 1)
½ cup brown sugar
1 cup flour
½ cup chopped nuts
¾ teaspoon baking powder
½ teaspoon salt
¼ teaspoon baking soda
Nut Topping*

Set Power Select at MEDIUM. Combine shortening, milk, egg, banana and sugar; add flour, nuts, baking powder, salt and baking soda, stirring only until flour is moistened.
Pour into greased 8-inch round baking dish; sprinkle with Nut Topping. Heat 9 to 10 minutes; let STAND, covered, 10 minutes. Store, covered, until ready to serve.

*Nut Topping: Combine ¼ cup brown sugar, ¼ cup chopped nuts, 2 tablespoons flour and ⅛ teaspoon ground cinnamon; blend in 1 tablespoon softened butter or margarine.

GRAHAM STREUSEL COFFEE CAKE

Power Select: HIGH
                    MEDIUM→STAND
Approx. Cooking Time: 18 minutes
Yield: about 10 servings

½ cup butter or margarine
1 cup graham cracker crumbs
½ cup brown sugar
⅓ cup chopped nuts
¾ teaspoon ground cinnamon
1 package (18½ oz.) yellow cake mix
3 eggs
1 cup water
¼ cup oil
Vanilla Glaze*

Set Power Select at HIGH. In small glass bowl, heat butter ¾ minute or until melted; stir in crumbs, sugar, nuts and cinnamon. Spread ½ cup crumb mixture into each of two 8-inch round baking dishes, bottoms lined with wax paper.
With electric mixer, blend cake mix, eggs, water and oil at low speed ½ minute; beat at medium speed 3 minutes. Pour 1½ cups batter into each dish; sprinkle with remaining crumb mixture. Pour in an additional ½ cup batter into each dish. Place one cake in refrigerator.
Set Power Select at MEDIUM. Heat cake 7½ to 8½ minutes; repeat procedure with refrigerated cake. Let STAND, covered, 10 minutes. With knife, loosen cake from sides of dish. Invert one cake onto serving platter; carefully peel off wax paper. Invert second layer onto paper plate;

carefully peel off wax paper. Cover until cool; just before serving, spread ½ Glaze on cake on serving platter; top with second layer. Drizzle with remaining glaze.

Vanilla Glaze: Combine 2 cups confectioners' sugar, 2 to 3 tablespoons water and 1 teaspoon vanilla extract.

HOLIDAY CRANBERRY COFFEE CAKE

Power Select: MEDIUM→STAND
Approx. Cooking Time: 11 minutes
Yield: about 8 servings

1 can (8 oz.) whole berry cranberry sauce
6 tablespoons sugar
¼ cup chopped nuts (optional)
1 tablespoon butter or margarine, melted
2 cups buttermilk biscuit mix
1 cup orange juice or apple juice
1 egg

Set Power Select at MEDIUM. Combine cranberry sauce, 4 tablespoons sugar, nuts and butter; spread into 8-inch round baking dish, bottom lined with wax paper.

Combine biscuit mix, juice, egg and remaining sugar, blending until smooth, about ½ minute. Pour batter over cranberry mixture; heat 10 to 11 minutes. Let STAND, covered, 10 minutes before inverting onto platter; carefully peel off wax paper. Store, covered, until ready to serve. If desired, drizzle with Glaze* just before serving.

Glaze: Combine 1 cup confectioners' sugar, 1 to 2 tablespoons water and ½ teaspoon vanilla extract.

MARMALADE GINGERBREAD

Power Select: MEDIUM→STAND
Approx. Cooking Time: 9 minutes
Yield: about 8 servings

1 package (14 oz.) gingerbread mix
¾ cup orange juice
½ cup orange marmalade

Set Power Select at MEDIUM. Combine gingerbread mix, orange juice and marmalade; blend according to package directions.
Pour into greased 8-inch round baking dish; heat 7½ to 8½ minutes. Let STAND, covered, 10 minutes. Store, covered, until ready to serve.

PROOFING (RAISING) FROZEN BREAD DOUGH

- At Power Select HIGH, in 4-cup glass measure, heat 3 cups hot water 5 to 6 minutes or until boiling.
- In well greased 8"×4"×2½" loaf dish, place 1 loaf (16 oz.) frozen bread dough; cover with wax paper.
- Arrange loaf dish in oven with hot water.
- At Power Select WARM, heat 20 minutes; let STAND, covered, (in oven) 10 minutes. Repeat procedure.
- Turn dough over and repeat procedure twice or until dough has doubled in size.
- Bake conventionally according to package directions.

Note: *Bread can be proofed in 9"×5"×3" loaf dish, but will not raise as high.*

PROOFING (RAISING) YEAST BREAD

Take your favorite yeast bread recipe and follow these basic directions for proofing dough.
- Prepare dough according to recipe directions. Do not select a recipe that yields more than two (9"× 5"×3") loaves.
- Fill a 4-cup glass measure with 3 cups water. Heat at Power Select HIGH 5 to 6 minutes or until water is boiling.
- Set Power Select at WARM. Place glass measure in corner of oven; place dough in medium glass bowl, covered with wax paper.
- Heat 20 minutes. Remove dough from oven; let stand, covered with wax paper, 20 minutes.
- Reshape dough as recipe directs; repeat proofing procedure, if required (per recipe).
- Bake conventionally according to recipe directions.

Sweets, everyone's weakness, are even more tempting when prepared with the speedy assistance of your microwave oven. You do not have to wait for a special occasion to make something special. Bake apples in 10 minutes while you eat dinner and treat yourself to something your Mom always made for you. We have selected recipes in this chapter to meet your every whim. Cakes from scratch or convenient mixes, candies, pies, bar cookies...the choice is deliciously yours.

HINTS FOR SUCCESSFUL CAKES AND CUPCAKES

Cake batters for layer cakes are best when baked in single layers, one at a time. The entire mix can be prepared in a greased large glass bowl, with an inverted glass in the center to form a tube shape, or in a 10 or 12-cup glass Bundt dish (be sure to also grease the glass "tube"). A microwave oven safe baking ring (6 cup) can be used to bake small "tube" cakes with 2 cups batter or single layer cake mixes. When baking cupcakes, use custard cups lined with cupcake paper or set cupcake paper in microwave oven safe muffin pan; fill paper only ½ full. Arrange cups on glass oven tray in circular pattern if not using a muffin pan. Follow these easy steps.

- Prepare batter according to package or recipe directions.
- Use glass baking dish, baking ring or cupcake paper lined container as indicated in charts or recipes.
- Use a large glass bowl with an inverted glass in the center or microwave safe Bundt dish when baking all the batter at one time.

- Grease and line bottom of baking dishes with wax paper if the cake will be inverted (layer cake, up-side down cake, etc.) DO NOT GREASE AND FLOUR DISHES.
- Grease the baking dish or ring or any container used for serve-from-dish cakes (brownies, etc.).
- Use 2 cups batter in each layer or in the 6-cup baking ring. Do not fill any container more than ½ full.
- Bake cupcakes with any remaining batter.
- Bake layers one at a time. IMPORTANT: Refrigerate any remaining batter until ready to heat.
- Test cake doneness with toothpick inserted near the center—it should come out clean. Cake should also pull away from sides of dish.
- Let stand on flat surface, covered, 10 minutes.
- Turn out of dish and carefully peel off waxed paper.
- Frost, if desired, when completely cooled.
- Store, covered, until ready to serve.

PREPARING CAKE MIXES

ITEM	CONTAINER	APPROXIMATE HEATING TIME at Power Select MEDIUM (in minutes)	STANDING TIME (in minutes)
Basic Cake (17 to 18½ oz.)	8 or 9-inch round or square cake dish (2 cups batter) or "tube" dish or 10 or 12-cup Bundt dish (all batter)	4 to 6 →	5
		12 to 14 →	10
Brownies (15 oz.) (cake-like or fudge-like)	9-inch round or square cake dish	8 to 10 →	10
Bundt-type cake (17 to 18½ oz.)	"tube" dish or 10 or 12-cup Bundt dish	12½ to 14½ →	10
Cake Mix with pudding mix included (18¾ to 20¼ oz.)	8 or 9-in. round cake dish (2 C batter)	6 to 7½ →	5
	"tube" dish or 10 or 12-cup Bundt dish (all batter)	13½ to 15 →	10
Cupcakes	Cupcake paper in individual custard cups or muffin pan		
	1	¾ to 1½	
	2	1 to 2	5
	4	2½ to 3½ →	
	6	3 to 4	
Mix-in-Dish Cake (15 oz.)	8 or 9-in. round or square cake dish	8½ to 10½ →	10

Pictured on the preceding page: Spice Cake (from mix), Chocolate Fudge, Peanut Brittle, Almond Butter Crunch, Coconut Lemon Meringue Pie, Baked Apples.

CAKES AND FROSTINGS ❦❦❦❦❦❦❦❦

APPLE SPICE TARTS

Power Select: MEDIUM→STAND
Approx. Cooking Time: 11 minutes per batch
Yield: 12 tarts

1 can (21 oz.) apple pie filling
¼ cup raisins (optional)
1 package (18 oz.) spice cake mix
2 eggs
1⅓ cups water
Sweetened whipped cream or whipped topping

Set Power Select at MEDIUM. In each of 4 greased custard cups (10 oz. ea.), spoon 1½ tablespoons pie filling and 1 teaspoon raisins.
Prepare cake mix according to package directions using eggs and water; spoon ½ cup batter in to each cup. Arrange on glass oven tray in circular pattern.
Heat 9½ to 10½ minutes or until tarts are done.
Let STAND, covered, 10 minutes. Repeat procedure twice with remaining ingredients. (Refrigerate batter between heating times). To serve, loosen edge of each tart and invert onto serving plate; garnish with whipped cream.

Variations:

For APPLE SPICE RING, *spoon ½ cup pie filling and ¼ cup raisins into greased 6-cup glass Bundt dish; use 2 cups cake batter. Heat 5½ to 6½ minutes.*

For APPLE SPICE CAKE, *spoon 1 cup pie filling and ⅓ cup raisins into greased 10 or 12-cup glass Bundt dish; use all the batter. Heat 13½ to 15 minutes turning dish once.*

BASIC BUTTER CAKE

Power Select: MEDIUM→STAND
Approx. Cooking Time: 9 minutes
Yield: 1 layer

⅔ cup sugar
¼ cup butter or margarine, softened
1 egg
⅔ cup milk
1 teaspoon vanilla extract
1 cup flour
1½ teaspoon baking powder
¼ teaspoon salt

Set Power Select at MEDIUM. Cream together sugar and butter; add egg, milk and vanilla. Add remaining ingredients, stirring until smooth. Pour batter into greased 8 or 9-inch round baking dish*. Heat 7 to 8½ minutes; let STAND, covered, 10 minutes. Store, covered, until cool.

*Hint: *If inverting cake before frosting, line bottom of dish with wax paper. Turn out of dish before storing, covered. Cool completely before frosting.*

CARAMEL CREAM FROSTING

Power Select: HIGH
Approx. Cooking Time: 2 minutes
Yield: to frost single layer

8 caramels
1½ to 2 tablespoons water
1 package (3 oz.) cream cheese, softened
2 cups confectioners' sugar

Set Power Select at HIGH. In medium glass bowl, heat caramel and 1 tablespoon water 1½ to 2 minutes; stir until smooth. With electric mixer, blend in cream cheese, then sugar; add ½ to 1 tablespoon water to reach desired consistency.

CARROT SPICE CAKE

Power Select: MEDIUM→STAND
Approx. Cooking Time: 12 minutes
Yield: about 8 servings

1¼ cups flour
1 cup brown sugar
1 teaspoon baking powder
1 teaspoon baking soda
1 teaspoon ground cinnamon
½ teaspoon ground allspice
½ teaspoon salt
1 cup shredded carrot
⅔ cup oil
2 eggs
½ cup crushed pineapple with syrup
1 teaspoon vanilla extract

Set Power Select at MEDIUM. Combine flour, sugar, baking powder, baking soda, cinnamon, allspice, salt and carrot; with electric mixer, blend in remaining ingredients and beat 2 minutes at medium speed. Pour batter into greased 6-cup glass Bundt dish or baking ring. Heat 10 to 11½ minutes; let STAND, covered, 10 minutes. Store, covered, until ready to serve.

CHOCOLATE POUND CAKE

Power Select: MEDIUM→STAND
Approx. Cooking Time: 15 minutes
Yield: about 12 servings

1 package (18½ oz.) chocolate cake mix*
1 package (4½ oz.) instant chocolate pudding mix*
4 eggs
1 cup water
¼ cup oil

Set Power Select at MEDIUM. In large bowl, combine all ingredients; with electric mixer, beat at medium speed 4 minutes. In greased 10 or 12-cup Bundt dish, pour batter; heat 13 to 15 minutes. Let STAND, covered, 15 minutes before inverting onto serving platter; let stand, covered, until cool.

*Variation: *Use yellow cake mix and instant lemon pudding mix for chocolate cake and pudding mixes.*

SWEETS AND TREATS

CIDER SPICE CAKE

Power Select: MEDIUM→STAND
Approx. Cooking Time: 15 minutes
Yield: about 12 servings

2¼ cups flour
2 teaspoons ground cinnamon
1 teaspoon ground cloves
1 teaspoon ground nutmeg
1 teaspoon salt
¾ teaspoon baking soda
1½ cups sugar
½ cup butter or margarine, softened
1 egg
1¼ cups apple cider or juice
1 cup raisins
2 tablespoons flour
Confectioners' sugar

Set Power Select at MEDIUM. Combine 2¼ cups flour, cinnamon, cloves, nutmeg, salt and baking soda. With electric mixer, cream sugar and butter; add egg. Alternately add flour mixture and cider, mixing until smooth; fold in raisins tossed with 2 tablespoons flour. In greased 10 or 12-cup glass Bundt dish, pour batter; heat 13½ to 15 minutes.
Let STAND, covered, 10 minutes, before inverting onto serving platter. Let stand, covered, until cool. Just before serving, sprinkle with confectioners sugar.

COCONUT NUT TOPPING FOR CAKE

Power Select: HIGH
Approx. Cooking Time: 6 minutes
Yield: about 2¼ cups

1 cup evaporated milk
1 cup sugar
½ cup butter or margarine
¼ cup flour
1⅓ cups flaked coconut
1 cup chopped nuts
1 teaspoon vanilla extract

Set Power Select at HIGH. In medium glass bowl, combine milk, sugar, butter and flour; heat 4½ to 5½ minutes or until mixture is thickened, stirring twice. Add remaining ingredients; cool until spreadable, stirring occasionally.

CREAMY CHEESECAKE

Power Select: MEDIUM
Approx. Cooking Time: 10 minutes
Yield: about 8 servings

1 package (8 oz.) cream cheese, softened
½ cup sugar
1 egg
1 teaspoon vanilla extract
1 cup sour cream
9-inch graham cracker crumb crust, baked
** (see page 131)**

Set Power Select at MEDIUM. Combine cream cheese, sugar, egg and vanilla until smooth; stir in sour cream. Pour mixture into prepared crust; heat 8 to 10 minutes or until center is almost set. Chill at least 3 hours or overnight.

Variations:
For CHOCOLATE Cheesecake, *add 1 packet (1 oz.) pre-melted unsweetened chocolate to cream cheese mixture; increase sugar to ⅔ cup.*
For FRUIT-TOPPED Cheesecake, *top chilled pie with canned fruit pie filling.*
For PRALINE Cheesecake, *brush top of chilled pie with maple syrup; garnish with chopped pecans.*
For PINWHEEL Cheesecake, *heat ½ cup raspberry jam ½ minute (at Power Select HIGH); swirl into pie before heating.*

DEVIL'S FOOD CAKE

Power Select: MEDIUM→STAND
Approx. Cooking Time: 9 minutes
Yield: 1 layer

¾ cup sugar
¼ cup butter or margarine, softened
1 egg
⅔ cup hot water
1 cup flour
¼ cup unsweetened cocoa
¾ teaspoon baking soda
½ teaspoon salt
½ teaspoon vanilla extract

Set Power Select at MEDIUM. With electric mixer, cream sugar and butter; add egg and water. Stir in remaining ingredients and blend until smooth. Into greased round 8 or 9-inch baking dish*, pour batter. Heat 7½ to 9 minutes; let STAND, covered, 10 minutes. Store, covered, until ready to serve.

***Hint:** If inverting cake before frosting, line bottom of dish with wax paper. Turn out of dish before storing, covered. Cool completely before frosting.*

FESTIVE RUM CAKE

Power Select: MEDIUM→STAND
Approx. Cooking Time: 18 minutes
Yield: about 12 servings

1 cup finely chopped pecans or walnuts
1 package (18½ oz.) yellow cake mix
1 package (3¾ oz.) instant vanilla pudding mix
4 eggs
½ cup water
½ cup oil
½ cup dark rum
Rum Glaze*

Set Power Select at MEDIUM. In generously greased 10 to 12-cup glass Bundt dish, sprinkle nuts. With electric mixer, combine cake mix, pudding mix, eggs, water, oil and rum; beat at medium speed 4 minutes. Pour batter evenly over nuts.
Heat 12½ to 14 minutes, turning dish once; let STAND, covered, 10 minutes. Prick top of cake; drizzle ½ Rum Glaze over cake (to absorb). Invert cake onto serving platter and prick top and sides of cake; drizzle cake with remaining glaze. Stored, covered, until reaby to serve.

*Rum Glaze
½ **cup butter or margarine**
1 **cup sugar**
¼ **cup water**
¼ **to ⅓ cup dark rum**

Set Power Select at HIGH. In 2-cup glass measure, heat butter ¾ to 1 minute or until melted. Stir in sugar and water and heat 2 to 2½ minutes or until boiling; stir in rum.

GERMAN CHOCOLATE UPSIDE-DOWN CAKE

Power Select: HIGH
          MEDIUM→STAND
Approx. Cooking Time: 9 minutes
Yield: about 8 servings

½ **cup brown sugar**
⅓ **cup butter or margarine**
Pecan halves
½ **cup flaked coconut**
2 **tablespoons milk**
Single layer chocolate cake mix*
Ingredients as cake package directs

Set Power Select at HIGH. In small glass bowl, heat sugar and butter ½ minute or until butter is melted; stir until smooth.
Into 8 or 9-inch round baking dish, bottom lined with wax paper, spread butter mixture; arrange pecans on top. Sprinkle with coconut and drizzle with milk. Prepare cake mix according to package directions; pour over coconut. Heat 6½ to 8 minutes at MEDIUM; let STAND, covered, 10 minutes. Invert onto serving platter; carefully peel off wax paper. Store, covered, until cool.

***Note**: *For HOMEMADE German Chocolate Cake, use Devil's Food Cake recipe (page 122); heat 9 to 10 minutes.*

Pineapple Upside-Down Cake, page 123

PINEAPPLE UPSIDE-DOWN CAKE

Power Select: HIGH
          MEDIUM→STAND
Approx. Cooking Time: 26 minutes
Yield: 2 (9-inch) layers

½ **cup butter or margarine**
1 **cup brown sugar**
1 **can (20 oz.) sliced pineapple, drained**
   (reserved syrup)
Maraschino cherries (optional)
1 **package (18 oz.) yellow cake mix**
Ingredients as cake package directs

Set Power Select at HIGH. In small glass bowl, heat butter 1 to 1½ minutes or until melted; stir in sugar. Into bottom of 2 (8 or 9-inch) round baking dishes, bottoms lined with wax paper, spread sugar-butter mixture; arrange pineapple and cherries.
Prepare cake mix according to package directions, using reserved syrup as part of water. Pour 2 cups batter into each dish. Place one dish in refrigerator. Set Power Select at MEDIUM. Heat other cake 10 to 12 minutes; repeat procedure with remaining cake. Let STAND, covered, 10 minutes. With knife, loosen cake from sides of dish; invert onto serving platter. Carefully peel off wax paper; store, covered, until ready to serve.

PLANTATION COCONUT CAKE

Power Select: MEDIUM→STAND
Approx. Cooking Time: 14 minutes
Yield: about 8 servings

1 **package (18½ oz.) yellow cake mix**
1 **package (3¾ oz.) instant coconut cream or toasted**
   coconut pudding mix
4 **eggs**
1 **cup water**
¼ **cup oil**
1 **jar (12 oz.) strawberry or raspberry preserves**
Creamy Glaze*
Flaked coconut

Set Power Select at MEDIUM. With electric mixer, combine cake mix, pudding mix, eggs, water and oil; beat at medium speed 4 minutes. In greased 10 to 12-cup glass Bundt dish, pour batter; heat 12½ to 14 minutes. Let stand, covered, 15 minutes before inverting onto serving platter. Let STAND, covered, until cool.
Split cake into three layers; spread preserves between each layer. Drizzle with Creamy Glaze and top with coconut. Store, covered, until ready to serve.

***Creamy Glaze:** *Blend until smooth 1½ cups confectioners' sugar, 2 to 2½ tablespoons milk and 2 tablespoons butter or margarine, softened. If desired, add 2 drops of red food coloring.*

STEAMED DATE-NUT PUDDING

Power Select: MEDIUM→STAND
Approx. Cooking Time: 10 minutes
Yield: about 8 servings

1¼ cups flour
½ cup each chopped walnuts, dates and raisins
1 teaspoon ground cinnamon
½ teaspoon baking soda
½ teaspoon salt
¾ cup hot water
½ cup molasses
1 egg
2 tablespoons butter or margarine, melted

Set Power Select at MEDIUM. Combine flour, walnuts, dates, raisins, cinnamon, baking soda and salt; stir in water, molasses, egg and butter. Turn batter into greased 6-cup glass Bundt dish or 2-quart glass bowl with inverted glass in center. Cover with plastic wrap; secure wrap with rubberband. Heat 8 to 10 minutes or until pudding is done. Let STAND, covered, 10 minutes. Invert onto serving platter; cover until cool.
Serve, if desired with Vanilla Sauce (page 30) flavored with whiskey or brandy.

SUPER CHOCOLATE FROSTING

Power Select: MEDIUM-LOW
Approx. Cooking Time: 8 minutes
Yield: about 1½ cups

2 squares (1 oz. ea.) unsweetened chocolate
1 can (14 oz.) sweetened condensed milk
1 tablespoon water
½ teaspoon salt
½ teaspoon vanilla extract

Set Power Select at MEDIUM-LOW. In medium glass bowl, heat chocolate 2 to 3 minutes or until melted; stir in milk, water and salt. Heat 3½ to 4½ minutes, stirring twice; stir in vanilla.
Place bowl in larger bowl filled with ice(or in sink with cold water). Beat until frosting is smooth and shiny; cool before frosting cake.

CANDIES

ALMOND BUTTER CRUNCH

Power Select: HIGH
Approx. Cooking Time: 11 minutes
Yield: about 1¼ pounds

½ cup butter or margarine
1½ cups sugar
3 tablespoons water
1 tablespoon light corn syrup
4 milk chocolate candy bars (1¼ oz. ea.)
½ cup finely chopped almonds

Set Power Select at HIGH. In 3-quart pyroceramic casserole dish, heat butter 1½ to 2 minutes or until melted; stir in sugar, water and corn syrup. Heat 8 to 9 minutes or until mixture reads 290°F (soft crack stage) when tested with candy thermometer*.
Pour onto well greased wax paper; let stand ½ minute. Arrange chocolate on candy; as chocolate melts, spread evenly over candy. Top with nuts, pressing nuts into chocolate. Chill until chocolate is set; break into small pieces.

***Important:** *Do not use candy thermometer in dish while operating the microwave oven.*

BUTTERSCOTCH FUDGE

Power Select: HIGH
Approx. Cooking Time: 11 minutes
Yield: about 3 pounds

3 cups sugar
¾ cup butter or margarine
1 can (5⅓ oz.) evaporated milk
1 package (12 oz.) butterscotch flavored pieces*
1 jar (7½ oz.) marshmallow creme
1 cup chopped walnuts
1 teaspoon vanilla extract

Set Power Select at HIGH. In 2½-quart casserole dish, combine sugar, butter and milk; heat 9 to 10½ minutes or until sugar is dissolved, stirring twice. Add remaining ingredients and stir until butterscotch is melted. Turn into well greased oblong baking dish. Cool; cut into squares to serve.

***Variation:**
For CHOCOLATE Fudge, *use 1 package (12 oz.) semi-sweet chocolate pieces.*

FAST FIXIN' CHOCOLATE FUDGE

Power Select: HIGH
Approx. Cooking Time: 6 minutes
Yield: about 3 pounds

2 packages (16 oz. ea.) confectioners' sugar
1 cup unsweetened cocoa
½ cup milk
1 cup butter or margarine
1½ cup chopped nuts (optional)
2 tablespoons vanilla extract

Set Power Select at HIGH. In large bowl, mix sugar and cocoa. Add milk and butter (do not stir). Heat 4½ to 6 minutes or until butter is melted; add nuts and vanilla, stirring until smooth. Spread into well greased square baking dish; chill until firm. Cut into squares to serve.

Note: For 1½ pounds Fudge, *follow above procedure. Halve all ingredients, heat 2 to 3 minutes; pour into greased loaf dish.*
Variation:
For ROCKY ROAD Fudge, *coarsely chop nuts and add 1 cup miniature marshmallows.*

PEANUT BRITTLE

Power Select: HIGH
Approx. Cooking Time: about 16 minutes
Yield: about 1½ pounds

½ cup water
2 tablespoons butter or margarine
1½ cups sugar
2 tablespoons molasses
1 jar (8¼ oz.) dry roasted peanuts (about 1½ cups), coarsley chopped
1 teaspoon baking soda

Set Power Select at HIGH. In 3-quart pyroceramic casserole dish, heat water and butter 1½ to 2 minutes or until boiling; stir in sugar and molasses. Heat 13 to 14 minutes or until mixture reads 300°F when tested with candy thermometer*.
Quickly stir in peanuts and baking soda, stirring until soda foams. Pour onto well greased cookie sheet; spread thin. Let stand until candy is hardened; break into small pieces.

*Important: *Do not use candy thermometer in dish while operating the microwave oven.*

PECAN PRALINES

Power Select: HIGH
Approx. Cooking Time: 9 minutes
Yield: about 1½ dozen

1 cup brown sugar
1 cup sugar
⅓ cup light corn syrup
¼ cup water
1½ cups coarsely chopped pecans
1 tablespoon butter or margarine
1 teaspoon vanilla extract

Set Power Select at HIGH. In medium glass bowl, combine sugars, corn syrup and water; heat 7 to 9 minutes or until mixture reads 238°F (soft ball stage) when tested with candy thermometer*. Stir in pecans, butter and vanilla. Let stand 2 minutes. Drop by tablespoonfuls onto well greased wax paper lined cookie sheet; chill until set.

*Important: *Do not use candy thermometer in dish while operating the microwave oven.*

RAISIN CLUSTERS

Power Select: MEDIUM-LOW
Approx. Cooking Time: 4 minutes
Yield: about 2 dozen

8 squares (1 oz. ea.) semi-sweet chocolate
⅔ cup sweetened condensed milk
1 cup raisins*

Set Power Select at MEDIUM-LOW. In medium glass bowl, heat chocolate 3 to 4 minutes or until chocolate is melted; stir in milk until smooth, then raisins. Drop by teaspoonful onto greased wax paper lined cookie sheet; chill.

*Variations:
For ELEPHANT Clusters, *use 1 cup unsalted peanuts for raisins.*
For CHINESE Clusters, *use 1 cup crisp chow mein noodles for raisins.*

SWEET SPICED NUTS

Power Select: HIGH
　　　　　　　HIGH→STAND
Approx. Cooking Time: 6 minutes
Yield: about 1½ cups

½ cup brown sugar
1½ tablespoons water
½ teaspoon salt
½ teaspoon ground cinnamon
¼ teaspoon ground allspice
⅛ teaspoon ground cloves
⅛ teaspoon ground nutmeg
1½ cups almond, cashew, pecan or walnut halves or combination

Set Power Select at HIGH. In 2-quart casserole dish, combine sugar, water, salt, cinnamon, allspice, cloves and nutmeg. Heat 1 to 1½ minutes or until sugar is melted; stir in nuts. Place nuts in wax paper lined oblong baking dish. Heat 3½ to 4½ minutes at HIGH or until syrup begins to harden; let STAND to completely harden. Break into small pieces and store in airtight container.

TOFFEE FONDUE

Power Select: MEDIUM
Approx. Cooking Time: 6 minutes
Yield: about 6 servings

1 package (14 oz.) caramels
¼ cup strong coffee
2 to 4 tablespoons milk
½ cup milk chocolate pieces (optional)
Dippers*

Set Power Select at MEDIUM. In medium glass bowl, combine caramels, coffee, milk and chocolate. Heat 5 to 6 minutes, stirring twice until smooth. Serve with assorted Dippers. If Fondue gets cool, reheat 1 to 2 minutes.

*Dippers: *Apple and pear slices, banana chunks, large marshmallows, angel food or yellow cake, cut into 1½-inch cubes.*

COOKIES ꜟꜟꜟꜟꜟꜟꜟꜟꜟꜟꜟꜟꜟꜟꜟ

APPLE FUDGE BROWNIES 🔲

Power Select: HIGH
                      MEDIUM→STAND
Approx. Cooking Time: 14 minutes
Yield: about 16 brownies

½ cup butter or margarine
2 squares (1 oz. ea.) unsweetened chocolate
1 cup brown sugar
½ cup applesauce
2 eggs
1 teaspoon vanilla extract
1 cup flour
½ teaspoon baking powder
¼ teaspoon baking soda
1 cup chopped apple (1 small) or chopped walnuts

Set Power Select at HIGH. In large glass bowl, heat butter and chocolate 1 to 2 minutes or until melted. Stir in sugar, applesauce, eggs and vanilla. Gradually add flour, baking powder and soda; stir in apple. Pour into greased 8-inch round baking dish.
Set Power Select at MEDIUM. Heat 10 to 12 minutes. Let STAND, covered, 5 minutes; cool uncovered, 10 minutes. Store, covered, until ready to serve.

CRISPY MARSHMALLOW TREATS

Power Select: HIGH
Approx. Cooking Time: 4 minutes
Yield: about 2½ dozen

1 package (10 oz.) marshmallows
¼ cup butter or margarine
5 cups toasted rice cereal

Set Power Select at HIGH. In large glass bowl, heat marshmallows and butter 3 to 4 minutes, stirring twice until smooth. Add cereal and stir to coat well. Press into greased oblong baking dish. Cool; cut into squares to serve.

Variation: *Stir in 1 cup salted peanuts or raisins with cereal.*

DOUBLE BUTTERSCOTCH BROWNIES 🔲

Power Select: HIGH
                      MEDIUM→STAND
Approx. Cooking Time: 14 minutes
Yield: about 16 brownies

¼ cup butter or margarine
1 cup brown sugar
1 egg
¾ cup flour
1 teaspoon baking powder
1 teaspoon vanilla extract
¾ cup chopped nuts
1 package (6 oz.) butterscotch flavored pieces

Set Power Select at HIGH. In medium glass bowl, heat butter 1 to 1½ minutes or until melted; stir in sugar, egg, flour, baking powder, vanilla and nuts. Pour batter into greased 8 or 9-inch round baking dish.

Set Power Select at MEDIUM. Heat 7 to 8½ minutes; let STAND, covered, 10 minutes.
Meanwhile, in small glass bowl, heat butterscotch 3 to 4 minutes or until melted; stir until smooth. Spread over brownies; cut into squares to serve. Store, covered.

MARBLE BROWNIES

Power Select: MEDIUM-LOW
                      MEDIUM
Approx. Cooking Time: 20 minutes
Yield: about 40 brownies

1 package (22½ to 23¾ oz.) fudge brownie mix
Ingredients as brownie package directs for fudge-type brownies
2 packages (3 oz. ea.) cream cheese
2 tablespoons butter or margarine
1 egg
¼ cup sugar
1 tablespoon flour
½ teaspoon vanilla extract

Set Power Select at MEDIUM-LOW. Prepare fudge-type brownies according to package directions. Spread 1 cup batter into each of 2 greased (8 or 9-inch) round baking dishes.
In small glass bowl, heat cream cheese and butter 1½ to 2 minutes or until softened; blend in remaining ingredients. Evenly divide cheese mixture into baking dishes; spoon remaining brownie batter on top. With knife, swirl gently to marble. Place one dish in refrigerator.
Set Power Select at MEDIUM. Heat other dish 7 to 8½ minutes; repeat procedure with remaining dish. Let stand, covered, until cool. Store covered, until ready to serve.

NUTTY CHIP CHEWS

Power Select: MEDIUM
Approx. Cooking Time: 9 minutes
Yield: about 8 bars

¾ cup brown sugar
½ cup butter or margarine, softened
1 egg
¼ cup milk
1 teaspoon vanilla extract
½ teaspoon baking powder
1¼ cups flour
½ cup chopped nuts
1 cup semi-sweet chocolate pieces

Set Power Select at MEDIUM. With electric mixer, cream sugar and butter; add egg, milk and vanilla. Stir in baking powder and flour until well blended; add nuts and ½ chocolate pieces.
Into greased 8-inch round baking dish, spread batter; top with remaining chocolate. Heat 7 to 8½ minutes or until center is almost set. Let stand, covered, until cool. Store, covered, until ready to serve.

QUICK BAR COOKIES (FROM MIX)

Power Select: MEDIUM
Approx. Cooking Time: 7 minutes
Yield: about 16 bars

1 package (12 oz.) chocolate chip cookie mix
Ingredients as package directs

Set Power Select at MEDIUM. Prepare mix according to package directions. Spread dough into ungreased 8 or 9-inch round baking dish. Heat 5½ to 6½ minutes. Let stand, covered, until cool. Store, covered, until ready to serve.

SIX LAYER BARS

Power Select: MEDIUM
Approx. Cooking Time: 12 minutes
Yield: 32 bars

½ cup butter or margarine, melted
1½ cups graham cracker crumbs
1 can (14 oz.) sweetened condensed milk
1 package (6 oz.) semi-sweet chocolate pieces (about 1 cup)
1 can (3½ oz.) flaked coconut (about 1 cup)
1 cup finely chopped nuts

Set Power Select at MEDIUM. In each of 2 (8-inch) square baking dishes, pour ¼ cup butter. Sprinkle with ¾ cup crumbs; pour ½ of condensed milk evenly over crumbs. Top with ½ of chocolate, coconut and nuts; press down slightly.
Heat, one dish at a time, 5 to 6 minutes. Let stand, covered, 5 minutes; chill. Cut into squares to serve.

S'MORES

Power Select: HIGH
Approx. Cooking Time: 1 minute
Yield: 4 cookies

8 graham cracker squares
2 milk chocolate candy bars (1¼ oz. ea.), halved
4 marshmallows

Set Power Select at HIGH. For each cookie, arrange 1 graham cracker in center of paper napkin or paper towel; top with chocolate and marshmallow. Cover with graham cracker and wrap in napkin. Arrange on glass oven tray and heat ¾ to 1 minute; let stand 2 minutes before unwrapping.

CUSTARDS AND PUDDINGS ❧❧❧❧❧❧

HEATING PUDDING AND PIE FILLING MIXES

- Combine ingredients according to package directions.
- Use a glass container twice the volume of the mix.
- Stir twice during heating time.
- Chill before serving (stirring rice and tapioca pudding occasionally).

ITEM	APPROXIMATE HEATING TIME at Power Select MEDIUM (in minutes)
Regular Pudding and Pie Filling 4 servings (3¼ to 3¾ oz.) 6 servings (4¾ to 5½ oz.)	 7½ to 9 11½ to 13
Egg Custard* (3 oz.)	7 to 8½
Rice Pudding* (3¾ oz.)	7½ to 9
Tapioca Pudding* (3½ oz.)	7 to 8½

Mixture will thicken as it chills.

BASIC EGG CUSTARD

Power Select: MEDIUM
⠀⠀⠀⠀⠀⠀⠀⠀⠀MEDIUM-LOW
Approx. Cooking Time: 14 minutes
Yield: 6 servings

2 cups milk
4 eggs, beaten
¼ to ⅓ cup sugar
½ teaspoon vanilla extract
Ground nutmeg

Set Power Select at MEDIUM. In 1-quart glass measure, heat milk 4 to 5 minutes or until scalded; quickly stir in eggs, sugar and vanilla. Pour into 6 greased custard cups (6 oz. ea.); sprinkle with nutmeg. On glass oven tray, arrange dishes in circular pattern.
Set Power Select at MEDIUM-LOW. Heat 7½ to 9 minutes or until custard is set. Let stand until cool.

Variation:
For CARAMEL CUSTARD, *in small glass bowl, heat ½ cup sugar and 3 tablespoons water at Power Select HIGH 4 to 5 minutes or until sugar is melted and light brown. Pour into greased custard cups, tilting cups to coat bottom. Proceed as directed above.*

Arrange food
in circular pattern

CHILLED CHOCOLATE ALMOND SOUFFLE

Power Select: MEDIUM-LOW
Approx. Cooking Time: 6 minutes
Yield: about 8 servings

1 envelope unflavored gelatin
¾ cup sugar
3 eggs, separated
1 cup milk
2 squares (1 oz. ea.) unsweetened chocolate, melted*
¼ teaspoon almond extract
1 cup whipping cream, whipped

Set Power Select at MEDIUM-LOW. In large glass bowl, mix gelatin and ½ cup sugar; stir in egg yolks beaten with milk. Heat 5 to 6 minutes or until gelatin is dissolved, stirring occasionally. With wire whip, stir in chocolate and almond extract; chill until mixture mounds slightly, stirring occasionally. Meanwhile, beat egg whites until soft peaks form; gradually add remaining sugar and beat until stiff. Fold in chocolate-almond mixture; fold in whipped cream.
Turn into small souffle dish with 2-inch collar or 6-cup bowl and chill until firm. Garnish, if desired, with slivered almonds and additional whipped cream.

*Hint: *To melt chocolate in your microwave oven, see Quick Tips, (page 140).*

QUICK RICE PUDDING

Power Select: MEDIUM
Approx. Cooking Time: 13 minutes
Yield: about 6 servings

3 cups milk
½ cup packaged precooked rice
1 package (3 oz.) vanilla pudding and pie filling mix
3 tablespoons raisins*
¼ teaspoon ground cinnamon or nutmeg*

Set Power Select at MEDIUM. In 2-quart glass measure or bowl, combine all ingredients; heat, covered with wax paper, 11 to 13 minutes or until pudding is thickened, stirring three times. Chill before serving.

*Variations *Use 1 tablespoon orange liqueur and ¼ cup chopped candied fruit for raisins and cinnamon.*

RAISIN BREAD PUDDING

Power Select: MEDIUM
Approx. Cooking Time: 25 minutes
Yield: about 6 servings

2 cups milk
¼ cup butter or margarine
5 eggs, beaten
1 cup sugar
1 teaspoon vanilla extract
4 cups cubed raisin bread (about 16 slices)
⅛ teaspoon ground cinnamon

Set Power Select at MEDIUM. In 1-quart glass measure, heat milk and butter 4½ to 5½ minutes or until milk is scalded; quickly stir in eggs, ½ cup sugar and vanilla.

Meanwhile, in 3-quart casserole with inverted glass in center, arrange bread cubes; sprinkle with remaining sugar and cinnamon. Pour milk-egg mixture over bread. Heat, covered, 17 to 19 minutes or until pudding is set. Serve warm or chilled.

SUPERB STRAWBERRY SOUFFLE

Power Select: MEDIUM
Approx. Cooking Time: 6 minutes
Yield: 6 to 8 servings

Water
2 packages (10 oz. ea.) frozen sliced strawberries in heavy syrup, thawed* and drained (reserve syrup)
4 eggs, separated
2 envelopes unflavored gelatin
6 tablespoons sugar
1 cup whipping cream, whipped

Set Power Select at MEDIUM. Add water to reserved syrup to equal 1½ cups; stir in egg yolks. In large glass bowl, mix unflavored gelatin and 4 tablespoons sugar; stir in syrup mixture.
Heat 5 to 6 minutes or until gelatin is dissolved, stirring occasionally. Stir in an additional 1 cup cold water. Chill until mixture mounds slightly, stirring occasionally. Fold in strawberries. Beat egg whites until soft peaks form; gradually add remaining sugar and beat until stiff. Fold in gelatin mixture, then whipped cream. Turn into small souffle dish with 3-inch collar or 6 cup bowl; chill until firm.

*Hint: *To quickly thaw frozen fruit, see page 139.*

FRUIT DESSERTS

BAKED APPLES

Power Select: HIGH→STAND
Approx. Cooking Time: 8 minutes
Yield: 4 servings

4 large baking apples (about 6 oz. ea.)
¼ cup brown sugar
2 tablespoons finely chopped nuts or raisins
¼ teaspoon ground cinnamon
2 tablespoons butter or margarine
¼ cup water

Set Power Select at HIGH. Core apples, leaving small plug in blossom end; peel skin 1-inch from top. Combine sugar, nuts and cinnamon; fill apples with mixture.
In baking dish, arrange apples; dot with butter and sprinkle with water. Heat, covered, 6 to 7½ minutes, turning dish once. Let STAND 5 minutes; serve warm or chilled, spooning sauce over apples.

Note: **For TWO servings,** *follow above procedure. Halve all ingredients; heat apples 3 to 4 minutes.*
For ONE serving, *heat apple 1½ to 2½ minutes.*

BAKED GRAPEFRUIT

Power Select: HIGH
Approx. Cooking Time: 5 minutes
yield: 4 servings

2 medium grapefruit
8 teaspoons brown sugar, granulated sugar or maple syrup
Ground cinnamon

Set Power Select at HIGH. With sharp knife, cut each grapefruit in half; remove seeds and cut around each section. On glass oven tray arrange grapefruit; sprinkle with brown sugar. Heat 3½ to 4½ minutes; sprinkle with cinnamon before serving.

Note: **For TWO servings,** *follow above procedure. Halve all ingredients; heat 2 to 3 minutes.* **For ONE serving,** *heat 1 to 2 minutes.*

BRANDIED PEACHES

Power Select: HIGH
Approx. Cooking Time: 4 minutes
Yield: about 4 servings

1 can (29 oz.) peach halves, drained (reserve ½ cup syrup)
⅔ cup peach or pineapple preserves
¼ to ⅓ cup brandy
1 teaspoon lemon juice
Toasted coconut*

Set Power Select at HIGH. In baking dish, arrange peaches. Combine reserved syrup, preserves, brandy and lemon juice. Pour over peaches; top with coconut. Heat, covered, 3 to 4 minutes or until heated through. Serve warm or chilled.

***Hint:** To toast coconut in your microwave oven, see Quick Tips, page 140.*

BREAKFAST FRUIT TART

Power Select: HIGH
Approx. Cooking Time: 6 minutes
Yield: about 4 servings

1½ cups flour*
½ cup oil
2 tablespoons milk
1 tablespoon sugar
1 teaspoon salt
⅓ cup apricot, peach or favorite preserves
Sliced fresh fruit or canned fruit, well drained

Set Power Select at HIGH. Combine flour, oil, milk, sugar and salt; pat onto bottom and sides of 9-inch glass pie plate. Prick with fork; heat 4½ to 5½ minutes; cool.
In small glass bowl, heat preserves ½ minute or until melted. Arrange fruit on tart shell; drizzle with preserves. Cut into wedges to serve.

***Substitution:** Use ¾ cup whole wheat flour and ¾ cup all-purpose flour for 1½ cups flour.*

CARAMEL APPLES

Power Select: HIGH
Approx. Cooking Time: 3 minutes
Yield: 4 to 5 servings

1 package (14 oz.) caramels
1 tablespoon hot water
4 to 5 medium apples
Wooden ice cream sticks
Finely chopped nuts

Set Power Select at HIGH. In 1½-quart casserole dish, heat caramels and water 2 to 3 minutes or until melted, stirring twice until smooth. Insert sticks into stem end of apples. Dip each apple into caramel mixture turning and tipping dish to coat apples; dip in chopped nuts. Place on greased waxed paper; store in cool place.

Tip: *If caramel mixture becomes too stiff while dipping apples, return to oven and heat ½ to ¾ minute.*

CHUNKY APPLESAUCE

Power Select: HIGH
Approx. Cooking Time: 9 minutes
Yield: about 4 cups

3 pounds baking apples, peeled, cored and sliced (about 4 cups)
¾ cup sugar or to taste
½ cup water
½ to 1 teaspoon ground cinnamon

Set Power Select at HIGH. In large glass bowl, combine all ingredients; heat, covered with wax paper, 7 to 9 minutes or until apples are soft, stirring once. Mash apples until chunky; serve warm or chilled.

Note: **For 2 cups applesauce**, *follow above procedure. Halve all ingredients; heat apples 4 to 5 minutes.*

CURRIED FRUIT COMPOTE

Power Select: HIGH
Approx. Cooking Time: 11 minutes
Yield: about 6 servings

1 can (17 oz.) apricot halves, drained (reserve syrup)
1 can (16 oz.) peach slices, drained (reserve syrup)
¼ teaspoon curry powder
¼ teaspoon ground cinnamon
1 tablespoon cornstarch
¼ cup water
½ cup raisins

Set Power Select at HIGH. In 2-cup glass measure, combine 1 cup reserved syrups, curry and cinnamon; heat 2 to 3 minutes. Stir in cornstarch blended with water and heat 1½ to 2 minutes or until slightly thickened, stirring occasionally.
In baking dish, combine apricots, peaches and raisins; heat 3½ to 4½ minutes or until heated through, stirring once. Pour sauce over fruit and heat 1 to 1½ minutes. Serve warm or chilled.

FRUIT COBBLER

Power Select: MEDIUM-HIGH
Approx. Cooking Time: 11 minutes
Yield: about 6 servings

Filling:
2 cans (30 oz. ea.) peach slices or other canned fruit*,
**   drained (reserve ¼ cup syrup)**
3 tablespoons flour
½ tablespoon lemon juice
½ teaspoon vanilla extract
½ teaspoon ground cinnamon

Topping:
1 cup buttermilk biscuit mix
¼ cup brown sugar
¼ cup butter or margarine, softened
2 tablespoons hot water

Set Power Select at MEDIUM-HIGH. In square baking dish, combine Filling ingredients. In small bowl, combine Topping ingredients, stirring until dough pulls away from sides of bowl and forms a ball. Gently spread topping onto filling (topping will spread slightly when heated). Sprinkle, if desired, with additional cinnamon. Let stand to cool.

*Variations:

For FRESH PEACH Cobbler, combine 1½ pounds peeled and sliced peaches and ¼ to ⅓ cup brown sugar; heat, covered, at Power Select HIGH 3½ to 4 minutes or until tender. Follow above procedure, omitting ¼ cup reserved syrup.
For QUICK Fruit Cobbler, substitute 2 cans (21 oz. ea.) fruit pie filling and ¼ cup water for Filling ingredients.

Steamed Date-Nut Pudding, page 124

GINGERBREAD PEAR COBBLER

Power Select: MEDIUM
Approx. Cooking Time: 13 minutes
Yield: about 6 servings

1 can (16 oz.) sliced pears, drained (reserve syrup)
½ cup raisins or chopped nuts
1 package (14 oz.) gingerbread mix
Water

Set Power Select at MEDIUM. Line bottom of 8 or 9-inch round baking dish with wax paper. Arrange pears on paper; top with raisins. Prepare gingerbread according to package directions using reserved syrup as part of water. Pour batter over pears. Heat 11½ to 13 minutes or until gingerbread is done. Let stand, covered, until ready to serve.

PEARS WITH CARAMEL SAUCE

Power Select: HIGH
Approx. Cooking Time: 12 minutes
Yield: 6 servings

6 large pears (6 oz. ea.)
1 tablespoon sugar
Dash ground cinnamon
½ cup water
30 caramels (about 10 oz.)
2 tablespoons butter or margarine
2 tablespoons rum (optional)
1 tablespoon water
½ teaspoon ground cinnamon
Sweetened whipped cream

Set Power Select at HIGH. Core pears and peel skin 1 inch from top. Combine sugar and dash cinnamon; sprinkle inside pears.
In oblong baking dish, arrange pears; sprinkle with water. Heat, covered, 8 to 9 minutes or until pears are tender, cool or chill.
Just before serving, in glass bowl, combine caramels, butter, rum, water and cinnamon; heat 2 to 3 minutes, stirring twice until smooth. Spoon sauce over pears; top with whipped cream.

SPICY APPLES 'N OATS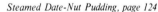

Power Select: HIGH→STAND
Approx. Cooking Time: 5 minutes
Yield: about 6 servings

4 large baking apples, peeled and sliced
**   (about 1¼ lb.)**
⅔ cup brown sugar
⅓ cup chopped nuts or raisins
1 teaspoon ground cinnamon
¼ teaspoon ground nutmeg
⅓ cup butter or margarine, softened
⅓ cup flour
⅓ cup old fashion or quick oats

Set Power Select at HIGH. In 8 or 9-inch round baking dish; layer ½ apples. Combine sugar, nuts, cinnamon and nutmeg; sprinkle ½ sugar mixture over apples. Top with remaining apples. Into remaining sugar mixture, blend in butter, flour and oats; sprinkle over apples. Heat 4 to 5 minutes or until apples are fork-tender. Let STAND 5 minutes; serve warm or cool.

PIES ❧❧❧❧❧❧❧❧❧❧❧❧❧❧❧❧❧❧❧

PREPARING PIE CRUSTS
(8 or 9-inch single crust)

- Lightly grease glass pie plate before lining with pastry.
- Before heating, prick bottom and sides of pastry with fork and brush with dark corn syrup (for sweet fillings); Worcestershire or soy sauce for savory fillings.
- If desired, substitute ½ cup whole wheat flour for ½ cup all-purpose flour when preparing pastry from scratch.
- For frozen crust, remove to 8 or 9-inch glass pie plate; heat ½ minute, then prick crust and brush as directed above.
- Recipe testing for graham cracker crust was prepared with ¼ cup butter (softened), 1¼ cup crumbs and ¼ cup sugar.
- Let stand to cool (chill crumb crusts).

ITEM	APPROXIMATE HEATING TIME at Power Select HIGH (in minutes)
From Scratch or Mix	3½ to 5
Frozen	4 to 5½
Graham Cracker or Cookie Crumb	1½ to 2

COCONUT LEMON MERINGUE PIE

Power Select: HIGH
Approx. Cooking Time: 10 minutes
Yield: about 8 servings

1 package (3⅜ oz.) lemon pudding and pie filling
¾ cup sugar
2¼ cups water
2 eggs, separated
9-inch pastry shell, baked (see chart)
1 egg white (optional)
⅓ cup toasted coconut*

Set Power Select at HIGH. In medium glass bowl, combine pudding mix and ½ cup sugar; stir in water and egg yolks. Heat 4½ to 6 minutes or until mixture is thickened, stirring twice; let cool 5 minutes. Pour pudding into prepared crust; let cool 10 minutes. Meanwhile, beat egg whites until soft peaks form, gradually add remaining sugar and beat until stiff. Spread meringue onto pie; sprinkle with coconut. Heat 3 to 3½ minutes or until meringue is set. Cool completely before serving.

*Hint: *To toast coconut in your microwave oven, see Quick Tips, page 140.*

CHOCOLATE ROCKY ROAD PIE

Power Select: MEDIUM
Approx. Cooking Time: 9 minutes
Yield: about 8 servings

1 package (3⅝ oz.) chocolate pudding and pie filling mix
1¾ cups milk
1 to 1½ cups miniature marshmallows
½ to 1 cup coarsely chopped walnuts
9-inch chocolate cookie crumb crust, baked (see chart)

Set Power Select at MEDIUM. In 4-cup glass measure, combine pudding mix and milk; heat 7 to 8½ minutes or until pudding is thickened, stirring twice. Cool 5 minutes; fold in marshmallows and nuts. Turn into prepared crust; chill until firm.

FRESH PEACH PIE

Power Select: HIGH
Approx. Cooking Time: 11 minutes
Yield: about 8 servings

2 pounds fresh peaches, peeled and sliced**
½ cup brown sugar
½ tablespoon cornstarch
2 teaspoons lemon juice
½ teaspoon ground cinnamon (optional)
9-inch pastry shell, baked (see chart)
Crumb Topping*

Set Power Select at HIGH. Toss peaches with sugar, cornstarch, lemon juice and cinnamon; arrange in prepared shell. Heat, covered, with wax paper, 4 to 6 minutes or until peaches are almost tender. Sprinkle with Crumb Topping; heat 4 to 5 minutes or until topping is set. Let stand until cool.

*Crumb Topping: *Combine ½ cup flour, ½ cup brown sugar, ¼ cup butter or margarine, softened, ⅓ cup finely chopped nuts (optional) and ¼ teaspoon ground cinnamon.*

**Variation:
**For FRESH APPLE PIE, *use 2 pounds apples for peaches.*

GRASSHOPPER PIE

Power Select: MEDIUM
Approx. Cooking Time: 5 minutes
Yield: about 8 servings

3 cups miniature marshmallows
½ cup milk or half 'n half
3 tablespoons creme de cocoa
3 tablespoons creme de menthe
1 cup whipping cream, whipped
9-inch chocolate cookie crumb crust, baked (see chart)

Set Power Select at MEDIUM. In large glass bowl, heat marshmallows and milk 3½ to 4½ minutes; stir until smooth. Stir in creme de cocoa and creme de menthe; chill until mixture mounds slightly. Fold in whipped cream and turn into prepared crust. Chill until firm.

GREAT GRAPE PIE

Power Select: HIGH
Approx. Cooking Time: 2 minutes
Yield: about 8 servings

1 envelope unflavored gelatin
¾ cup water
1 can (6 oz.) frozen grape juice concentrate
1 cup whipping cream, whipped
9-inch graham cracker crumb crust, baked*
  (see page 131)

Set Power Select at HIGH. In large glass bowl,
sprinkle unflavored gelatin over water; heat 1¼ to 1¾
minutes or until gelatin is dissolved, stirring twice.
Stir in grape juice concentrate until melted; chill until
mixture mounds slightly, stirring occasionally.
Fold in whipped cream; turn into prepared crust and
chill until firm. Garnish, if desired, with sugared grape
clusters.

*Hint: *When preparing ingredients for crust, add ¼ cup
finely chopped nuts and ¼ teaspoon each ground
allspice, cinnamon and nutmeg.*

MAMA'S CHESS PIE

Power Select: MEDIUM
Approx. Cooking Time: 10 minutes
Yield: about 8 servings

1 cup brown sugar
½ cup sugar
3 eggs
½ cup evaporated milk
½ cup chopped walnuts (optional)
1 teaspoon vanilla extract
⅛ teaspoon lemon extract
9-inch pastry shell, baked (see page 131)
Sweetened whipped cream or whipped topping

Set Power Select at MEDIUM. Combine sugars, eggs,
milk, walnuts, and extracts; pour into prepared shell.
Heat 8½ to 10 minutes or until center is almost set.
Let stand, covered with wax paper, until cool. Just
before serving, top with whipped cream.

ORCHARD FRUIT PIE

Power Select: MEDIUM-HIGH
Approx. Cooking Time: 8 minutes
Yield: about 8 servings

1 can (21 oz.) favorite pie filling
¼ cup raisins (optional)
1 teaspoon lemon or orange juice
⅛ teaspoon ground cinnamon
8 or 9-inch pastry shell, baked (see page 131)
½ cup flour
¼ cup brown sugar
¼ cup butter or margarine, softened

Set Power Select at MEDIUM-HIGH. Combine pie
filling, raisins, lemon juice and cinnamon; pour into
prepared crust. Blend together remaining ingredients;
crumble over filling. Heat 6 to 8 minutes or until
heated through; cool before serving.

ORANGE MANDARIN CHIFFON PIE

Power Select: MEDIUM-LOW
Approx. Cooking Time: 6 minutes
Yield: about 6 servings

1 envelope unflavored gelatin
⅓ cup sugar
4 eggs, separated
1 can (11 oz.) mandarin orange sections, drained
  (reserve ⅔ cup syrup)
2 tablespoons lemon juice
½ teaspoon grated lemon peel
½ cup sugar
9-inch graham cracker crumb crust, baked
  (see page 131)

Set Power Select at MEDIUM-LOW. In medium glass
bowl, mix gelatin and ⅓ cup sugar; stir in egg yolks
blended with reserved syrup, lemon juice and lemon
peel. Heat 5 to 6 minutes or until gelatin is dissolved,
stirring twice.
Chill until mixture mounds slightly, stirring occasionally. Meanwhile, beat egg whites until soft peaks form;
gradually add ½ cup sugar and beat until stiff. Fold in
gelatin mixture and ½ oranges; turn into prepared
crust. Chill until firm; garnish with remaining oranges.

PECAN PIE

Power Select: MEDIUM
Approx. Cooking Time: 9 minutes
Yield: about 8 servings

1 cup dark corn syrup
¼ cup brown sugar
3 eggs
2 tablespoons butter or margarine, melted
1 teaspoon vanilla extract
¾ cup chopped pecans
9-inch pastry crust, baked (see page 131)

Set Power Select at MEDIUM. Combine syrup, sugar,
eggs, butter and vanilla; stir in pecans. Pour into
prepared crust. Heat 7 to 9 minutes or until pie is set.
Let stand until cool. Garnish, if desired, with
sweetened whipped cream.

PUMPKIN PIE

Power Select: MEDIUM
Approx. Cooking Time: 22 minutes
Yield: about 8 servings

1 can (16 oz.) cooked pumpkin
1 cup evaporated milk
2 eggs
½ cup sugar
¼ cup brown sugar
½ teaspoon salt
1 teaspoon ground cinnamon
½ teaspoon ground ginger
¼ teaspoon ground cloves
9-inch pastry shell, baked (see page 131)

Set Power Select at MEDIUM. Combine pumpkin, milk,
eggs, sugars, salt and spices. Pour into prepared shell.
Heat 20 to 22 minutes or until center is almost set.
Let stand, covered with wax paper, until cool.

You have come to the most unique section of this cookbook! Meals are meals......and they are delicious when prepared in your microwave oven. But making holiday ornaments, brewing fruit flavored liqueurs...... now that is special! Read on and explore the "extra" benefits that come with being a microwave cook.

- Blanching Fresh Vegetables for Freezing
- Bread Dough Art
- Dried Flowers
- Jams and Jellies
- Liqueurs and Brandies

BLANCHING FRESH VEGETABLES

A special at the market on your favorite green vegetable? Use your microwave oven to blanch vegetables for freezing, preserving that garden-fresh flavor to enjoy at a later time. This method is also ideal when freezing vegetables from your garden. You can blanch small quantities when the vegetables are at their peak...not when there are enough to make it worth your while.
Follow the guidelines and heating times below. You will be surprised how easy it is.

TO BLANCH:
- Wash vegetables; sliced or chop as directed.
- Measure amount according to chart into 2-quart casserole dish; add water if directed.

Set Power Select at HIGH; heat, stirring once. Vegetables will be an even bright color throughout.
- Plunge vegetables immediately into ice water. Blot dry on paper towels to remove excess moisture.
- Package in freezer containers or plastic bags suitable for freezing. Label and date; freeze immediately.

TO PREPARE:
- Empty vegetables into casserole dish; break up if possible.
- Set Power Select at HIGH; heat, covered, stirring once.
- Let stand, covered, 3 minutes; season to taste.

VEGETABLE	AMOUNT	WATER	APPROXIMATE HEATING TIME TO BLANCH VEGETABLES (in minutes) at Power Select HIGH	APPROXIMATE HEATING TIME TO COOK (in minutes) at Power Select HIGH
Asparagus Cut into 2-inch pieces	1 lb.	¼ cup	2 to 2½	5 to 6
Beans, Green Cut into 2-inch pieces	1 lb.	¼ cup	5½ to 6	5 to 6
Broccoli Chopped or cut into Spears	1 to 1¼ lb.	¼ cup	4 to 4½	5 to 6
Brussel Sprouts	10 oz.	¼ cup	3½ to 4	5 to 6
Cauliflower Cut into flowerets	1½ to 1¾ lb.	¼ cup	3½ to 4	4 to 5
Spinach, leaves	1 to 1¾ lb.	———	2½ to 3	6½ to 7½
Zucchini Cut into ½ to ¾-in. pieces	1 lb.	¼ cup	3 to 3½	6½ to 7½

Pictured on the preceding page: Liqueurs and Brandies, Bread Dough Ornaments, Jams and Jellies, Dried Flowers.

JAM AND JELLY JAMBOREE

With the help of your microwave oven, you can escape the toil associated with preparing these special sweets. Many of the jam basics will remain the same as you change to the microwave way. Just follow each recipe and the hints below to insure your first microwave jam will be the best ever.

- Use a large glass bowl or casserole dish (4 or 5-quart).
- Stir mixture two or three times during first third of heating to dissolve the sugar.
- Wait until the mixture comes to a full rolling boil as the recipes direct. Be patient!
- Stir and skim foam off mixture, if necessary, (5 to 7 minutes)
- Ladle into hot sterilized glasses or jars. Seal with thin (⅛ to ¼-inch) layer of parafin.
- Properly sealed and stored (in a cool, dry place) jams and jellies will keep at least 1 year.

Important Note: *In hot and humid climates, the U.S. Department of Agriculture recommends storing jams in jars with two-part lids and processing in hot water bath for 5 to 15 minutes. (This can NOT be done in microwave ovens!) Contact your local extension service for specific details.*

APRICOT PINEAPPLE JAM

Power Select: HIGH→MEDIUM
                HIGH
Approx. Cooking Time: 28 minutes
Yield: about 6½ cups

¼ pound dried apricots, finely chopped
1 can (20 oz.) crushed pineapple, drained (reserve syrup)
Water
6½ cups sugar
½ cup lemon juice
½—6 ounce bottle liquid pectin

Set Power Select at HIGH. In 4-cup glass measure, combine apricots and reserved syrup; heat 1 to 2 minutes.
Set Power Select at MEDIUM. Heat 3 to 4 minutes or until apricots are soft. Add pineapple and enough water to equal 3½ cups. In large bowl, thoroughly combine fruit mixture, sugar and lemon juice.
Set Power Select at HIGH. Heat 19 to 21 minutes or until mixture comes to a full boil, stirring occasionally during first 7 minutes. Heat an additional 1 minute. Stir in pectin and skim off any foam; stir and skim foam for about 7 minutes. Ladle into glasses; seal with parafin.

GRAPE JELLY

Power Select: HIGH
Approx. Cooking Time: 19 minutes
Yield: about 3 cups

2 cups grape juice
3½ cups sugar
½—6 ounce bottle liquid pectin

Set Power Select at HIGH. In large glass bowl, thoroughly combine juice and sugar. Heat 10 to 12 minutes or until mixture is boiling, stirring twice during first 4 minutes of heating. Stir in pectin and heat 4 to 6 minutes or until mixture comes to a full boil. Heat an additional 1 minute; skim off any foam. Ladle into glasses; seal with parafin.

PEACH JAM

Power Select: HIGH
Approx. Cooking Time: 18 minutes
Yield: about 9 cups

4 cups peeled, sliced fresh peaches (about 3 lb.)
7¼ cups sugar
¼ cup lemon juice
½—6 ounce bottle liquid pectin

Set Power Select at HIGH. In large glass bowl, thoroughly combine peaches, sugar and lemon juice. Heat 15 to 17 minutes or until mixture comes to a full boil, stirring occasionally during the first 5 minutes. Heat an additional 1 minute. Stir in pectin and skim off any foam; stir and skim foam for about 7 minutes. Ladle into glasses; seal with parafin.

STRAWBERRY JAM

Power Select: HIGH
Approx. Cooking Time: 23 minutes
Yield: about 6½ cups

4 packages (10 oz. ea.) frozen strawberries in heavy syrup, thawed
5 cups sugar
2 tablespoons lemon juice
½—6 ounce bottle liquid pectin

Set Power Select at HIGH. In large glass bowl, thoroughly combine strawberries, sugar and lemon juice. Heat 20 to 22 minutes or until mixture comes to a full boil, stirring occasionally during first 7 minutes. Heat an additional 1 minute. Stir in pectin and skim off any foam; stir and skim foam for about 7 minutes. Ladle into glasses; seal with parafin.

BREAD DOUGH ORNAMENTS

Want to work on a project that will give you the "I made it myself" satisfaction without it taking days of effort?

With a few ingredients and simple tools, in an afternoon you will create numerous Bread Dough Ornaments so popular now. What makes this all possible in such a short time? The MEDIUM-LOW power setting on your microwave oven.

Most drying of bread dough ornaments in conventional ovens takes one-half to one hour. With the assistance of your microwave oven, most ornaments will be dry in about 3 minutes, ready for painting as soon as they cool, about 10 minutes.

The Ingredients

> 2 cups all-purpose flour
> 1 cup salt
> 1 cup water*

Combine flour and salt. Gradually add water, stirring to form a ball of dough.

On a lightly floured surface, knead dough 7 to 10 minutes or until dough is smooth, but firm.

You might need to add a bit more water, depending upon the humidity. Do not go overboard and add too much—a little at a time.

- Do not use self-rising flour.
- Wrap dough in plastic wrap or keep in a plastic bag when not using. This keeps dough smooth and workable.
- If dough does dry out—work a bit of water into it. If dough is too sticky—knead in a small amount of flour.

The Tools

- A piece of cardboard, preferably corrugated (cut to fit the tray of your microwave), covered with wax paper. Remember to leave the oven glass tray in place while drying ornaments.
- A rolling pin or something similar.
- Things to be used to shape, mark and mold your ornament-to-be.

> cookie cutters   nails and screws
> pizza cutter   meat mallet
> garlic press   toothpicks
> fork   toothbrushes

The Creating

The easiest way to start designing an ornament is with a cookie cutter. Always work on a lightly floured surface to prevent the shape from sticking; roll a small amount of dough ¼-inch thick. Keep unused dough wrapped airtight.

Puncture, pinch, dab—just do not build up too much. If joining two pieces of dough, moisten your fingers with water and press dough together.

For best results, keep beginning work simple. Our initial shapes were done with 2 to 3-inch cookie cutters and 3-inch high rope initials.

Make a hole in the top of the ornament for the string before baking. Be careful not to close the hole when painting or finishing.

The Drying

Using a pancake turner, carefully transfer ornament to the wax paper-covered cardboard; place cardboard on glass oven tray.

Set Power Select at MEDIUM-LOW. Heat each piece about 3 to 4 minutes, turning over once during heating (when possible).

If a piece bubbles as it dries in the oven, make a hole in the ornament with a pin. If a flat piece curls, weigh down that area with a microwave oven-safe glass and heat 30 seconds. Remove glass and continue drying. Some bubbles add interest to the piece.

The Extra Shapes

To Make Beads: Shape dough around a plastic straw and lay the straw between the edges of a baking dish. Heat 4 beads about 2 minutes. If the weight from the beads causes the straw to bend, insert a wooden skewer through the straw to hold it straight.

To Make Free-Form Designs: Roll or shape dough as desired. Start heating about 2 minutes and continue adding 30 seconds until piece is dry. From experience, you can see when the piece has dried completely. Turn the piece over once, if possible. Popular free-form designs include rope initials and napkin rings as well as abstract figures. More advanced projects can include wreaths for candles and small picture frames.

The Finishing

The only essential thing that needs to be done is to apply a coat or two of shellac, varnish, acrylic sealer, etc.—something to protect the ornament from moisture and humidity. (Two coats are best— and produces a shiny finish.) What you do before that is up to you. The ornaments can be painted, glittered, stained, even shoe-polished, to achieve the look you want.

Even the natural dough color, after sealing, looks attractive. Be sure to let ornaments dry completely in between finishing treatments.

DRIED FLOWERS

Preserve the beauty of the seasons by drying fresh flowers with the speedy assistance of your microwave oven.

Additional Material Needed

Drying agent to absorb moisture of the flowers
   a. Uncolored kitty litter—can be reused
   b. Silica Gel—available in craft and hobby stores
   c. Fine white sand

Method

1. Cut flower stem ½-inch long.
2. Spread ¾-inch layer of drying agent in proper size container.
3. Place flower bloom-up in container.
4. Carefully spoon additional drying agent between and over petals. Cover flower completely.
5. Place the container and a 2-cup glass measure filled with water in microwave oven.
6. Set Power Select at MEDIUM-HIGH. Heat a few minutes depending upon size of flower (see HINTS).
7. Let stand 8 hours or overnight.
8. Carefully remove flowers. loosening and removing all drying agent.
9. Bend floral wire fishhook style and thread through base of flower; wrap wire with floral tape.
10. To preserve dried flowers, spray with dried flower spray.

HINTS: Choose brightly colored flowers that are half open and firm. Flowers already in full bloom lose their petals very easily. White and pastel colored flowers may turn brown or gray; deep colors may look black. Yellow, rust and blue flowers do very well. Use this guide in selecting timing (approx. time given in minutes) for single flowers:

DAISIES	½ to 1
DAISY MUMS (pom poms)	1½ to 2
CARNATIONS	2 to 2½
CORNFLOWERS (bachelor buttons)	¾ to 1
MUMS (small)	2 to 2½
ROSES	2 to 3
STAR MUMS	1¼ to 1¾

LIQUEURS AND BRANDIES

APRICOT BRANDY

Power Select: MEDIUM→WARM
Approx. Cooking Time: 40 minutes
Yield: 2 cups

½—16 ounce package dried apricots, chopped
2 cups sugar
2 cups vodka

Set Power Select at MEDIUM. In medium glass bowl, thoroughly combine all ingredients. Heat 10 minutes or until sugar is dissolved, stirring twice.
Set Power Select at WARM. Heat 30 minutes, stirring twice. Cover and let stand 3 to 4 days. Strain before serving.

COFFEE LIQUEUR

Power Select: HIGH
                MEDIUM→WARM
Approx. Cooking Time: 40 minutes
Yield: 2 cups

1½ cups hot water
2 cups sugar
⅓ cup freeze-dried coffee
2 cups vodka
1 vanilla bean

Set Power Select at HIGH. In large glass bowl, heat water 3 to 4 minutes or until boiling. Stir in sugar and coffee until dissolved; add remaining ingredients.
Set Power Select at MEDIUM. Heat 5 minutes.
Set Power Select at WARM. Heat 30 minutes, stirring twice. Cover and let stand 3 to 4 days. Strain before serving.

PEACH LIQUEUR

Power Select: MEDIUM→WARM
Approx. Cooking Time: 40 minutes
Yield: 2 cups

1½ pounds fresh peaches, peeled and sliced
1½ cups sugar
4 strips lemon peel
3 whole cloves
2 cinnamon sticks
2 cups bourbon

Set Power Select at MEDIUM. In medium glass bowl, thoroughly combine all ingredients. Heat 10 minutes or until sugar is dissolved, stirring once.
Set Power Select at WARM. Heat 30 minutes, stirring twice. Cover and let stand 3 to 4 days. Strain before serving.

PLUM BRANDY

Power Select: MEDIUM→WARM
Approx. Cooking Time: 40 minutes
Yield: 2 cups

1½ pounds fresh plums, halved (remove pits)
2 cups sugar
2 cups gin

Set Power Select at MEDIUM. In medium glass bowl, thoroughly combine all ingredients. Heat 10 minutes or until sugar is dissolved, stirring once.
Set Power Select at WARM. Heat 30 minutes, stirring twice. Cover and let stand 3 to 4 days. Strain before serving.

 APPENDIX

Heating Frozen Convenience Foods

ITEM	POWER SELECT	APPROXIMATE HEATING TIME (in minutes)	SPECIAL HINTS
APPETIZERS			
Bite Size	MED. HIGH	2½ to 4½	Heat 12 at a time on paper towel lined paper plate or microwave oven roasting rack. Brush pastry items with Worcestershire sauce.
MAIN DISH			
Hearty T.V.-Style Dinner (17 oz.)	MED. HIGH	8 to 10	If container is ¾-inch deep, remove foil cover and replace foil tray in original box.
Regular T.V.-Style Dinner (11 oz.)	MED. HIGH	5 to 7	
Entree			For containers more than ¾-inch deep, remove food to similar size glass container; heat covered if no top crust. Stir occasionally, if possible.
(8 to 9 oz.)	MED. HIGH	6 to 8	
(21 oz.)		15 to 17	
(32 oz.)		17 to 19	
Macaroni and Cheese (8 oz.)	MEDIUM	8 to 10	
Pot Pie (8 oz.)	MEDIUM	9 to 11	Brush top of pot pie with Worcestershire sauce.
Breakfast Entree (4 to 5 oz.)	MED. HIGH	1½ to 2½	
French Toast	MEDIUM		
2 pieces		1 to 2	
4 pieces		2 to 3	
Waffles	MEDIUM		
2 pieces		1½ to 2½	
4 pieces		3 to 4	
Fried Chicken	MED. HIGH		Arrange on paper towel lined paper plate, cover with paper towel.
2 pieces		4 to 5	
4 pieces		5 to 6	
6 pieces		7 to 8	
Fried Fish Fillets	MED. HIGH		
2 fillets		2 to 3	
4 fillets		3½ to 4½	
Fish Cakes	MED. HIGH		
4 cakes		3½ to 4½	
Pizzas (individual)	MED. HIGH		Arrange on microwave oven roasting rack.
1		1½ to 2½	
2		3 to 4	
4		5 to 6	
Pouch Dinners	MED. HIGH		Pierce pouch, set on saucer.
(5 to 6 oz.)		4 to 5	
(10 to 11 oz.)		7 to 8	
SIDE DISHES			
Baked Stuffed Potatoes	MED. HIGH		Heat in original containers and box. Let STAND 5 minutes after heating.
2		10 to 12	
4		15 to 17	
Vegetables in Pouches	HIGH	7 to 9	Pierce pouch, set on saucer.
Frozen Potato Puffs (10 oz.)	MED. HIGH	2 to 3	Heat on paper plate, covered with paper towel, stirring once.
BAKED GOODS	DEFROST		
Brownies (13 oz.)		2 to 3	Remove from original container; arrange on serving plate. Let stand 5 minutes after heating (to defrost).
Cupcakes (6) (10 to 11 oz.)		1½ to 2½	
Cheese Cake (17 oz.)		3½ to 4½	
Layer Cakes (17 to 18 oz.)		1½ to 2½	Add an additional 1 to 1½ minutes to serve warm.
Pound Cake (10¾ oz.)		1 to 2	
Coffee Cake (11 to 12 oz.)		3 to 4	

ITEM	POWER SELECT	APPROXIMATE HEATING TIME (in minutes)	SPECIAL HINTS
BAGELS	DEFROST		
2		2 to 3	
4		3 to 4	
DANISH	DEFROST		
1		½ to 1	
2		1½ to 2	
4 (9 oz. package)		2½ to 3½	
6 (13 oz. package)		3½ to 4½	
Dinner Rolls (6)	DEFROST	1½ to 2½	
Donuts	DEFROST		
Plain or Sugar coated			Each individually wrapped in a paper towel (for 1 or 2). Arrange on paper plate; cover with paper towel (for 4 or 6).
1		¾ to 1	
2		1 to 1½	
4		2½ to 3	
6		4 to 4½	
Hard Rolls (1 to 1¼ oz. ea.)	DEFROST		
1		½ to ¾	
2		1 to 1½	
4		2 to 2½	
MISCELLANEOUS (TO THAW)			
Frozen Juice Concentrates	MEDIUM		Remove lid. If container is foil lined, remove to pitcher.
(6 oz.)		¾ to 1¼	
(12 oz.)		1½ to 2½	
Non-Dairy Creamer	DEFROST		Open carton. Let STAND equal time after heating.
(16 oz.)		9½ to 10½	
Pancake/Muffin Batter	DEFROST		
(10 oz.)		4 to 5	
Whipped Topping (9 oz.)	DEFROST	2 to 3	Heat in original plastic tub. Let STAND 5 minutes.
Frozen Mixed Fruit	DEFROST		Pierce pouch or remove metal lid; set on saucer. Let STAND 5 minutes.
(10 oz.)		4½ to 5½	
Frozen Vegetables	DEFROST		Pierce box; set on saucer. If box is foil wrapped, remove foil. If vegetables are in pouch, pierce pouch. Let STAND 5 minutes.
(6 oz.)		3 to 4	
(10 oz.)		5 to 6	

Heating Canned Goods 🔲

- Empty contents of can into serving dish
- Heat, covered, at Power Select at MEDIUM→STAND
- Stir occasionally during heating

ITEM	APPROXIMATE HEATING TIME (in minutes) at Power Select MEDIUM-HIGH	STANDING TIME (in minutes)
Baked Beans (8 oz.)	1½ to 2½	3
(15 to 16 oz.)	3½ to 4½	3
Chow Mein (15 to 16 oz.)	3 to 4	3
Corned Beef Hash (15 oz.)	3 to 4	3
Macaroni and Cheese (15 oz.)	4 to 5	3
Sloppy Joe (15 oz.)	4½ to 5½	3
Ravioli (15 oz.)	4 to 5	3
Vegetables (8 oz.)	2 to 3	3
(16 oz.)	3 to 4	3

Quick Tips

To further illustrate the versatility of your microwave oven, here are some of our favorite tips to help you save more time, even when doing the little things. All times given are approximate.

- SOFTEN CREAM CHEESE, cheese spread or a stick of BUTTER. At Power Select LOW 3 oz. package cream cheese or ¼ pound butter will be spreadable in ½ to 1 minute.

- FRESHEN a STALE ROLL. Wrap in wax paper or paper napkin and heat about ¼ to ½ minute at Power Select MEDIUM LOW.

- HEAT PANCAKE and other SYRUPS. Heat at Power Select HIGH in a glass pitcher or bottle (remove metal cap) for 1 to 2 minutes (depending upon quantity).

- HEAT CITRUS FRUITS ½ to 1 minute at Power Select MEDIUM. They will be easier to squeeze; giving you more juice.

- DRY LEMON and ORANGE PEELS in your microwave oven for your own bottled grated peel. Place grated peel in small glass bowl. Heat at Power Select HIGH ½ to 1 minute or until dry, stirring once.

- REMOVE OVEN ODORS easily. Combine water with the juice and peel of a lemon in a small glass bowl. Heat at Power Select HIGH 5 minutes; wipe oven interior with damp cloth.

- Have FRESH COFFEE all day. Refrigerate what is not used at breakfast. Reheat by the mugful 1½ to 2 minutes at Power Select HIGH.

- REHEAT COLD FRUIT PIE ¼ to ¾ minute at Power Select MEDIUM-HIGH for fresh from the oven flavor.

- HEAT BABY BOTTLES or jars of baby food; remove cap on bottle and metal lid from jars. Heat at Power Select MEDIUM HIGH (with milk-MEDIUM) ½ to 1½ minutes or until warm.

- DRY HERBS quickly in your microwave oven. Place a few sprigs or ½ cup leaves between paper towels and heat 2 to 3 minutes at Power Select HIGH or until dry and crumbly. Timings may vary with different herbs.

- For CAREFREE BARBECUES, partially cook chicken, ribs, etc. in the microwave oven. Season and finish on the grill.

- QUICK COOK CHICKEN pieces at Power Select HIGH when you need cut-up, cooked chicken for salads, sandwiches or casseroles.

- SEPARATE COLD BACON slices easily. Heat package at Power Select HIGH ¼ to ½ minute.

- Heat LIQUEURS for FLAMING DESSERTS in a glass measure at Power Select HIGH 15 to 30 seconds. Pour over dessert and ignite.

- SOFTEN HARD ICE CREAM for serving or molding at Power Select WARM. Heat ½ gallon 3½ to 5 minutes.

- DRY BREAD for croutons or bread crumbs. Two cups bread cubes, in shallow glass dish will dry in 3 to 4 minutes, at Power Select HIGH, stirring occasionally.

- BLANCH NUTS by heating in boiling water at Power Select HIGH ½ to 1 minute. Drain and slip skins off by rubbing between paper towel.

- SOFTEN DRY FRUIT. In small glass bowl, sprinkle fruit with water and heat, covered, at Power Select HIGH ½ to ¾ minutes.

- SOFTEN HARD BROWN SUGAR. In glass dish, place sugar and slice of fresh bread or apple wedge; cover and heat at Power Select HIGH. One cup sugar will soften in ½ to 1 minute.

- MELT BUTTER or CHOCOLATE for cooking. Heat butter (¼ lb.) 1 to 2 minutes and chocolate (1 oz.) 2 to 3 minutes at Power Select MEDIUM-LOW. Chocolate will not lose its shape when melted, so check before adding extra time.

- Toast COCONUT easily at Power Select HIGH. In small glass bowl, heat ⅓ cup for 1 to 1½ minutes, or until golden brown, stirring twice.

- Roast NUTS quickly at Power Select HIGH. In small glass bowl, heat 1½ cups for 3 to 4 minutes, stirring twice.

- Toast SESAME SEEDS at Power Select HIGH. In small glass bowl, heat ¼ cup for 2½ to 3½ minutes, stirring twice.

For Your Information

HIGH ALTITUDE COOKING

Different cooking times are not necessary when cooking at high altitudes. However, because the possibility of shrinkage is greater, meats, fish and poultry should be loosely covered when heating. For baked goods, follow high altitude directions for preparing batter. Cover loosely with wax paper and watch heating carefully. Cutting heating time back slightly and wrapping slightly cooled baked goods in foil will help create a satisfactory product. Check with the Home Services Department of your local utility company or with your county Extension Service for additional help.

INGREDIENT SUBSTITUTION

It is always best to use the exact ingredients called for in any recipe, but we have all found ourselves in the "I thought I had..." situation. The following is a list of foods and acceptable substitutes for those emergencies:

Baking powder (1 t.) ...¼ teaspoon baking soda *plus* ½ teaspoon cream of tartar

Buttermilk (1 cup) ......1 cup milk *plus* 1 tablespoon vinegar OR lemon juice; let stand 5 minutes.

Chocolate, Semi-Sweet (2 oz.) ......⅓ cup semi-sweet chocolate pieces

Chocolate, Unsweetened (1 oz.) ...3 tablespoons cocoa *plus* 1 tablespoon shortening

Corn Syrup (½ cup)......½ cup sugar *plus* 2 tablespoons liquid

Cornstarch (1 T.) ....2 tablespoons flour

Cake Flour (1 cup) ..... ¾ cup plus 2 tablespoons all-purpose flour

Garlic (1 clove)............⅛ teaspoon dried garlic flakes OR garlic powder

Grated Fresh Fruit Peel (1 t.) ....½ teaspoon dried grated peel

Green Pepper (2 T. chopped) ....1 tablespoon dried green pepper flakes

Herbs, Fresh (1 T.) ......1 teaspoon dried

Honey (1 cup) ....1¼ cups sugar *plus* ¼ cup liquid

Milk (1 cup) ....½ cup evaporated milk *plus* ½ cup water OR ⅓ cup instant non-fat dry milk *plus* 1 cup minus 1 tablespoon water

Onion (¼ cup chopped) ....1 tablespoon dried onion flakes OR 1 teaspoon onion powder

METRIC CONVERSION CHART FOR WEIGHTS AND MEASURES:

The United States is currently going through the transition to the Metric System. The following metric equivalents are for converting ingredients that may be purchased by metric measures. Also included are temperature equivalents.

1 teaspoon..................5 milliliters (ml)
1 tablespoon ....15 milliliters
½ cup ....125 milliliters
1 cup ....250 milliliters
1 quart ....1 liter (1000 milliliters)
1 ounce ....30 grams (g)
1 pound ....455 grams
2.2 pounds ....1 kilogram (kg) (1000 grams)

Fahrenheit	Celsius
115°	46°
130°	55°
145°	63°
160°	70°
175°	80°

OTHER MICROWAVE COOKBOOKS AVAILABLE

Benoit, Jehane Mme., Microwave Cook Book (Toronto, Canada; McGraw-Hill Ryerson Limited) 1975.
Better Homes and Gardens Microwave Cook Book (Meredith Corporation) 1976.
Culinary Arts Institute Microwave Cooking: Adventure in Cooking Series (Melrose Park, IL: Culinary Arts Institute) 1977.
Harris, Barbara, Let's Cook Microwave (Portland, OR: Microwave Cooking Consulting Service) 1975.
Methven, Barbara, Basic Microwaving, (Publication Arts, Inc., 5700 Green Circle Drive, Minnetonka, MN 55343.) 1978.
Methven, Barbara, Microwaving Meats, (Publication Arts, Inc., 5700 Green Circle Drive, Minnetonka, MN 55343.) 1979.
O'Connor, Hyla, The Miracle Microwave Cookbook (New York, N.Y.: The Benjamin Company, Inc.) 1976
Sadlack, Janet L., Enjoying Microwave Cooking (Burnsville, MN Recipes Unlimited, Inc.) 1975.
Scribner, Ginger, The Quick & Easy Microwave Oven Cookbook (Los Angeles, CA: Brooke House) 1976.
Stehle, Audrey P., Southern Living Microwave Cooking Made Easy, (Oxmoor House, Inc., P.O. Box 2463, Birmingham, AL 35202.) 1978.
Sunset Microwave Cook Book (Menlo Park, CA: Lane Publishing Co.) 1976.
Wasser, Barbara, Microwave Cooking (New York, N.Y.: Grosset & Dunlap) 1976.

Results may vary when using recipes from other microwave cookbooks since these recipes have not been tested in our microwave ovens.

PRINTED IN U.S.A.